THE POLITICAL ELEMENT
IN THE
DEVELOPMENT
OF ECONOMIC THEORY

A*

THE POLITICAL ELEMENT
IN THE
DEVELOPMENT
OF ECONOMIC THEORY

by

GUNNAR MYRDAL

**TRANSLATED FROM THE GERMAN
BY PAUL STREETEN**

HARVARD UNIVERSITY PRESS

CAMBRIDGE, MASSACHUSETTS

1965

Printed in Great Britain

PREFACE
TO THE ENGLISH EDITION

ALMOST a quarter of a century has passed since the original Swedish version of this book was written and published. It is perhaps understandable that, when the author is faced with the task of adding some prefatory notes to the present English edition, the thoughts that come to his mind are all in the nature of excuses, explanations, and qualifications.

Excuse and explanation are due first because, apart from a few cuts and minor editorial rearrangements, the English edition is an unrevised translation of the original version. To bring it up to date would have meant writing a new book. I would, among other things, have had to take into account the economic literature of the last twenty-five years. Apart from personal circumstances which have made such an undertaking impossible, I believe that this would not have added much to the value of the book.

After Pigou's welfare treatises the economic writings on the basic value problem have remained mostly eclectic. Compared with the works of Sidgwick, Edgeworth and other economists among their contemporaries, these later writings are usually less careful in their reasoning and less conscious of their doctrinal antecedents. The most distinguished accomplishments of our generation of economists lie in other fields. The note at the end of this volume by Mr. Paul Streeten on *Recent Controversies* is, as I read it, well suited to demonstrate that the 'new' welfare theory provides not even new wine for the old bottles. Meanwhile most economists, whether they participated in the new welfare discussion or not, have, as the economists in the generations before them, on appropriate occasions, spelled out in not greatly improved language the venerable formulae inherited from Senior and J. S. Mill about the boundary line between economic science and politics, and have then continued to harbour in their thinking the old unsolved conflict

v

between scientific aspirations and normative practice. This book, written twenty-five years ago, is, therefore, not very much out of date. A new book, like the old one, would have had to go back to the thought of a time when the value problem, which is still with us, was given a more explicit and penetrating treatment.

But the rewriting of the book would have permitted adjusting the arguments to the present world setting and to the practical problems which economists are facing now and which give direction to their scientific and methodological interests. This leads me to my second explanation: why, and in response to what scientific controversy, the book was originally written.

The setting was the Swedish economic discussion in the late 'twenties, the last quasi-normal period in our generation. On the whole, the years preceding the crash on the New York Stock Exchange in September 1929 was a time of confidence in restored stability and progress. Particularly after Knut Wicksell's death in 1926, a very uncompromising laissez-faire doctrine dominated the teaching of economics in Sweden. Gustav Cassel, Eli F. Heckscher and other Swedish economists who are less well known abroad (e.g. Sven Brisman and Gunnar Silverstolpe) were prolific writers. They also wrote popular books and they contributed to the daily press. They had an enormous influence, in Cassel's case far beyond Sweden. This book was planned as a frontal attack on the dogmas of the older generation and it was originally meant to be a popular exposition.

Books have, however, their own destinies even while they are being written. In the course of my work, which took the better part of two years instead of the two months I had set aside for the purpose, I gradually lost interest in our passing controversies of the day and, particularly, in the policies and doctrines of my older colleagues, which I had set out to refute. There were much clearer formulations to be found further back in the history of economic thought and in other countries. Above all, they were founded on more consistent and more elaborate theories and, ultimately, on the great philosophies of natural law and utilitarianism, which fascinated me. The purpose of the book thus became gradually, first, to understand economic doctrines as a coherent, growing body of thought, closely integrated into the entire setting of contemporary ideas and aspirations, and, second, to apply to them an immanent method of criticism and to lay bare the specific fallacies which, according to my initial proposition, must be found some-where between, on the one hand, statements of facts and theoreti-cal analysis and, on the other hand, political conclusions.

The third explanation which I owe, is a qualification. Re-writing the book would also have forced me to make it conform more closely with the views on the value problem which I have reached after further experience and study. I might here be per-mitted to refer in particular to '*Das Zweck-Mittel-Denken in der Nationalökonomie*' (*Zeitschrift für Nationalökonomie*, vol. IV, no. 3, 1933) and to the methodological appendices to *An American Dilemma — The Negro Problem and Modern Democracy* (New York, 1944). By presenting the book in its original form I have abstained from making it conform to my present position. Instead, I should like to add to the references just given a few remarks of self-criticism.

The book is devoted almost entirely to criticism. The suggestions in the last chapter for a positive solution of the problem, on how to introduce valuations into economic analysis and thus make it possible to draw political conclusions on a scientific basis, are very sketchy, although I still believe that they point in the right direc-tion; these ideas have been further developed, particularly in *An American Dilemma*. I still consider the criticism correct and worth doing. But throughout the book there lurks the idea that when all metaphysical elements are radically cut away, a healthy body of positive economic theory will remain, which is altogether indepen-dent of valuations. Political conclusions can then be inferred simply by adding to the objective scientific knowledge of the facts a chosen set of value premises.

This implicit belief in the existence of a body of scientific know-ledge acquired independently of all valuations is, as I now see it, naïve empiricism. Facts do not organize themselves into concepts and theories just by being looked at; indeed, except within the framework of concepts and theories, there are no scientific facts but only chaos. There is an inescapable *a priori* element in all scien-tific work. Questions must be asked before answers can be given. The questions are an expression of our interest in the world, they are at bottom valuations. Valuations are thus necessarily involved already at the stage when we observe facts and carry on theoretical analysis, and not only at the stage when we draw political infer-ences from facts and valuations.

I have therefore arrived at the belief in the necessity of working always, from the beginning to the end, with explicit value premises. The value premises cannot be established arbitrarily: they must be relevant and significant for the society in which we live. To begin with, they must be made concrete in terms of economic interests actually pursued by groups of people, and of real human attitudes to social processes. Under no circumstances should the value premises in realistic research be represented by the sort of general and abstract principles of which the economists in our great tradition of natural law and utilitarianism avail themselves to bridge the gulf between objective science and politics. This is why the immanent criticism of economic doctrines, contained in the present volume, remains not only valid but relevant and useful, in spite of my philosophical naïveté in the wider question of how to base objective research on subjective valuations.

The original Swedish edition has been for some time out of print. The unsold stock of copies of the German edition, (*Das Politische Element in der nationalökonomischen Doktrinbildung*, Junker und Dünnhaupt Verlag, 1932) which has served as the basis for the translation into English, went up in flames after one of the bombing raids on Leipzig during the last war. The English edition will therefore also serve the purpose of keeping the book available for the public. The late Professor Karl Mannheim, then editor of *The International Library of Sociology and Social Reconstruction*, took the initiative ten years ago in arranging an English version of the book. I am grateful to the publishers who have waited for so long. I am very much indebted to Mr. Paul Streeten of Balliol College, Oxford, who has made the translation and contributed the Appendix in which he surveys critically more recent discussions of the value problem.

GUNNAR MYRDAL

Geneva, February 1953

PREFACE
TO THE SWEDISH EDITION

THE present work is based on a series of lectures delivered at the University of Stockholm during the Spring Term of 1928. Its purpose is to give the reader, in broad outline, a historical and critical account of the part played by political speculation in the development of economic theory.

Since the theme is so vast, a good deal of pruning and condensing has had to be done. A considerable number of generalizations are left less completely verified than would have been possible and doctrines dealt with have been chosen as typical examples only. I have sought, throughout, to concentrate on the essential ideas in the development of economic theory. Especially in the treatment of modern doctrines I have attempted, whenever this was possible without blurring the picture, to criticize fundamental notions as such without complicating the issues by focusing too much interest on specific formulations recorded in individual works. In selecting writers representative of the views discussed, I have tried to find the theorists whose thought is most lucid and who have exercised the greatest influence on the development of economic theory: criteria which go together often but not always. Notes and references have been reduced to a minimum. It was hoped that a broad general survey of this kind might serve as a useful introduction to economic studies, together with books on positive theory as well as more encyclopaedic reviews of the evolution of economic thought. I have tried to make my exposition as direct and simple as the subject permits and I have dared to hope that the book may reach the broad public interested in the validity of economic arguments in political discussion.

One limitation of scope should perhaps be indicated at the outset. The book discusses only the political doctrines that have developed within the province of economic theory proper; in other

words, within the line of economic thinking which started with
the Physiocrats, proceeded via the classical school, and finally
branched out in the several variants of neo-classical marginalism.
'Scientific socialism' and related doctrines of the German historical and juristical schools have only received such brief mention
as was desirable to ensure continuity of the theme and to fill in the
background.

This method of approach gives us a fairly homogeneous pattern
of ideas. At the same time, the ideas analysed are those of maximum significance, at least in contemporary Sweden. As for 'scientific socialism', its most important doctrines have already undergone a thorough analysis and critique at the hands of liberal
economists. Even apart from this external onslaught, 'scientific
socialism' may be said to be disintegrating—its rate of decay is
roughly proportional to the strength of working-class representation in the parliaments of the Western world. The 'ethically
attuned' historical school (*Kathedersozialismus*) is likewise in a
state of dissolution. This process is hastened both by the increased
German interest after the Great War in economic theory and
by the perceptive criticism furnished by Max Weber and his
disciples.

This book is thus concerned with the history of ideas. In actual
fact we cannot pretend to understand completely, or even to
define logically, the economico-political speculation of recent times
except in the perspective of historical evolution. We must look
upon the majority of modern economic doctrines as modified
reminiscences of very old political thinking, conceived in days
when a teleological meaning and a normative purpose were more
openly part of the subject-matter of economics. True, many problems of our own day are of quite a different character and it has
become necessary to modify the old political doctrines before they
are applied. Moreover, they are rarely represented in logical isolation but usually as apparently less essential components together
with empirical material and with purely scientific analyses of such
material. Often they are only present as tacit assumptions, implicit in the conclusions. Also, with the growth of statistical knowledge, the refinement of economic analysis, and the evolution of
ever more intricate and specialized forms of economic organization, both our practical economic problems and the elements of
political doctrine lurking in accepted solutions have become highly

complex. Even so, once these political elements have been isolated and defined by logical analysis, it is usually possible to trace them back several generations. Even their wording, when they are made explicit, has often remained practically unchanged.

From this point of view, the political speculation which has permeated economics from the very beginning is found to be crystallized around three main foci: the idea of Value; the idea of Freedom; and the idea of Social Economy or collective housekeeping (*Volkswirtschaft*). These three notions, variously combined, have given economic doctrines their political content. Naturally, the three main normative ideas cannot be kept separate and distinct; as a matter of fact they are closely related logically. Nevertheless, it will be found that this book deals with each of them in turn.

The general nature of the problem is outlined in the first chapter and the second gives a historical sketch of the ideological background. The two following chapters on the classical and neo-classical theories of value are primarily devoted to an analysis of the idea of value itself, which lies at the root of our present problem. The fifth chapter on economic liberalism is concerned with the idea of freedom and its development. The idea of the social household (*Volkswirtschaft*) and the related doctrine of social value (or general welfare) are dealt with in the sixth chapter. The seventh chapter is a continuation of the same theme but with reference to a special problem, the theory of public finance. The last chapter discusses briefly how economics can be rendered useful without becoming a theory of objective politics.

In the attempt made in this book to provide a logical critique of certain normative speculations, the ideas under consideration are analysed in so far as they purport to serve as scientific premises for, or inferences from, economic theory, not as the expression of someone's personal political opinion. Even if it can be shown that such ideas lack not only scientific objectivity but also logical coherence, this means only that they are deficient for the purpose of scientific reasoning. To anticipate a theme touched upon at the end of the book, it is an illusion to imagine that the political attitude of an individual or a group can (and should) be logically reduced to the form of mutually compatible statements, capable of being subordinated to a set of first principles. The illusion consists not only in the ancient belief in the existence of such first prin-

ciples as objective norms. It also includes the unwarranted notion
that people's political valuations form a logical system; an idea
which, of course, could be upheld even though the objectivity of
the first principles were given up. This conception is based on a
false analogy which confuses the emotional sphere with the intellectual. Incidentally, it is an analogy which stems from the over-
intellectualized interpretation of human life characteristic of
modern Western civilization. In any case, our criticism is levelled
at the use of normative ideas as links in a scientific argument and
not as expressions of personal political opinions.

This book is therefore entirely non-political although it deals
with the frontier between politics and economics and tries to chart
the proper relationship between the two regions. A little outside
the scope of my study, I would like to express my conviction—
which I cannot prove, at least not here—that the practice of ex-
pressing political attitudes only through the medium of purportedly
objective arguments and scientific theories is probably in the long
run highly injurious to the actual policy that one wishes to support. Quasi-scientific rationalization of a political endeavour may
be an effective propaganda weapon; yet its effect at the crucial
time, when the ideal has acquired enough political backing to be
transformed into practical action, is in a democratic setting almost
always inhibitory and disintegrating. I make an exception for
completely conservative strivings which seek nothing more than
the preservation of the *status quo*; from such a political standpoint
doctrinaire thinking may be less dangerous. Discussing the intellectual bankruptcy of the German Marxists, when they were un-
expectedly confronted, during the winter of 1918–19, with a chance
of realizing in practice their policy, Egon Wertheimer wrote: "The
curse of all dogma is that one cannot touch a single stone without
threatening the whole doctrinal structure."[1] How right he was! By
'dogma', as used in this context, he meant the rationalization of a
political attitude.

Finally, it should be stressed that the acceptance of the following critique by no means shatters the foundations of economics as
a science. Those writers who have insisted on placing normative
devices, e.g. the theory of value, at the very basis of economics
have done our science an ill service. It does not, however, alter the
fact that these devices are entirely unnecessary for economic

[1] Egon Wertheimer, *Portrait of the Labour Party*, 1929, p. 19.

theory which after their rejection stands as firm and unshaken as before. Nor is the practical usefulness of the results of our research thereby diminished.

If the critique is justified, it will serve to eliminate a lot of dead-weight. The superfluous metaphysical ballast which burdens the brains of our science, which makes economic theory unnecessarily difficult to grasp for the beginner and the layman, which checks scientific progress by distorting and hiding the multitude of real problems, may then be thrown overboard. With it will go the quasi-scientific dogmas in the political sphere which now serve as powerful obstructions to clear and realistic thinking in practical questions.

Every economist is painfully aware that there exists widespread doubt about the supposed 'scientific' character of economics. The distrust is, indeed, well founded. A branch of knowledge which works with a whole set of premises missing is hardly reliable. To the ordinary citizen this methodological defect is not apparent; it actually conforms with his own ways of thinking. But what he can notice, whether he is versed in modern scientific methods or not, is the conspicuous lack of agreement among the various writers on the economic aspects of practical and political problems.

This inability of economists to agree has almost become pro-verbial. The late Hjalmar Branting, the great Swedish socialist leader who had the background of an astronomer, once exclaimed: 'Economics is not like the natural sciences, in which what one investigator has demonstrated to be true cannot be questioned by another authority, since the critic would then simply show that he is ignorant of the facts. In the field of economic science we still see school ranged against school; while the number of authentically recognized general truths is, unfortunately, still very small.'[1] True, this last statement is grossly exaggerated if it is intended to include purely scientific economic research, a province where economics has advanced quite far. But Branting's indictment is a perfectly accurate description of the political doctrines foisted into economics.

At this point we may refer to a discussion of Wicksell's. Some twenty-five years ago, Wicksell delivered his inaugural lecture at the University of Lund on 'The Ends and Means of Political

[1] Hjalmar Branting, *Samlade Skrifter*, Stockholm, 1927, p. 189.

Economy'.[1] He began by pointing out that economics, 'like
theology and for *approximately the same reasons*',[2] had hitherto failed to
arrive at generally accepted results. We cannot mention a single
doctrine which is not flatly contradicted by the diametrically opposite view, also put forward as scientific truth by writers of good re-
pute. Now it is certainly the case, Wicksell continued, that conflicting views are also to be met with in other sciences. Indeed, some such
antagonisms are natural and even necessary for the further growth
of knowledge. The history of science is a history of scientific controversy. In other disciplines such warfare of ideas usually leads to
some definite result. Theories are refuted, hypotheses become obso-
lete, the frontiers of knowledge are pushed forward. Outworn
conceptions die out with the generation that accepted them. Thus
a natural course of events brings continual renewal to research and
releases fresh energy. 'The Copernican idea of the universe, the
Newtonian system, the theory of blood circulation, and the phlogi-
ston theory in chemistry once found both adherents and opponents.
. . . Nowadays these theories are either universally believed or dis-
believed—provided, in the latter instance, that they have not
simply been forgotten.'

In economics, on the contrary, *all* doctrines live on persistently.
No new theories ever completely supplant the old. Every new
hypothesis that is not a mere restatement of a formerly held belief
adds to the confusion. 'The Malthusian theory of population has
now been debated for more than a hundred years; yet we have still
not arrived at a settled view. Some economists still regard an un-
restrained growth of the population as a grave national *calamity*;
whereas others look upon such an increase as the greatest *good
fortune* and regard any restriction upon it as *disastrous*. The controversy as to the *best* foreign trade policy has an even longer
ancestry. This, indeed, is a dispute which had apparently been
settled finally fifty years ago. But no, it flares up again, some
economists maintaining that national boundaries should be abol-
ished in the economic field so that the natural resources of the
whole world may be shared by all its peoples, and others striving
to reinforce such boundaries with the steepest possible walls.'[2]

Wicksell's criticism is fully justified. We dwell upon his analysis
here because he gropes for an explanation of the exceptional
position of political economy in a way typical of the old school. He

---

[1] K. Wicksell, *Ekonomisk Tidksrift*, 1904, pp. 457 ff.   [2] My italics.

first asserts that the problems of economic science are unusually difficult. Now this proposition must be qualified. They are scarcely more difficult in themselves than the problems handled for instance by pure mathematics, colloid chemistry, or atomic physics. It is reasonable to assume that research in every subject continually pushes back the boundaries of the unknown with a speed proportionate to the amount of intelligence available. In any case, Wicksell does not attach much importance to his first argument. For him the most powerful cause of dissension in economic science lies elsewhere, in the 'divergent views and a more or less acute sense of what *ought to be the goal* of the economic evolution of society'.

After this the reader of Wicksell's lecture would perhaps expect the following conclusions: since the evil is caused by the varying political attitudes of the economists, the radical cure must lie in research without preconceived normative ideas. Instead, Wicksell's own conclusion is an obscurely worded plea for a *particular* political valuation: for his own view of what the goal should be for social evolution. Wicksell's thought, elsewhere so lucid, becomes here extremely difficult to follow. He finally expresses the hope that we shall all ultimately realize 'that our goal here on earth is to give the greatest possible measure of happiness to all human beings—of whatever class, race, sex, language or creed'. Then, he believes, we shall make a pleasant discovery: that the method and results of political economy are attuned precisely to this social ideal.[1]

No one could feel less inclined than I to voice scepticism by deriding the faith and personal dedication which Wicksell expresses in this quotation and which governed his whole life. Yet, in the first place, the goal of social evolution, as formulated by Wicksell, is surely not very clearly defined. The terms of reference of his valuation are so wide that they cover almost any and every kind of sincere political striving in a democracy, however mutually antagonistic on concrete issues. One might also say that the ulti-

---

[1] Wicksell never gave up this view of what economics as a science really amounted to: 'As soon as we begin seriously to regard economic phenomena *as a whole* and to seek for the conditions of the welfare of the whole, consideration for the interests of the proletariat must emerge; and from thence to the proclamation of *equal* rights for all is only a short step. The very concept of political economy therefore, or the existence of a science with such a name, implies, strictly speaking, a thoroughly revolutionary programme.' *Lectures on Political Economy*, Vol. I, p. 4, London, 1934.

mate aim of all policy is the public weal. But what does this mean? If it is a truism it says nothing, if it says anything it is not a truism. The sceptic might therefore further contend that if Wicksell's formulation really does define the goal, however vaguely, and really does outline a concept, however feebly, this ideal nevertheless remains extremely ambiguous since it will still embrace a motley jumble of political valuations, and its pretension to objectivity is unfounded.

For Wicksell himself his formulation of the socio-political ideal did carry a definite meaning as is shown by the very precise conclusions at which he arrived with its aid when investigating various questions of economic policy. He doubtless also regarded his political valuation as objective truth, a conviction prompted by his utilitarian religiosity. Meanwhile, his curiosity and his genius led him to important discoveries in many branches of economics. His ultimate goal, however, was to be able to lay down the rules of right conduct and to furnish the rational reasons why men should follow them. But he merely arrived at rationalizations.

GUNNAR MYRDAL

Washington, D.C.
31 December 1929

CONTENTS

Chapter 1

POLITICS AND POLITICAL ECONOMY

THE task of economic science is to observe and describe
empirical social reality and to analyse and explain causal
relations between economic facts. Our scientific goal is to
achieve a knowledge of the world in which we live, sufficiently
adequate to enable us to forecast future events and thus to take pre-
cautions and fulfil our wishes rationally. To determine what our
fears and wishes ought to be is, however, outside the realm of
science. Many different types of societies are brought to light as we
cast our view back in history and over different regions and cul-
tures. An important step in our analytical work is to invent and
analyse imaginary societies of many kinds, to construct theoretical
models built upon abstract assumptions. But the proposition that
one state of society, actual or imagined, is politically preferable to
another can never be inferred from the results of scientific work.

This does not imply, of course, that the results of economic
research are of no importance for the formation of political
opinions. Such opinions relate to the actual state of society. They
involve wishes and plans for the preservation of this state or its
change in various ways and directions. All political discussion
implies, therefore, certain beliefs about the facts and the causal
relations between them. Economic problems take an important
place in political controversy and economic arguments are constantly employed. In contrast to the elements of valuation that are
also present in political opinions, these arguments are susceptible
to objective criticism and can, by scientific analysis, be shown to be
either true or false. And all of them, without exception, need
supplementing.

In laying this foundation for political opinion science does not
trespass beyond its boundaries. Logically, no valuations are involved. The fact that valuations nevertheless do play a part,
psychologically, in the formation of our notions about reality is

one more reason for insisting on strictly scientific criticism. The emotional colouring of our image of reality is what the scientists call a 'subjective source of error', which results in bias.

Who can doubt that political discussion ought to be made more rational in this sense? By subjecting to impartial criticism those arguments in political controversies which concern the facts and the causal relations between them, economic science can make an important contribution in the political sphere. As often as not, conflicting political opinions spring not so much from divergent valuations about the best possible future state of society and the proper policy for securing it, as from subjectively coloured and therefore distorted beliefs regarding actual social conditions.

Furthermore, it is often perfectly possible to make scientific predictions about the likelihood of achieving a certain political end by resort to a given means. It is also of the utmost importance that the subsidiary effects produced by a given political measure should not be overlooked. In the social flux every phenomenon is somehow connected with every other phenomenon. The causal relations involved are so elusively intertwined, so difficult to grasp directly, that they are often revealed in the scientific analysis as something quite different from what they appear to be. Thus a political measure which seems entirely justified as long as the indirect effects are disregarded, often turns out to be absurd from the standpoint of the same set of political valuations when *all* its economic effects are taken into account.

Politics is an art which is circumscribed by the Actual and the Possible, and precisely for this reason can it look to economic science for assistance. The politician may reasonably expect of the economist that he should explain the actual situation and state the effects of different possible modes of action in relation to the same initial situation. But the scientist must not venture beyond this. If he wishes to go further he needs another set of premises, which is not available to science: an evaluation to guide him in his choice of the effects which are politically desirable and the means permissible for achieving them.

The epistemological approach suggested here is not, of course, peculiar to the present writer. On the contrary, it represents what has actually been the official view in economic theory for roughly a century. In the fifth of the brilliant essays which he wrote as a young man, 'On the Definition of Political Economy and on the

Method of Investigation proper to it',[1] John Stuart Mill wanted to restrict the scope of economic science to the study of the factual and the probable. Senior had forcibly argued for the same view in his inaugural lecture[2] when he succeeded to the newly created Oxford professorship in economics, and he never tired of reiterating the same thesis in his later writings.[3] He expressly stated that the economist's 'conclusions, whatever be their generality and their truth, do not authorize him in adding a single syllable of advice'.[4]

Cairnes, the last of the great classical writers, put the point even more vigorously.[5] The end of political economy, Cairnes said, is 'not to attain tangible results, not to prove any definite thesis, not to advocate any practical plan, but simply to give light, to reveal laws of nature, to tell us what phenomena are found together, what effects will follow from what causes'.[6] He held the view that in its relation to politics, economics is neutral and therefore not bound to one or other of the various 'competing social schemes'. It is neutral in the same way as the study of mechanics is neutral in relation to alternative methods of building railways, or in the same way as chemistry remains neutral in the face of various sanitary projects. The writer who does not bear these principles steadily in mind 'labours under a constant temptation to wander from those ideas which are strictly appropriate to his subject into considerations of equity and expediency. . . . Instead of addressing himself to the problem, according to what law certain facts result from certain principles, he proceeds to explain how the existence of the facts in question is consistent with social well-being and natural equity; and generally succeeds in deluding himself with the idea that he has solved an economic problem, when, in fact, he has only vindicated, or persuaded himself he has vindicated, a social arrangement.'[7]

Similar views are expressed by Bagehot,[8] Sidgwick,[9] John Neville Keynes,[10] and other authors. Formulated in various ways, we find much the same attitude in present-day manuals of economics, even in those of more popular appeal. At bottom this attitude reflects an honest ambition common to all economists, the desire to see their work recognized as a true science.

Unfortunately, the fact that in principle economists commonly seem to be in complete agreement about the limitations of political economy as a science, far from clarifying the issue, only leads to further perplexity. We are only too well aware that throughout the past century economists, speaking in the name of their science, have been airing views on what they considered to be socially imperative. They have proceeded to calculate, *immediately on the basis of their scientific findings*, the course of action which is economically 'desirable' or 'right', just as they have also opposed certain policies on the ground that their realization would decrease the general 'welfare' or imply the 'neglect' (or even the 'infringement') of economic laws. Even when the claim is not explicitly expressed, the conclusions unmistakably imply the notion that economic analysis is capable of yielding laws in the sense of *norms*, and not merely laws in the sense of *demonstrable recurrences and regularities of actual and possible events.*

Thus the theory of 'free competition' is not intended to be merely a scientific explanation of what course economic relations would take under certain specified assumptions. It simultaneously constitutes a kind of proof that these hypothetical conditions would result in maximum 'total income' or the greatest possible 'satisfaction of needs' in society as a whole. 'Free competition' thus on logical and factual grounds becomes more than a set of abstract assumptions, used as a tool in theoretical analysis of the causal relations of facts. It becomes a political *desideratum*. In a similar way the capital movements and the distribution of labour between districts or countries have been discussed from the point of view of the 'common good', 'general welfare', or 'world economy'. Theories have been devised to establish the 'population optimum'. Principles have likewise been framed for the 'right', 'just', or 'equitable' distribution of taxation. Indeed, the theory of public finance is still commonly expounded as a body of doctrines which lays down what system of taxation we *ought* to impose.

We are here selecting our examples from that school in economics which will continue to be our chief concern in this book. But the German historical school attempted similarly to frame an objective social policy. The criticism launched by this school against economists in the classical tradition was directed against their abstract *a priori* way of reasoning and against the specific normative attitudes adopted by the classical writers, rather than against the establishment of norms *per se*. This applies equally to the adherents of the modern institutionalist school in the United States. These writers have taken up again the criticisms voiced by the historical school. They criticize nearly everything in the classical heritage—except the basic normative approach. Without being quite clear about it themselves they are as much dominated by the general welfare concept as the classical writers.

There is an obvious lack of agreement between the principles of research in economics and its practice. On the one hand, it is emphasized that economic science only observes social life and analyses what can be expected to happen in different circumstances, and that it never pretends to infer what the facts ought to be. On the other hand, practically every economist draws such inferences. And the various specific economic theories are most of the time arranged for the very purpose of drawing them. The result is political precepts of a supposedly scientific and objective nature. It would seem as if the terms 'observations' and 'facts' do not mean the same things in economics as they do elsewhere in scientific terminology. Economists appear to have access to *a sphere of values which are both objective and observable*. Perhaps we were wrong when we spoke of epistemological principles that can boast a hundred years of continuous recognition. Perhaps it is only the words that are identical while their meaning is different.

But what then *is* the meaning of these denunciations of the possibility that economic science can arrive at political conclusions? If an objective sphere of values is believed to exist within the compass of observable phenomena, why then should writers be at such pains to emphasize that the sole concern of science is with observation and explanation of the factual or factually possible world, and that it is beyond its power to frame political precepts? If there really are such things as scientifically ascertainable social values, why should science not give the inquirer an objective grasp of what is economically desirable?

Clearly, the situation cries out for a conceptual analysis. The only proper method involves tracing the historical development of the ideas concerned, step by step, from their inception. We shall attempt this later in our analysis of specific doctrines. For the moment we seek only a broad perspective.

The Physiocrats and Adam Smith share the honour of having first visualized economic theory as a logically coherent system of causal relations. The prime objective of their analysis was the 'natural state': an ideal model (*Idealtyp*) of the actually existing society and at the same time a definition of the society which they held *ought* to exist. Because of this identification, the formulation of normative rules was for them one of the central functions of theoretical analysis. This explains why they attempted no demarcation of their science from rational politics.

Ricardo's analysis, it is said, marked an advance towards a more modern conception of economic science. He held that the principal problem in economics is to determine the laws which regulate the distribution of income.[11] And yet, Ricardo's theory also was fundamentally based on the philosophy of natural law. It is true that Ricardo's use of the term 'natural law', as compared with the sense in which Adam Smith used similar concepts, is more akin to the sense in which it is used in the natural sciences and less to notions of normative teleology. This change of emphasis is already apparent in the works of the French writers who followed the Physiocrats: Garnier, Canard, and, in particular, J. B. Say. It is well known that Ricardo had studied these authors and that he was also indirectly indebted to them, chiefly because of the counsel of James Mill who, with his wider reading and his more trenchant powers of analysing the principles involved in philosophical issues, became in this field the mentor of his older friend, although he was Ricardo's pupil in economic theory.

The disregard shown by this early generation of the classical economists for the problem of delimiting the science of economics from politics is perhaps nowhere more apparent than in the introductory chapter of James Mill's admirable *Elements of Political Economy*.[12] In it he tried to show that political economy is to the state what domestic economy is to the family. Anyone controlling the economy of his family is obliged to adjust the supply and demand of goods and services which cannot be obtained cost-free. According to James Mill, political economy is the art of achieving the same end within the larger framework of a national economy. This is merely a modified version of Adam Smith's celebrated pronouncement.

Nevertheless Ricardo was responsible for a radical change in the theory of the relation between science and politics, although this was not so much an intentional endeavour but rather the incidental result of his way of reasoning. Ricardo took greater pains than his predecessors to define the premises which limited his analysis. In addition his analysis was far more abstract. Because he worked with a set of clearly stated abstract premises, it became necessary for his successors to distinguish between two branches of economics, viz. the 'science' and the 'art'—terms which roughly correspond to the German conceptions of 'theoretical' and 'practical' science. Our previous quotations from Senior, John Stuart Mill, Cairnes, Bagehot, etc., are meant to be valid only as far as theoretical economic science is concerned. The distinction was originally suggested by J. B. Say, whose train of thought was taken up, in Germany, by Rau.[13] In England the idea was pursued further by Senior and John Stuart Mill in works to which we have already referred.

It is important to realize the precise meaning of this distinction and, perhaps even more, *why* it was drawn. After Ricardo and until the reaction under the auspices of the historical school, economic theory was generally conceived as an extremely abstract device. It is true that Malthus and Tooke, to name but two, were interested in historical and statistical studies and that their work in this field was both detailed and extensive. But, for this very reason, such achievements were considered not to belong properly to the school of Ricardo. The method appropriate to economic theory was held to be deductive and *a priori*. All its theorems could be derived by logical procedure from a small number of postulates or axioms. Thus Senior recognized only four. While it constituted the strength of the theory, it also restricted its significance. Malthus (and many authors after him) must have had this method in mind when he observed that economics is a science of 'tendencies' which in a given case might be counterbalanced by other causes not accounted for in the theory.

John Stuart Mill developed this theory of method in his fifth essay and later defined it more exactly in Book VI of his *System of Logic*, where he dealt with the 'Moral Sciences'. Senior's principles of method were essentially the same. The differences between the two writers were mainly formal. John Stuart Mill and subsequently Cairnes, both of whom were better versed in philosophy than Senior, were eager to stress that economic theory is a 'hypothetical science'. The truth of any deduction was supposed to depend upon the adequacy of the assumptions. Senior, on the other hand, stressed that the assumptions need not be arbitrarily chosen. Instead, valid generalizations ought to be formulated on the basis of empirical reality.[14] Senior believed that his four assumptions were generalizations that fitted reality fairly closely.

Apart from this difference of emphasis, they all fully agreed upon the undesirability of drawing rash conclusions from abstract theory. Indeed, they warned against this danger in no uncertain terms. The reason why they urged caution in matters of policy was, however, only that political economy as a theoretical and abstract science lacked some of the *empirical data* required for direct political inferences.[15]

Admittedly, Mill also said that 'science' is distinguishable from 'art' in much the same way that comprehension is distinguishable from volition, or the indicative from the imperative. The former is concerned with facts, the latter with precepts.[16] But it should be remembered that the quintessence of utilitarian moral philosophy, which at that time constituted the basis of economic thought, was the conviction that the will both can and should be rational even with respect to the end towards which it is directed.[17]

The point under debate, therefore, was not the establishment of a line of demarcation between science and non-science. At that time and in that particular circle the premises for such a distinction were altogether lacking. The point at issue was rather the delimitation of two different types of science. Conscientious study of the texts will corroborate this interpretation. And it should be noted that this conception persisted in the work of the later classical and neo-classical writers. It persists even to-day in the writings of most authors in the great theoretical tradition.

In other words, the distinction was not one of principle. It was dictated entirely by expediency. That this was the sole motivation was, indeed, sometimes explicitly stated.[18]

It was thus regarded as both natural and highly desirable that political economists should venture beyond the frontier line. The only qualification was that they then no longer practised economic theory in the narrow sense but became the spokesmen of the superimposed science of 'moral philosophy'. As matters then stood, this extension of their task was not particularly exacting. The objective social philosophy of utilitarianism, of which economic science was but one specific elaboration, was both easy to grasp and readily accessible.

When, therefore, John Stuart Mill later tackled a more comprehensive task he had only to tack on to the title of his book a phrase to make it plain that he was dealing with a field wider than that of pure economic theory.[19] For Sidgwick, the whole question of demarcation was reduced to a problem of classification. The student who is familiar with his *Principles of Political Economy* or, better, with his *Elements of Politics*, will know that the author did not regard it as impossible to discuss political issues and decide upon them from a scientific standpoint—or, as he himself says, 'from a purely economic or utilitarian point of view'. It is only difficult to understand why Sidgwick and many other writers should have made such a fuss about a relatively insignificant problem of classification.

It must further be borne in mind that economic theory became increasingly concerned with concrete problems. This was undoubtedly due in part to the criticism levelled against the classical texts by economists of the historical and institutionalist schools. In part it was the result of the fact that more and more historical and statistical material, both from public and private sources, had become available and was being collected and analysed. From the later years of John Stuart Mill onwards, and particularly since Cairnes, Bagehot, and Jevons, most economists endeavoured to make their theory more concrete. Marshall became the chief proponent of this ambition.

As we have shown, the division of the 'science' from the 'art' was regarded as a necessary result of the Euclidean abstractness of classical theory. The theory of knowledge familiar to the economists had never drawn a clear distinction between facts and ideals. Occasional hints that values cannot be objectively ascertained were not voiced with much conviction and were in conflict with the basic philosophy. Therefore, the system of thought based on classical authority, which was somehow still felt to be relevant, was found to lack sound foundations.

It continued to remain the fashion, however, for economists to repeat in their introductory paragraphs the conventional phrases about the non-political character of political economy. But it is clear that this was usually done more as a polite bow to a venerable tradition and as a reminder of the writer's familiarity with philosophical subtleties. The authors concerned could not reasonably attribute any great importance to the old stock phrases, particularly when it came to specific items of theoretical research which were no longer tackled in the *a priori* fashion of the classical school, but were thoroughly impregnated with, and often verified by, purely empirical research.

C

Unfortunately, the increasingly empirical nature of the study of special problems led also to reduced interest in the fundamental questions of methods and principles which in turn made it easier for logical contradictions to persist. Thus we find a theorist like Pigou advancing the thesis that economics is a positive science concerned with things as they are and not a normative science concerned with things as they ought to be—and yet at the same time devoting a not inconsiderable part of his work to the problem of rationally calculating that mode of political action which is the best possible from an economic and utilitarian point of view.[20] To give another example: the whole theoretical objective of J. B. Clark may be summed up as an attempt to prove the thesis that, given free competition, price-formation will meet the requirements of equity, inasmuch as each man's income must then correspond to the value to society of his productive contribution. Yet Clark, too, took it upon himself to stress that economic science as such had nothing to do with the question of the relative justice or injustice of existing institutions, laws, or customs. The same dual attitude is apparent in the majority of neo-classical theorists.

However, such equivocation has been countered by a constant flow of criticism. The eminent Dutch economist Pierson produced an analysis of this issue which must be recognized as irrefutable as long as one accepts his premises. Pierson's real aim was to get rid of the distinction altogether. He held that the older definition of economics as the science which lays down what rules men must observe if they are to ensure their material progress, was not, after all, so very wide of the mark.[21] In supporting such a definition, Pierson not only sided with the oldest classical writers and many of their followers who never drew the distinction; he also vindicated what was the practice of all other theorists. He himself clearly realized and stressed this. His only concern was to get a common and widespread practice recognized as a permissible scientific method.

Pierson believed that the supposedly 'scientific' character of economics stems from the habit of presenting logical imperatives as grammatical indicatives. The imperative is implicit in such indicatives as 'something is of value' or 'something is harmful'. He asked whether it can be of any real significance whether the practical conclusion of a study takes the form of a statement that protectionism is injurious, or of a recommendation to abstain from protectionist measures. No author, he maintained, has ever explained the economic effects of various monetary systems, agrarian constitutions, agricultural methods, or principles of foreign trade, without turning his results into precepts for political conduct. And why not, since those precepts are nothing else, and can be nothing else, than a recapitulation of his scientific results?[22]

As a concession to logic, though a trivial one, Pierson admitted that all ideas about what ought to be are in a sense conditional. The political imperatives which are implied by the contention that a certain course of action increases material welfare are, of course, only valid on the assumption that we really desire material welfare. Pierson also admitted that it is possible to envisage other social goals for political action. But the boundary he imposed between the 'economic' and the 'social' is not a boundary between science and politics. Rather, as he emphasized, is it a boundary between two *political* sciences. Moreover the boundary is fluid— more fluid than Pierson himself supposed. However, considered on the basis of his own premises, his criticism was entirely correct. It is not possible to draw a theoretical line between economics and politics in the manner and with the significance so much stressed by most economists in their methodological discussions. To insist on such a boundary would, at best, be tedious pedantry. It is understandable that economists should prefer positive assertions and a minimum use of exclamation marks. But if we have no other grounds for calling our work scientific, we might as well drop this as a piece of fraudulent snobbery. Pierson was merely voicing the common-sense protest of many economists—both now and earlier —against combining the view that economics is a purely positive science with the attempt to find norms for economic policy.

Pierson's logic is irrefutable but his premises are untenable. If it were true that we were cognizant of a sphere of social values which is accessible to research, our science would be able to furnish politicians with objective norms for economic policy, and economists would have no reason to try to cover up this fortunate state of affairs by maintaining the contrary. If we could really lay down scientifically the postulates required for an optimum population, if we could determine the principles of establishing a just distribution of the tax-burden, if we could formulate the conditions for the maximum social utility accruing from production and exchange, if this and much else were within our reach, then our science would be normative. But it is precisely such questions

as these that we cannot answer. A misunderstanding of this fundamental point of epistemology explains much of that uncertainty
in matters of principle which still tends to undermine the basis of
economic science. We must not be reconciled to half-measures.
The belief that it is possible to arrive at a happy compromise in
this issue is mere self-deception.

This source of error in the approach to the study of social
reality must infect the logic and invalidate the analysis. It should
be admitted, however, that as a result of the incessant endeavours
of several generations of economists to reach norms for economic
policy, a nucleus of positive theory has been developed and
gradually perfected. It is true, as Menger observed, that economics has been brought to birth and nurtured by scholars who
often grudged themselves the leisure to reflect upon their own
research and to subject it to logical analysis. In the present state of
economics, however, it may not be a waste of labour to go over the
old ground and to try to reassess the fundamental issue. To-day, we
have accumulated an almost unmanageable quantity of empirical
data and endless reams of theoretical analysis, while at the same
time we have only a very vague idea of the true significance of our
knowledge and of the best way to exploit it for the purpose of
grappling with the immense political problems which now loom
larger than ever.

Max Weber, that great scholar who made lasting contributions
in so many fields of social research, was also one of the first to
stress forcefully the principle that economics, if it is to be scientific,
must be kept *wertfrei*, i.e. free of values.[23] His fundamental critique
is transcendental and based upon modern German logic. His
views are set forth mainly in his critical commentary on the
Marxian conceptions of history and society, and on the German
socio-political school of economists. As a result of the efforts of
Schmoller, Schäffle, and Wagner, this school had become increasingly normative with a bias towards reforms. In the course of time
it had also become doctrinaire, though this fate had threatened it
from the start.

It is not surprising that Weber never proceeded to a critique of
the political speculation in classical and neo-classical economic
theory. Economic theorizing was not encouraged in Germany in
his days. Indeed, it continued to be regarded as only remotely

interesting until very recently, when a fresh start in theoretical research was made; this reawakening of interest was due, in no small measure, to the influence of Cassel's *Theoretische Sozialökonomie* published at the end of the Great War. Moreover, Weber was more of a sociologist and historian than an economic theorist.

In Sweden Axel Hägerström has on general philosophical grounds criticized decisively normative social science. His interest has been directed mainly at the normative and teleological notions which, originally founded on primitive magic, are still present in modern jurisprudence. Hägerström's main thesis has, however, a much wider relevance. There are no values in the objective sense, only subjective valuations. These should be distinguished from perceptions of reality. This idea is the central point of view of the present critical analysis of economic theory.

Our task in the following chapters will be to criticize the economico-political doctrines in the inherited body of economic thought on their own premises. The general thesis that economic science, if it is to be scientific, should refrain from attempting to establish political norms, has been accepted by leading economists for about a hundred years and is a commonplace to-day. But the full significance of this postulate is apparently not generally grasped and the political doctrines are still with us. They were originally formulated by men who believed in their objectivity and who attempted to prove them scientifically. Some economists to-day are equally explicit in their use of normative methods. More often, however, the norms are suppressed and appear only implicitly in the specific political recommendations presented as results of economic analysis. This is certainly not an advance in scientific methodology. We must therefore probe deeper and attack the normative and teleological system of economic thinking from within. The tenability of a given theory must be tested on the basis of its own premises. Only a critique which is immanent in this sense can carry conviction. We must make explicit and then scrutinize the long chain of premises and inferences which underlie the glibly accepted formulae of political economy.

We have already traced in the broadest outline the historical evolution which ideas about the aims and limitations of economics as a science have undergone since the earliest classical writers. By way of introduction a few general remarks should be added about the economic doctrines themselves.

They do not show complete homogeneity but display considerable differences in content. The degree of uniformity which nevertheless prevails and which facilitates systematic treatment is largely due to the common legacy from the moral philosophies of natural law and utilitarianism from which economic speculation branched out.

The first basis upon which a system of economic theory was constructed was the philosophy of natural law. The substitution, later, of utilitarian philosophy for the philosophy of natural law did not occur suddenly and did not cause a revolution. It was a gradual process of extending and reinforcing the old basis. This, at least, is the interpretation suggested by the evolution of economic theory. First, the logical distance between the ultimate normative premises and the practical political conclusions is increased by the insertion of additional steps. Second, attention is focused on these additional steps—these are the utilitarian elements which are added—while the ultimate premises—which are still the aprioristic notions of natural law—are kept in the shadow. Bentham inveighed against the circular reasoning in all arguments based on natural law, to the effect that something is 'right' merely because it is 'natural', or sometimes even more simply because it is 'right'. But the result of his own endeavours was, as we shall find, only to increase the diameter of the logical circle.

The economic doctrines take their normative aim, their main categories of thought, and their methods of proof from the philosophy of natural law and utilitarianism. Some latitude of movement, and hence divergent political conclusions, are made possible through certain logical defects in the normative reasoning contained in these two philosophical systems. Logical fallacies are inevitable when economic theory attempts the logically impossible feat of arriving at political conclusions without political premises. Within the latitude which the normative reasoning allows, the results are determined psychologically by the political biases of the period, the social setting, and the prejudices of the author. The arbitrariness implicit in the normative method of the two underlying philosophical systems is not known to the authors under consideration. Their loose thinking is performed in good faith. Their doctrines are what is nowadays called 'rationalizations'.

While, for instance, many economists, especially in earlier times, have felt called upon to demonstrate the equity or expediency of the prevailing distribution of income and wealth, others have tried to prove the contrary and to indicate reforms which, if adopted, would replace the ruling system by a more equitable one. In later decades economists often attempted to sidestep the whole issue, for instance by assuming the existence of an equitable distribution of property and income. This premise is sometimes also made to embrace all 'non-economic' valuations about distribution for those who distrust a 'purely economic' solution of the problem of the correct distribution. The assumption is stated in order that the theorist shall be left free to establish rules for exchange, production, taxation, and all matters which, as he thinks, can be isolated from the problem of distribution and thus rendered independent of political premises.

In spite of the many divergent inferences, economic doctrines possess a morphological unity, which is most obvious in the theory of *Value*. The whole history of economic thought is stamped by the notion that by recourse to purely logical operations it is possible to construct on the basis of empirical observations the concept of a kind of 'value' which is somehow profounder than mere exchange-value or price. It is believed that this concept must be the starting-point for all economic analysis which really tries to probe beneath the surface. It is also commonly believed that the theory of value has a central significance for the construction of economico-political doctrines. As a matter of fact, the value theory is always implicit in the political results, even where it has not figured explicitly among the premises.

The classical concept of *Real Value* is derived from the philosophy of natural law. It is based upon the labour-value and property theories of Hobbes and Locke. Under the influence of utilitarian philosophy, the classical writers infused a psychological element into value theory. The neo-classical theory of *Subjective Value* or the theory of marginal utility was from its inception purely psychological. It is really just an elaboration of Bentham's hedonistic pleasure-pain calculus.

Modern psychological research has completely abandoned this type of explanation of what goes on in the human mind, and with it the whole approach of associationist hedonistic psychology. The upholders of the theory of subjective value in economics have therefore tried to make their value concept appear less objectionable by purporting to eliminate psychological hedonism. This tendency was already present in the work of the earliest proponents of marginal utility theory; in Jevons and Walras, to some degree also in Menger, and certainly in Böhm-Bawerk. Gradually, the subjective value theory was reduced to an empty formula with an absolute minimum of psychological content. With great theoretical ingenuity nothing more was accomplished than an elaborate formulation of a tautology based upon circular definitions. It was the function of this very complicated modern theory of value, as it had been of its simpler, openly hedonistic predecessor, to mask the specific logical errors which permit the inference of political norms.

But as soon as the theory of value is given a psychological foundation by the neo-classicists it becomes purely individualistic. By itself it does not permit political conclusions. The norms, on the other hand, must indicate what is valuable for society as a whole. Hence the subjective theory of individual value requires to be transformed into a theory of *Social Value*. The actual expression 'social value' is generally avoided. Only an occasional dour theorist is consistent and persistent enough to develop the concept. Nevertheless it is an ubiquitous notion, even though it is expressed in many different ways. *'General Welfare'* is one of the synonyms. It is identical with the notion of the economic process as a form of collective housekeeping in the interests of society (*Volkswirtschaft*).

The analogy between society and the economy of a patriarchal family had already been developed by Adam Smith. Even he was merely reformulating ancient beliefs which had been systematized in the course of the seventeenth and eighteenth centuries, particularly by the Cameralists. We have already had occasion to refer to an exposition of the theme by James Mill. As a definition of theoretical economics, the analogy with a socially operated economy was first criticized by John Stuart Mill. In his attempt to draw a dividing-line between theoretical and practical political economy he chose to begin with a critique of his father's views on this very issue.[24] Nevertheless he continued to regard the notion of a socially operated economy in the old sense as valid for the more comprehensive discipline of practical economics.

The idea of a socially operated economy and that of general

welfare, defined as the interest of society as a whole, as something which can be observed and known objectively, were given new life by the subjective theory of value. Jevons, who of all the early marginalists put the matter most lucidly, wrote as follows:

'The problem of economics may, as it seems to me, be stated thus: Given a certain population, with various needs and powers of production, in possession of certain lands and other sources of material; required, the mode of employing their labour which will maximize the utility of the produce.'[25]

The idea that the economic process represents the economy of a personified society which tries to make the best of the available resources, thus working towards a common goal, remained the generally accepted form of reasoning in economics and governed the formulation and proof of its political doctrines. For it will be found that in essence all such doctrines serve to indicate what is most 'economic' from the standpoint of society.

During its development economic theory became increasingly isolated from other social sciences. The effects of this evolution have been harmful, particularly because economic research is bound to touch constantly upon psychology, jurisprudence, sociology, epistemology, and philosophy.

We have noted that there was no isolation initially. The whole theory of economics, as well as the other social sciences, was an offshoot of philosophical speculation in France and England during the eighteenth and nineteenth centuries. However, the intimate connection between political economy and related disciplines was not maintained. Economists clung too tenaciously to the philosophical foundations upon which their science had first been built. At about 1870, just at the time when psychology was beginning to take its modern empirical form, we find economists perfecting their theory as an explanation of economic behaviour in general. Only at this late stage was the ancient ideal that economics should become an accomplished, all-embracing 'calculus of pleasure and pain' realized. If the moral philosophy of the utilitarians still survives in a fairly systematic shape, it owes this to the loving care with which it has been preserved in economic theory.

Utilitarian influence reached its peak with the introduction of the theory of marginal utility. Afterwards, the circle from tacit premise to normative conclusions tended to become narrower again. Once again natural law made its influence felt more directly. Never properly eliminated, the idea of natural law was revived. We find it particularly in popular expositions which require the compression of arguments. In modern writings which most clearly bear the stamp of natural law philosophy, the utilitarian element is often reduced to a loosely attached assertion that the 'natural' state, the 'state of equilibrium' or whatever other phrase is used to cover the inserted norm, is bound to lead to 'the maximum satisfaction of human needs'. In effect, if not in actual phraseology, this simply echoes the contention of many economic writers in the eighteenth century *prior* to the utilitarian school. As we would expect, we find that the more conscientious theorists deplore such a 'watering down' of economic theory. This refusal to accept the superficiality of natural law philosophy has, indeed, always lent a particular impetus to the utilitarian creed. [26]

In attempting to characterize the morphology of economic doctrines we shall come across a circumstance whose logical necessity will only gradually become apparent as our investigation proceeds. In those cases where a real effort has been made to furnish a detailed and explicit proof of a specific political doctrine, it will be seen that this proof regularly assumes the form of a logical deduction from certain abstract principles which on closer inspection are revealed as purely formal, i.e. as intrinsically meaningless. The dilemma facing normative science is the following: For the sake of scientific 'objectivity' the fundamental normative principles involved must be formulated in such a way that they have no content; whereas they can be given content only by the underhand insertion of tacit premises, that is to say, of concrete valuations derived from other sources. This suggests a methodological rule for our critique in the following chapters. We must try to lay bare the specific logical errors resulting from the insertion of valuations. These insertions are due to the logical impossibility of deriving positive political conclusions from mere premises of facts (together with a value premise devoid of content which, as a result of its lack of content, can be regarded as irrefutable, i.e. as 'objective').

The difference between the various doctrines is to be found largely in the number of logical steps between the ultimate formal premises and the specific final conclusions. The more conscientious the thinker, the greater, usually, is this distance.

In texts where economic policy is discussed in practical terms adapted to concrete problems, we usually find that the elements of specific political doctrines are introduced as simple assertions, without the paraphernalia of proof which the writers concerned undoubtedly feel they could easily supply if required. And we could hardly expect anything else. The doctrines are used in much the same way as we employ familiar formulae for converting expressions in mathematical analysis, formulae that we know by name and which have been proved once for all. Nor could we object to such a practice, provided that proof were really rendered elsewhere. The layman who tries to follow such a practical argument remains often quite unaware of the doctrinal elements, which may be masked as apparently innocent and self-evident expressions or even omitted altogether in the chain of reasoning. It frequently requires a trained eye to detect them at all. They have, as it were, entered into the logical method employed in economics, have become an integral part of the manner in which we 'think in economic terms'.

In attempting to explain the extreme conservatism, the faithfulness to defunct philosophical methods, apparent in economic theory, it should not be forgotten that, from the very first, the whole terminology of economics has been permeated with the maxims of natural law philosophy and, later, of utilitarianism. The linguistic forms which tradition offers to the economic theorist ensnare him at every turn in their old-accepted associations. They continually tempt him to propound valuations and rules of conduct when he should only describe and explain disinterestedly. Westergaard, the Danish economist, historian, and statistician, once spoke about economics as 'a science where expressions and metaphors readily engender supposed proofs' and says that the 'power of the words to shape thoughts' has been strong in our science.[27]

Nearly all the general terms current in political economy, and in the social sciences generally, have two meanings: one in the sphere of 'what is', and another in the sphere of 'what ought to be'. The word 'principle', for instance, means, on the one hand, 'theory', or 'basis of a theory', or 'working hypothesis within a theory'. 'Theory' means a systematic understanding of certain objective regularities. Thus Cassel, for example, says that the theory of price-formation rests on the 'scarcity principle', or again he completes his system of simultaneous equations with a series of equations which fall under the heading 'principle of costs'. But the word 'principle' may also mean an 'aim of conscious striving' or 'chief means for attaining a postulated end' or a 'general rule of action'. The dual meaning of our terms is not accidental; it is the expression of the normative-teleological way of thinking, traditional in the social sciences and, indeed, programmatic in the philosophy of natural law upon which they were founded. The very method of this philosophy is, in one sense, a systematic sliding between the two meanings of the terms.

From a scientific point of view, nearly all our terms are for this reason 'value-laden'. The danger to the unsophisticated theorist, of sliding into normative habits without stating his value premises explicitly, is aggravated by the fact that the same thing is done habitually in popular reasoning. Without being aware of the logical process, he tends to bolster up the objectivity of the 'principle' in the sense of a norm, by its objectivity as an element of theory. The norm thus acquires an air of being founded upon the 'nature of things'. This precisely is the circular reasoning inherent in the philosophy of natural law.

Other such terms with a double meaning are, for instance, 'productivity', 'equilibrium', 'balance', 'adjustment', etc. The harmless term 'function' also becomes dangerous if it is not stated in relation to what end or purpose the 'function' is defined. It may, for instance, be said that it is the 'function of the entrepreneur to shoulder the risks' or 'to combine the factors of production' or 'to direct production'. These are teleological figures of speech, by themselves just as innocent as those which adorn primers of biology in which it is explained that the function of the heart is to act as the pump of the blood-system. But in economics it is, as we know, so fatally easy to proceed as follows: 'As a reward for performing this function, he receives a profit', and thereafter to go further and regard the fact that the entrepreneur fulfils a 'function' as constituting some kind of justification for the profit he receives.

Figuratively speaking, we may also say that the price fulfils the 'function' of restricting demand and stimulating supply, thus ensuring equilibrium in the market. Such a choice of phraseology may be warranted on stylistic grounds since it adds a lively touch to the exposition. But with the metaphor 'function' is associated the old idea that in equilibrium the price is the 'right' one and that 'the factors of production are put to the most economic uses'. We are then well away in normative-teleological thinking. The statement is not just false but, strictly speaking, meaningless. And the matter cannot be mended by the addition of the further postulate that the statement applies only 'from the standpoint of the valuation prevailing in the market' or 'in society'. For there does not exist such a 'valuation' (in the singular) in the market or in society. There are as many valuations as there are persons engaged in exchange. The valuations are determined partly by the economic position in which each individual finds himself. But this situation, in turn, is governed by the course of the whole process of price-formation and is thus partly determined by the valuations themselves. Moreover, scientifically speaking, valuations as such are incommensurable. The covert introduction of a uniform social valuation into explanations of economic phenomena conceals all these difficulties and impossibilities.

So far we have not mentioned the directly normative concepts occupying a central place in economic theory. These are best eliminated altogether, for it is hardly possible to make them useful for economic analysis, no matter how we modify our definitions. I refer to terms such as: *utility*; *value*—in meanings other than exchange-value; *real* or *subjective costs*; *welfare*; *social utility*; *real national income*—in the sense of quantities of subjective utility added together to form a social sum total; *minimum social sacrifice*; *economy* —directed to a social end (*Volkswirtschaft*); and many others, not to speak of such expressions as what is *economical*, *right*, *natural*, *equitable*, etc.

This question of terminology should not be passed over lightly. The terms have a peculiar significance in the social sciences. They represent involved structures of metaphysical ideas which are firmly anchored in our tradition of thought. They have developed within this tradition and have been moulded by it. The tradition is both persistent and elastic.

Once the vagueness of the ultimate philosophical premises is tolerated, it becomes possible to ward off a critic by granting him the most generous concessions in matters of principle, while at the same time not changing anything in substance and practice. At most we may achieve the suppression of a few particularly easily exploded formulations.

From sheer familiarity and established reputation the implicit teleological and normative methods have, as it were, acquired the character of immediate evidence. The student of economics is taught 'to think in economic terms'. This means chiefly—or so we are repeatedly told—that he should cultivate the ability to see and understand economic phenomena, rapidly and exactly, in a specific light, i.e. observe them from a particular point of view and classify them according to certain theoretical categories. The actual choice of viewpoint and categories will, of course, depend, in the last resort, on the underlying epistemological approach. Once one has grown accustomed to thinking within the frame of the inherited normative system, which offers the assurance of a 'beaten track', it becomes difficult to step aside and inspect the system from the outside, in the same way as it is difficult for creatures living two-dimensional lives on the surface of a sphere, to cite Einstein's famous example, to suspect the existence of a third dimension.

One tends to overlook the premises on which the system is founded. The results seem to be independent of all extra-scientific assumptions. Indeed, they appear to be scientific. Hence the belief, commonly voiced nowadays, that the fundamental arguments of social philosophy may safely be by-passed and that the economist may justly proclaim the independence of his science from political premises even when he actually ventures over the border into political speculation. As economic theory has grown more subtle and elaborate, as it has absorbed an ever-increasing number of experimental data, as it has been adapted to social conditions of ever-greater complexity—in short, as its reputation was strengthened by continued usage, by empirical verification, and by successful applications—it has become easier to disregard those speculations, rooted in social philosophy, which historically constituted and logically still constitute the basis of many of its conclusions. Such an attitude would, of course, have been more difficult at the time when the pioneers of our science were beginning to map out the frontiers of economic theory.

Chapter 2

THE IDEOLOGICAL BACKGROUND

For an understanding of the origin and the meaning of the political doctrines which pervade the theory of political economy, it is essential to remember that this theory, like other political 'systems' and utopias, has grown out of the philosophy of natural law and was developed under the powerful influence of utilitarian social philosophy. These two main influences upon economic theory have been very similar. Indeed, utilitarianism may be considered as an English offshoot of the philosophy of natural law. In so far as there are divergencies, they are typical of the general differences between English and Continental thought.

It is a commonplace that Continental thinkers are readier to use abstractions. They prefer to choose as premises general ideas which they believe to be derived directly from reason. These concepts are supposed to be self-evident because they are 'natural'; they are supposed to follow necessarily from the laws of thinking; to be innate; to be corollaries of the presuppositions of a Free Will, of a Rational Universe, of a creating and preserving Deity, etc. There are many ways of presenting this *a priori* social philosophy, but the differences are not important for our purpose.

British thought, on the other hand, has, since Bacon, been largely empirical. Just as British empiricists attempt to derive all knowledge from sense experience, so they try to construct a system of social ethics on the same empirical basis. They do not judge conduct to be right or wrong because it springs from a will which is good or bad in itself, but in virtue of its results, which they assume can be determined objectively as good or bad. The 'interest of the community' is postulated as the supreme norm. It is interpreted as an arithmetic sum of the satisfactions of individuals. Welfare is conceived as a psychological entity and thus psychology becomes the basis of morality. This line of argument was still used by J. S.

Mill in his *Utilitarianism* and by Sidgwick in his *Methods of Ethics*. Spencer also used it, although in a somewhat modified form in accordance with his idea of evolution. In some form or other it still appears in the most up-to-date versions of British and American philosophy. Yet, it is clear that such an empirical derivation of social ethics must fail. A study of empirical reality can never lead to an insight into the *summum bonum*, i.e. to a social value judgement which is objectively true. The utilitarian empiricists must somewhere or other have recourse to those *a priori* 'higher principles' which they denounce so vehemently.

It is significant that the utilitarians only gradually became aware of their conflict with the philosophy of natural law. Not until Bentham was the break explicit. Bentham was not the creator of utilitarianism as a philosophical system. His contribution was primarily his opposition to the doctrines of natural law, and thus the clear separation of the two systems. For Bentham, all talk of 'natural rights' was nonsense. He attacked violently the two great contemporary declarations of human rights: the *Declaration of Independence* of 1776 and the *Declaration des droits de l'homme* of 1789. They are, he said, metaphysical works—'the *ne plus ultra* of metaphysics. Let the articles be what they may, I will engage they must come under three heads—1. Unintelligible; 2. False; 3. A mixture of both.'[1] Speculations of this kind are, he said, at best tautological: but since such solemn declarations are always made with the intention of saying something meaningful, they are also false. Bentham's approach was, in modern economic terminology, pragmatic-institutionalist or functionalist. In his view, institutions cannot be justified merely in virtue of their existence, nor can they be defended merely on the ground that they are ordained by 'the nature of things'.

Following Hume, Bentham distinguished between 'real entities' and 'fictitious entities' in social life and attacked the tendency to mistake fictions for realities. 'Obligations, rights and similar words' designate, he held, such fictitious entities. They are merely metaphors. The proposition that somebody is 'obliged' to do something means no more than this: should he prefer not to do it, certain known conditions will make sanctions probable which will ultimately cause pain. Such words as 'duty' or 'obligation' contain a fiction to which an anticipation of pleasure and pain corresponds in the world of realities. This is the basis of Bentham's system.

'Nature has placed mankind under the governance of two sovereign masters, *pain* and *pleasure*. It is for them alone to point out what we ought to do, as well as to determine what we shall do.'² With these magnificent, much-quoted words, Bentham begins his *Introduction to the Principles of Morals and Legislation*.

Yet, let us note already at this stage, the distinction is not nearly so fundamental as Bentham would have us believe. Utilitarianism, like any other system of positive social ethics with a claim to objectivity, resembles the philosophy of natural law in that it purports to provide a basis for objective political norms, i.e. moral rights and duties from which ideal political conditions can be deduced and, therefore, the existing social order scientifically criticized. In the light of these objective norms one can determine whether institutions are right, just, or—to use the stock phrase— whether they promote the interest of the community. Bentham was convinced that politics should be a kind of utilitarian arithmetic and that one could always ascertain the appropriate line of action by purely logical and mathematical operations. This, indeed, was Bentham's main interest. He was above all a passionate social reformer and only in the second place a speculative thinker. It is characteristic of him that he spoke condescendingly of those curious people who ponder 'whether this table exists outside them, inside them, or not at all'. He believed that he had sidestepped this problem altogether.

Both the philosophers of natural law and the utilitarians attempted to arrive at practical rules of conduct through theoretical speculation, and both, therefore, lacked a sense of historical relativity. The philosophy of natural law lacked this sense because of its rationalist basis and origin. But why the utilitarians? According to their avowed programme, the calculation of social utility must be repeated time and again so as to take account of ever-changing social conditions. Indeed, the utilitarians stressed this difference when they contrasted their own philosophy with that of the school of natural law. In spite of this, they never paid more than lip-service to that part of their programme. This is mainly due to the logical difficulties which they encountered whenever they were faced with the problem of actually calculating social utility. They lapsed either into antiquated notions of natural law or into sheer arbitrariness; for not only 'rights' and 'duties' but also the 'common interest of the community', the 'general welfare',

are fictitious entities. Another reason why utilitarians never carried out their avowed programme was their firm belief in the universal and eternal uniformity of human nature. They had taken over this belief from the eighteenth-century philosophy of natural law and had never really abandoned it, although they denied it officially. It is this belief, and the maxims derived from it, which gave the social philosophy of, say, J. S. Mill unmistakably the stamp of the Age of Enlightenment.

Thus, utilitarians and natural law philosophers resembled each other not only in so far as both deduced ethical norms for which they claimed objective validity. The content of their doctrines too, and even their form, betrayed their close affinity. Indeed Paley, next to Bentham, may be considered as the founder of utilitarianism proper. He attempted to solve moral problems by testing various lines of action for their tendency to increase or to reduce social utility. Yet, he still distinguished between 'natural rights' and 'adventitious rights'. The former are universally valid since their observance increases utility, irrespective of the political institutions and other social conditions which happen to exist at the time. Whether the observance of adventitious rights on the other hand increases or diminishes utility depends upon these historical, and to some extent arbitrary, conditions. The right to property as such, for example, is a natural right, for private property is always useful, because of its tendency to encourage effort and thrift. Actually prevailing ownership rights, on the other hand, were defended more indirectly by Paley by pointing to the general increase in utility derived from obedience to the existing laws of a country. Similarly, monogamy is a principle of universal validity whose observance is required always and everywhere by the general principle of utility. It follows from the nature of things or rather from the fact that divine Providence decrees that men and women shall be born in approximately equal numbers.

It is true that Bentham and the later utilitarians no longer accepted such very general arguments of the natural law type. Nevertheless, whenever they descended from the most general principles to current issues, they argued curiously like their precursors. In some especially solemn context, utilitarians may also be found to speak occasionally of the 'eternal and natural right to own private property', and although such ideas are rarely expressed explicitly, they are frequently implied. The summation of pleasures and pains to estimate social utility or general welfare is usually carried out, or rather evaded, by suitable assumptions of a general nature, not unlike the *a priori* notions of the natural law doctrine. These operations do not become logically sound simply because Bentham had rejected some of the *a priori* speculations as 'fictions'. The only practical result of the utilitarian revolt was the somewhat more flexible treatment of those notions of natural law which no longer conformed with current political and social convictions. But even the natural law school itself had been quite generous in this respect. The abstract formulae could be used to lend the authority of 'naturalness' to almost any political belief or ideal. In practice, the utilitarians did not change radically the content of the time-honoured norms but merely presented them in a somewhat different guise.

Legal historians have stressed the fact that utilitarianism as a legal philosophy is just a new cloak for the teaching of natural law. It is part of the thesis of this book that in economics too, the direct contribution of utilitarianism amounted to little more than a more elaborate formulation of the natural law doctrines. Jurisprudence and economics were the two branches of social theory which were most directly influenced by utilitarianism. Nowadays modern psychology rejects the mechanistic, intellectualistic, and rationalistic approach of psychological hedonism. This deprives utilitarianism of its empirical basis, a grievous blow for a social doctrine which, from the outset, purported to be empirical. Finally, logical criticism has brought to light the fallacies which are the inevitable outcome of the conflict between its basic empiricist concepts and its metaphysical aspirations to be an objective philosophy of morality.

Not only can no clear theoretical line be drawn between the two main influences on economic theory, but their historical delineation also is blurred. Their close affinity is perhaps most apparent in the deistic arguments of the earlier utilitarians, particularly the theological utilitarians Tucker, Priestley, and Paley. For them the ethical standards of utilitarianism are 'natural' at least in the sense that they are part of the wise and benevolent intentions of divine Providence. Because these divine intentions are assumed to be good and rational, they can be discovered by subjecting human conduct to the utilitarian criterion: what promotes the welfare of society? Moral conduct, in the view of these earlier utilitarians, is conduct in harmony with 'the natural order', 'the demands of reason', or 'divine intention'. It is, therefore, the task of moral philosophy 'to discover the will of God by studying the effects of human actions upon the general well-being of society'. By rejecting the theological sanction, later utilitarians create a gap in their reasoning between the empirical fact of pleasure and pain and the binding nature of morality. They then attempt to bridge the gap by a rather forced argument, viz., the doctrine of the universal harmony of interests.

This is not the place to discuss at length the philosophy of natural law. Historically, it goes back to the theological speculations of the Middle Ages and the reawakened interest in Roman legal sources and thus indirectly to Roman jurisprudence, and to Stoic, and to some extent Epicurean, philosophy. Ultimately, its ancestors are certain ideas in pre-Platonic thought which occasionally contains allusions to objective laws, held to be both necessary and rational, both natural and divine.

In the course of time the same idea took on a number of different forms and was used for different purposes. All kinds of social conditions have been justified as natural and rational. The rosiest radical utopias and the most diehard conservative apologias have been vindicated by the same type of argument. What unites these divergent views is not an identical political bias, but the philosophical method employed. The peculiarity of the philosophy of natural law is not that it attempts to *derive* moral laws from the natural order of things, an 'ought' from an 'is'. If this were the essence of the doctrine of natural law, almost every type of objective moral philosophy and, as we have seen, utilitarianism in particular, would be a natural law doctrine. Its peculiarity is rather its attempt to *identify* 'is' and 'ought', the actual and the obligatory, directly and without lengthy proofs; it simply equates reason and nature. Notions of the philosophy of natural law in this latter sense have markedly influenced the Physiocrats.

The physiocratic study of the *ordre naturel* has the merit of being the first attempt to grasp the economic order as a unified whole and to comprehend all its manifestations in a logically coherent system. It is the beginning of a general economic theory in the modern sense. The ancient philosophers occasionally pronounce opinions on economic questions. But their comments are incidental and often no more than commonplaces. There is more substance in the writings of some medieval schoolmen, above all Thomas Aquinas. But the doctrinaire approach of the scholastic social philosophers and their purely theological orientation prevent them from looking at economic events as causally interconnected and from studying them empirically. The Cameralists and Mercantilists make indeed empirical observations but they do not succeed in formulating a general theory.

Most of the physiocratic system has fallen into oblivion but some of its ideas have survived and crop up in modern discussions of economic problems. In the following we shall draw attention to the relationship between those ideas and the philosophy of natural law on which the doctrine of the Physiocrats is based.

First, then, there is the teleological nature of their theoretical speculations. As true representatives of their century, they were more interested in reforming the world than in describing and explaining it. They admitted that the 'natural' system (*ordre naturel*) which they postulated does not coincide with the existing system (*ordre positif*), but they claimed that the former contains the code of rules for economic policy which can be derived from the nature of things. These rules are supposed to be immediately evident in virtue of their rationality. Being 'natural', they are also 'real': they constitute the 'true' or the 'real' reality from which the accidental, actual reality is distinguished by its 'non-natural' component. Hence these rules are also immutable and universally valid.

Out of the concept of a 'natural order' and its identification of value and fact grew the doctrine of laissez-faire. It was supposed to become immediately apparent from a study of the nature of economic life: it was held to be at once a scientific 'law' and a political postulate. It followed from their premises that their maxims require no proof. The Physiocrats did little more than paraphrase their assumption; but this of course does not detract from the merit of their criticism of mercantilism.

It is interesting to note nevertheless that the Physiocrats, like their utilitarian successors, based their doctrine of free trade and laissez-faire ultimately on the assertion that men try to serve their own interests. Quesnay already gave this idea the hedonistic stamp which, later, became so important for economic theory: every man's behaviour is naturally directed towards securing a maximum of satisfaction or a minimum of sacrifice. He goes on to argue that the state should not interfere with the individual in his quest for happiness. The happiness of the community will be maximized by allowing each to exercise his will freely within the 'natural bounds' since the interests of different individuals were assumed to be in natural harmony. As long as no obstacles are created, everyone, by acting selfishly, promotes the happiness of all. Thus individual interests are harnessed to serve the interests of all. Mercier de la Rivière was the most eloquent exponent of this doctrine of the harmony of interests which was to play such an important part in economics.

The principle of laissez-faire is, of course, not confined to economic policy. The ideal state is held to be the state of justice (*Rechtsstaat*) and the art of government is the art of refraining as much as possible from governing. If there must be laws, let them be 'natural laws'. But on the whole, natural laws need not be enacted since they are also the laws of nature. This identification is peculiar to the philosophy of natural law. Let everything take its course, confine yourself to the protection of life, limb, and property, and the natural laws will be obeyed automatically. The conservative bias of the system of the Physiocrats stemmed from their acceptance of the prevailing distribution of property as, on the whole, 'natural'. But this bias was not essential to the natural law method. The Physiocrats differed from other contemporary or later Rousseauesque socialists and anarchists mainly by their interpretation of what constitutes a 'natural order', especially with respect to property.

The idea of a 'social contract', which plays such an important rôle in the philosophy of natural law, does not seem to have been of great importance to the Physiocrats. Occasionally, they even opposed it explicitly. Yet, a more searching analysis shows that it was one of their implicit assumptions. They opposed not so much the contract idea itself as the revolutionary implications emphasized by the Radicals. As we shall elaborate in Chapter 7, the idea of a social contract, either as a historical fact or as a fiction, has decisively influenced the theory of public finance. Thus the body of normative doctrines in the theory of taxation known as the principle of advantage, or benefit, or interest, is rooted in the eighteenth-century notion of a contractual relation between the citizens in the state. The utilitarians and modern value theorists only added a more erudite terminology and a more elaborate casuistry.

In spite of its normative bias the system of the Physiocrats represented a considerable advance in the development of positive economic theory. It might be asked why just the Physiocrats, amongst so many contemporary schools, should have become the founders of economic theory. It was probably because of their conservative views on the distribution of private property. The physiocratic system was scientifically more valuable than its contemporary radical rivals which were equally imbued with the philosophy of natural law, because its political implications were less revolutionary and because it was biased in favour of the prevailing social order. Like all their contemporaries, the Physiocrats tried to interpret the 'natural order' of human society. But they, unlike the more radical schools of thought, looked upon the existing order as a fairly close approximation to this ideal natural order. It only had to be freed from the mutilating fetters of government intervention. Their analysis thus applied to a social order which was relevant to existing economic conditions, i.e. the order which would exist if all 'interventions' were removed. Now luckily for the Physiocrats it so happened that their political ideal turned out to represent a theoretical abstraction which proved useful for dealing with problems of positive economics. At certain stages of our analysis we are bound to adopt this abstraction quite irrespective of our views about its political desirability. The radical utopian systems which grew from the same idea of natural law but which required more fundamental social changes to attain the 'natural order' have fared less well in the history of economic thought because their policy recommendations provide methodologically less suitable abstractions. Conservatism thus profited from its 'realism'.

Although the Physiocrats applied the notion, that economic relations were governed by laws, only to the natural order which they chose to study, they introduced it thereby for the first time into economic thinking. In the framework of the natural order events were viewed as causally connected. The interests of individuals gave direction and cohesion to economic life, just as the force of gravitation held the planetary system together, an analogy which was popular at the time. Probably inspired by the idea of the social contract, the Physiocrats represented the 'circular flow' of economic life as a series of exchanges between individuals and classes. Their analysis was rudimentary and in nearly all respects inadequate but they bequeathed to modern theory the basic idea that prices, costs, and incomes can be explained by a general analysis of the processes of exchange.

What is true of the Physiocrats has been true of other contributions throughout the history of economic thought. Economists have repeatedly attempted to prove certain systems as 'right' or 'correct'. All such attempts are doomed to failure. But the by-products of those attempts have often been scientifically useful and entirely independent of the objectives which they were meant to serve.

In the course of time the physiocratic analysis of 'natural' price formation became even more fruitful by being linked with the idea of equilibrium. The Physiocrats themselves had already touched upon the thought that there is an equilibrium position towards which actual conditions always tend to move. Adam Smith fairly consistently identified natural price and normal price. Later stages in the development of this doctrine were Walras's *equilibre général*, Marshall's theory of normal price, and J. B. Clark's theory of static and atomistic price formation as the virtual equilibrium of the process of actual price formation. The concept of equilibrium which was taken over from the natural sciences has proved to be a convenient tool for the elaboration of subtle and elegant theories, although it failed to deal adequately with time and in particular with inertia and expectations. It has always been full of normative implications of the natural law type. Its danger lies in allowing economists to slide too easily from positive theory into ethical and political speculation.

The Physiocrats and, through them, the philosophy of natural law thus gave an initial impetus to economic theory. Since Adam Smith, it has come under the strong, almost exclusive influence of Anglo-Saxon thought. Between Adam Smith and the general acceptance of the marginal utility theory, the main contributors were Ricardo, Malthus, James Mill, Senior, John Stuart Mill, and Cairnes. J. B. Say and other French economists since Adam Smith followed faithfully in his footsteps. The only exception was the ingenious Cournot, and he was entirely ignored by his contemporaries. When Jevons rescued Cournot's work from oblivion, he confined himself to Cournot's marginalism and neglected the facts that he had been the first to criticize value premises in economics and had based his analysis of price formation on empirical concepts, i.e. supply, demand, and price.

German writing of the first half of the nineteenth century was prolific but again it was so faithful to Adam Smith and his disciple J. B. Say that large portions were almost copies of the sources. There were, however, a few notable exceptions and some original theoretical contributions. But the promising first analytical efforts were nipped in the bud by the often justified criticism of the historical school. Since this school was critical not only of the classical theory but also of abstract analysis as such, it had hardly any direct influence on the further development of theory. But, as has often been stressed, the indirect effect of its criticism was much more important. Henceforth the main interest of German economists lay in very useful detailed historical and sociological descriptions. Of course, the literature also contains 'theory' of a sort. The writers could not refrain from drawing conclusions, from making generalizations, and from looking for explanations. But their theorizing was less valuable than their historical research. They generalized too hastily from inadequate statistical and historical data, they speculated from metaphysical premises and, for the rest, they enumerated and classified ceaselessly without always distinguishing between important and unimportant, or dependent and independent variables. They then often added some not very clearly thought out reflections on the sociological setting. In so far as one can discover any unifying point of view, it is the apotheosis of social power or of the 'organic' structure of society. Often one is reminded of Nietzsche's complaint in *Die fröhliche Wissenschaft* that mystical explanations often pass for profound, when in fact they are not even superficial.

Much more important for the development of economic theory was the reaction of the marginal utility theorists against the classics. Hardly any idea has been so fertile as the notion that price is determined at the margin. Together with the equilibrium concept, it forms the basis of modern price-formation theory. Equilibrium theory could not be developed properly until the discovery of marginal analysis. The marginal utility school should not, of course, be given all the credit for this discovery. The classical theory of rent had made use of the idea of the margin, which was then applied to ever-wider fields, and the later classicists were on the brink of formulating a general marginal theory of supply and production. But the marginal utility school treated the demand side analogously and thus made a coherent and systematic theory of price formation possible. Modern equilibrium analysis substituted inter-dependent functional relations for one-way causal connections.

The marginal analysis for which the ground had thus been pre-pared and which had been partly anticipated by earlier authors, started simultaneously in three places. There were Menger in Austria, Walras in Lausanne, and Jevons in England. Menger founded the Austrian school, Walras's disciples were Pareto, Fisher, Cassel, and others, and Jevons's theory developed under the more eclectic influence of Marshall and his British and American followers.

For our purposes the marginal utility theory can be looked upon as a product of British thought. The opposition of the marginalists to the British classics was not so fundamental as they themselves made out. The idea of the margin, though still vague, had been familiar to Bentham and other utilitarians. After all, the theory of marginal utility is nothing more than a refinement of psychological hedonism. And psychological hedonism dominated nineteenth-century British thought, was elaborated carefully, and incor-porated into academic associationist psychology (James Mill, Alexander Bain, and others).

For our problem it is of the greatest importance that modern economic theory had its origins in Britain. This explains its utilitarian and hedonistic stamp. Continental philosophy had a negligible influence upon the further development of economic theory. The only rather unfortunate exceptions were certain developments in the theory of public finance which were domina-ted by the concepts of state and duty.

As we have seen, the characteristic feature of utilitarian moral philosophy is its strong empirical bent, typical of British thought in general. Continental thinkers have always sensed more or less clearly the epistemological difficulty of basing ethics on experience. In Kant this scepticism towards experience found its maturest expression. The British, on the other hand, had for centuries directed their scepticism against reason as the source of ethics. They had been less critical of experience and still less of its use as a basis for ethics than for theoretical knowledge.

First, a few words about the earlier phases of British moral philosophy. One could go back to Francis Bacon, but his main interests lay in other directions and his writings did not give rise to any important ethical discussions. Hobbes was much more decisive for later developments. He had no very close relation to Bacon, but was strongly influenced by the Continental philosophy of natural law. Important for our problem is his ethical egoism based on his materialistic sensory psychology.

According to Hobbes, all psychological phenomena are the outcome of bodily conditions. All actions of an individual are naturally—and ought to be rationally—directed to promote his interests, to preserve his life, to increase his pleasant and to reduce his painful experiences. Hobbes's philosophical egoism was the foundation of his theory of the state and society and of his social ethics.

Hobbes displayed many rather un-English traits. Prone to paradox, occasionally bizarre, and ruthlessly logical, he did not fear logical challenges. But precisely because of his shocking extremism he became a powerful influence. The controversies which he provoked contributed to the gradual crystallization of the utilitarian doctrine. Later generations rejected, on the whole, his pure egoism, or at least softened its nasty implications by the assumption of interest harmony. But they retained his psychological foundation of ethics and his empirical method.

It would certainly be false to say that utilitarianism has ever completely dominated British moral philosophy. There have always been aprioristic intuitionists. In the seventeenth century Cudworth, to some extent Henry More, and other members of the Cambridge school protested against Hobbes and opposed empiricism with Platonic, neo-Platonic, and Cartesian ideas. Later Samuel Clarke followed in the same tradition, and others like Cumberland, Locke, Shaftesbury, Butler, Hutcheson, Hume, Adam Smith, etc., blended empirical and utilitarian with *a priori* arguments.

The peculiar assumption of a harmony of interests made this blend of empiricism and intuitionism logically acceptable. This construction, of which more will be said later, became particularly popular after Shaftesbury, Butler, and Hutcheson. Even the intuitionists had used often purely hedonistic arguments which they integrated into their systems by assuming a harmony of interests. It is therefore difficult to classify the doctrines according to the methods used. The question is rather *to what extent*, in any particular case, one method or the other is employed. The point is whether the maximization of happiness is considered to be a *result* of moral conduct or as the *ground* for its being right. Here, again, the various authors were neither consistent nor very clear.

Hume laid so much stress on the empirical component that it was no longer possible to blend and confuse it with the intuitional. Thus English moral philosophy was gradually split into two schools. A contradiction, originally latent, gave rise to opposed schools of thought. On the one hand there were the more aprioristic intuitionists Price, Reid, Stewart, Whewell, and others; on the other hand, Tucker, Priestley, Paley, and Bentham evolved a full-blooded utilitarianism. They were followed by James Mill, J. S. Mill, Sidgwick, and Edgeworth, and the exponents of associationist psychology, first systematized by James Mill on Hartley's foundations.

In the course of this development, there was little Continental influence on British moral philosophy. Hobbes, it is true, drew fairly heavily on the philosophy of natural law. Bentham was influenced by Helvetius and Beccaria, Whewell by Kant, and J. S. Mill, in his later life, by Comte. Coleridge, Carlyle, and other romantic, historical, and metaphysical writers had read and admired the Germans, but their impact on English moral philosophy was slight. By and large, the controversy remained insular. Later historians noted with surprise the small part played in it by Kantian arguments and post-Kantian epistemological discussions. This insularity made for a stronger cohesion of British moral philosophy than would otherwise have been possible, and this cohesion further strengthened the influence of philosophical thought upon other branches of learning. This fact is particularly important for our inquiry.

So much for the historical development of utilitarianism. Our next task is to clarify the ideas which determined the development of economic theory in its classical and neo-classical phases. We can ignore the intuitionists, for the decisive stimuli are exclusively utilitarian. We can also ignore most of the aprioristic ideas which occasionally turn up in the writings of utilitarians. They are lapses and inconsistencies. It is a very pure form of utilitarianism which has been incorporated in economic theory. Particularly significant is the utilitarianism presented by its purest exponents Paley and Bentham, and later by J. S. Mill, Sidgwick, and Edgeworth.

Our first task is thus to analyse the utilitarian ideas which inspired economic inquiry and, above all, their philosophical *method*. For economic theory adopted not so much particular moral or philosophical postulates of utilitarianism, as its method. The doctrines of economics themselves became the most consistent formulation and application of utilitarianism as a system of positive social ethics. They gave it concrete meaning and *content*.

We shall in the following analysis often stress aspects of utilitarian moral philosophy which differ from those usually emphasized in ethical discussions. Philosophical critics and historians of philosophy have tended to pay more attention to problems which are not always identical with those which will concern us.

The starting-point of utilitarianism is that conduct should be judged morally according to its results, or, more specifically, according to its effects upon the balance of general human happiness. This is reminiscent of the old idea of a *bonum communionis* as opposed to a *bonum suitatis*. The *bonum communionis* is interpreted by the utilitarians as an arithmetical sum of happiness of all individuals. This idea is related to the economic concept of 'national income' as the sum of subjective utilities.[3] We shall meet it time and again in one form or another. It is a popular utilitarian device for drawing political conclusions from theoretical analysis.

Let us suppose, for the sake of the argument, that the happiness of the individual is a definite psychological quantity. Let us further suppose that it is possible to add up individual quantities and that the maximization of this sum is the moral and political optimum. Has the concept of a sum of the happiness of *all* a clear meaning?

First it should be noted that with the development of utilitarianism there has been a continuous extension of the meaning of 'all individuals'. Not only the nation but humanity as a whole, not only the living but future generations were included.[4] But this problem need not concern us here because economists have usually stated explicitly whether they were concerned with the nation only or with humanity as a whole. On the other hand, they have tended to neglect the interests of unborn generations. 'Organic' philosophers have not failed to point out this omission.[5]

Much more interesting is another ambiguity in the concept.

Suppose we have decided upon a definite population, either a nation or humanity as a whole. But clearly for certain purposes the relevant size is still indeterminate. Consider the much-discussed problem of the optimum population.

The logical difficulty lies precisely in the utilitarian formula: the greatest happiness of the greatest number. This criterion for the political ideal has the mathematical peculiarity that it postulates the simultaneous maximization of two magnitudes which are not independent of each other. Strictly speaking, it is meaningless, as Sidgwick pointed out in another connection.

The nature of the interdependence of these two variables is analysed by Malthus in his law of population. He says that an increase in population beyond a critical point will reduce the level of happiness. The same proposition appears in Ricardo's theory of rent and more generally in the law of diminishing returns.

On the other hand, what matters according to the classical utilitarian solution is the sum total of happiness, irrespective of how many share in it. This solution corresponds to Bentham's method of taking the number of individuals as one 'dimension' or one 'element' of happiness in the calculus. Paley had already declared that a larger population with moderate average happiness is preferable to a smaller population with greater average happiness, if the sum total is greater in the first case. The same notion underlies the work of Malthus, although it is never explicitly stated. It appears perhaps most clearly when he repudiates the attempts of some of his supporters to use his theory as propaganda for contraception.

J. S. Mill defined the optimum population in a different manner. Although it is nowhere very clearly stated, it can be shown that his ideal is a population in which average happiness per head is maximized. This view, which is older than Mill, was later developed by Wicksell. In England it is attributed to Cannan. In America population problems and hence the theory of an optimum population were not much discussed until after the First World War. American writers then usually followed Mill.

The adherents of this doctrine tended to present it either as self-evident or at any rate as deeply rooted in Western thought. But this was a curious claim. It would exclude from Western tradition all the early utilitarians as well as Sidgwick and Edgeworth. For Sidgwick demonstrated that a rigorous analysis of the problem leads to a different conclusion. He defined maximum happiness and hence the political optimum as the mathematical product of the number of persons and their average happiness.[6] Edgeworth considered this to be one of the most important contemporary discoveries in the social sciences and developed it later in his *New and Old Methods of Ethics* and *Mathematical Psychics*.

In criticizing the claim of self-evidence for one definition of optimum population we do not want to plead for the other definition. Both are, of course, equally arbitrary. There is an infinite number of other possible ways of 'solving' the problem of double maximization. But one of them has to be chosen in order to make the solution determinate. Whatever solution is chosen, an *a priori* principle is implied and the empirical programme of utilitarianism is violated.

We are not here concerned with an examination of the population problem. But we may note in passing that while the older theory of the optimum population was associated with conservative political views, the later formulation (maximum average happiness) had a radical tinge. It was also used as an argument for birth control. But there is by no means a necessary connection between the latter definition and this particular political view. Thus if its proponents should, later on, faced with a falling birth rate, change their political views, the theory could equally well be used to advocate larger families. As a political doctrine it is entirely flexible since no one has yet succeeded in applying it to a concrete situation, and to show what the optimum population would be. Moreover, there is always the alternative definition of the optimum (viz. maximum total happiness). It is equally plausible and, according to it, optimum population must certainly be *larger* than on the first definition (maximum average happiness), however ignorant we are about its exact size. One might add that the theory of the optimum population, from John Stuart Mill on, is frequently associated, at least implicitly, with the idea of freedom and that it has thus become almost a part of economic liberalism. If everybody could be educated to act rationally, it was held, the optimum population would be brought about automatically; in particular, as soon as birth control propaganda had been successful in the lower income groups. This view has, however, remained a vague belief and a strict proof has never been attempted.

.   .   .   .   .

Our first conclusion is this: in order to transform the utilitarian maxim from a popular slogan into an unambiguous proposition which could be used by economic theory, the meaning of 'the sum of all' had to be clarified. Even at this preliminary clarification empirical ethics had to fall back on dubious 'first principles'.

In the following we shall assume, in order to avoid a wreckage of the whole system, that the meaning of 'the sum of all' has somehow been determined satisfactorily. We also leave open for the moment the question of the meaning of individual sums of psychic quantities. We shall examine only the logical operation by which individual quantities of happiness are added to a social sum which is to be maximized.

The principle on which the addition is carried out is, of course, that everyone counts for one and no one for more than one. This principle 'is involved in the very meaning of Utility, or the Greatest-Happiness Principle. That principle is a mere form of words without rational signification, unless one person's happiness, supposed equal in degree (with the proper allowance made for kind), is counted for exactly as much as another's.'[7] And '. . . equal amounts of happiness are equally desirable, whether felt by the same or by different persons. . . . If there is any anterior principle implied, it can be no other than this, that the truths of arithmetic are applicable to the valuation of happiness, as of all other measurable quantities.'[8]

This is a popular utilitarian line of thought. It can also be found, for instance, in the belief that an impartial observer, who views situations objectively, not letting himself be enticed to prefer one person's happiness to another's, would necessarily arrive at a utilitarian conclusion. But it would be a mistake to consider that this can provide a logical basis for utilitarianism. It already presupposes that quantities of happiness can be measured and compared and that the concept of a social sum of pleasures is logically possible. In point of fact, however, no one is a disinterested observer of the course of social events. We all have our political convictions. Only with those convictions can we ever arrive at concrete political conclusions. If we attempted to view social conditions 'impartially' by abstracting from our convictions, we would abandon the possibility of making moral or political decisions. Such decisions can only spring from an interested point of view. The 'disinterestedness' of the utilitarian observer must mean that a particular partial interest is implied from the beginning and is somehow endowed with objectivity and impartiality. Otherwise it could not lead to any conclusions. The whole idea of 'impartiality' in estimating social utility cannot be criticized in detail here because we have, for the sake of the argument, assumed that the concept of the 'sum total' and the notion of individual utilities as measurable quantities are meaningful and unambiguous. If we further suppose that it has been proved that 'society' is necessarily and unconditionally the subject of moral purpose, the egalitarian pooling of utilities follows from the logical procedures and the moral maxims which we have assumed to start with. 'Impartiality' would then be meaningful. But the assumptions are, as we shall see, not tenable.

The assumption of a summation of happiness implies that it is possible to define an objectively correct social distribution of happiness. Later utilitarians have stressed that the distribution of happiness must be distinguished from the distribution of the means to happiness, i.e. from the income and property distribution. But the second problem arises as soon as the first is solved. The correct distribution of happiness is, of course, that which maximizes the sum total of happiness. Hence an unequal distribution of happiness is better than an equal distribution, if it increases the sum total of happiness. The principle of equal distribution is therefore secondary to the principle of maximizing utility. The utilitarian equality is only a plea for the fair or equitable computation of social utility, so that every individual's happiness is given its correct weight. The fact that there are other interpretations of the principle of equality, or rather of equity, is never brought out. If utilitarians nevertheless recommend occasionally equal distribution of happiness and even of income and wealth, this is, as we shall see in Chapter 5, partly an inference from the law of diminishing utility and partly a relic of the natural law idea that all men are originally equal and hence equally capable of enjoying happiness.

Let us consider next the assumption of commensurable individual amounts of happiness. Utilitarians have maintained that this assumption can be empirically verified. In order to prove it, they have had recourse to a proposition which had been formulated by the ancient Greeks and had never been completely abandoned later: every conscientious and rational individual always acts in such a way as to minimize his pain and maximize his

E

pleasure. Pain and pleasure had then to be rendered comparable for the purposes of psychology and ethics, no matter how incommensurable they might be for other purposes. Hence the law can be formulated more simply and consistently in this way: individuals always try to maximize the net balance of pleasure. If it were otherwise, the utilitarian definition of optimal behaviour would be ambiguous, even intra-personally.[9] But the comparability of pain and pleasure must be possible not only *intra*-personally but also *inter*-personally.

'Happiness' is thus defined as the algebraic sum of positive pleasures and negative pains. This definition is the cornerstone of the whole system. Pleasures and pains are only different according to their (positive or negative) sign, and, according to Bentham's famous classification, which was never abandoned, according to 'intensity', 'duration', 'certainty or uncertainty', and 'propinquity or remoteness'.

The last four qualities were called the 'dimensions' or 'elements' of value in a pleasure or a pain. Then there was 'fecundity', i.e. its capacity to engender similar experiences, its 'purity', i.e. the absence of consequential experiences of the opposite kind, and finally its 'extent', i.e. the number of persons affected by it. Strictly speaking only this last case adds another 'dimension'.

The computation of the individual experiences into individual sums of happiness, and then into a total sum for society, is carried out by first adding the quantities in the various individual dimensions for each individual (with due regard to sign) and then adding up the results. It was, of course, realized that this method could not be directly applied to every practical problem. But this was due to lack of empirical data. The aim was to collect as many data as possible in order to come as near as possible to the ideal calculus. Utilitarians had no doubt that they were dealing with commensurable psychological quantities which could, in principle at least, be observed, in spite of any practical difficulties. Any doubt about this would have undermined their whole system.

Inquiries into the emotional aspects of mental activity which could be considered to be empirical psychology in any modern sense are very rare in utilitarian writings. Psychological interest was focused on the problems of the association of sensations and ideas into higher and more complex phenomena. This elaborate theory of association gave nineteenth-century British academic psychology its conceptualist and intellectualist stamp.

Hedonistic psychology became a logical premise of utilitarian moral philosophy and was incorporated into economic theory at an early stage. Later, the marginal utility theorists elaborated and refined the hedonistic principle much more consistently than professional psychologists had done before. Economic theory was conceived of as a calculus of pleasure and pain, and the subjective theory of value as the realization of this ideal. It represents the most complete development of the psychological basis of utilitarianism.

For a closer analysis of the utilitarian method we should now have to examine the neo-classical theory of value. This analysis will be postponed until Chapter 4, but we shall anticipate for our present purpose two of its conclusions.

First there is a growing tendency of the subjective theory of value to interpret the hedonistic principle tautologically. Since no empirical element is introduced into the argument, it revolves in circles. The hope to gain an empirical basis by such logical acrobatics is, of course, vain.

Second, in the course of a careful analysis of the hedonistic calculus, the marginalist school was forced to admit that comparisons of pleasure and pain, of happiness, utility, and value, even if possible for one and the same person, are impossible between persons. They are quantities *sui generis* and cannot be compared or added. On no other point is there the same unanimity amongst the writers of the marginalist school. Yet, they are not prepared to draw the conclusions from this true proposition.

The logical difficulty of computing individual quantities of happiness into a social sum is the key to the understanding of the utilitarian argument of the harmony of interests. This argument was most clearly stated by earlier authors, but modern economists also use it, although more often tacitly. If it were true that the interests of individuals are always and everywhere harmonious, so that everyone, by promoting his own interests, promotes automatically the interests of all, there would be no need for a social summation. It would not be required for the determination of social utility. The doctrine of the harmony of interests is an escape both from the necessity of calculating social utility and, consequently, from our criticism. However the computation is carried

out, maximum social welfare would be obtained simply by a complete realization of laissez-faire. After our discussion in the earlier
part of this chapter, it is not surprising that this conclusion is akin
to the ideas of the philosophy of natural law. And we must bear
this in mind when we attempt to account for the extraordinary
vitality of the liberal doctrine in economics.[10]

Utilitarian philosophers have therefore always had a strong bias
in favour of the assumption of social harmony, if only because of
their desire to avoid logical difficulties. Similarly, the doctrine of
free competition has gained support as a result of these logical
difficulties. They would have become more conspicuous had that
doctrine not occupied such a prominent place in the system. There
is still another reason for the assumption of harmony. It over-
comes an even more deeply rooted difficulty, by endowing morality with that objectivity which utilitarians presuppose. Its central
idea is that both actual and moral conduct can be explained in
terms of pleasure and pain. This is essentially an idea of the natural
law type; the natural is used to identify the factual and the ideal.
It would contradict the utilitarian premise to assume that somebody may have to act against his own interests in order to act
morally.

These two logical difficulties make the doctrine of harmony a
desirable, and indeed a necessary, utilitarian assumption. Various
attempts have been made to prove it. Occasionally the old sophis-
tical argument is used that individual interest, as the subordinate
concept, is included in the collective interest as the higher concept. By increasing one's own happiness one increases simultaneously the happiness of society as a whole, just as an increase in
a part simultaneously increases the whole. The possibility of conflicts of interest is simply ignored.

But this type of argument was too transparent and too silly to
have been accepted by British philosophers, renowned for their
common sense. Yet in a somewhat subtler form it has been more
persuasive. The argument runs roughly as follows. We live in
society and depend on each other's services. (We shall find the
same argument in Adam Smith's theory of the division of labour.)
These services are rendered most efficiently if we allow free play
to self-interest. Acquisitiveness is a force which Providence has
planted into our nature. Its fruits accrue to the benefit of all, if
only we let it move without hindrance. Whenever someone in-

creases his income, all benefit. For he can only succeed by offering to his fellows better and cheaper services than his rivals; hence consumption guides and directs production.

Thus the spontaneous harmony of enlightened self-interest seems to have been established. For the classical economists this argument had an almost religious character. Adam Smith gave it immortal expression in the words that the individual is 'led by an invisible hand to promote an end which was no part of his intention. . . .'

Mandeville, no doubt, was among the first to have exposed this fiction. In his *Fable of the Bees, or, Private Vices, Publick Benefits*, he destroyed the unqualified doctrine of harmony as far as British moral philosophy is concerned, although it survived in economics. The fable attempts to show that social welfare depends upon private vices, even though individuals may derive personal satisfaction from their virtues. The prosperity of a nation depends upon the acquisitive efforts of its citizens. But acquisitiveness has its roots in such immoral qualities as the desire for power, ambition, the love of luxury, etc.

The British, who are rather sensitive in matters of morals, were irritated by this paradoxical presentation. It was objected that the qualities which Mandeville brands as 'vices' are not really immoral as such. Nobody put this better than Adam Smith in his *Theory of Moral Sentiments*. Nevertheless, it was felt that we do value such virtues as generosity, self-sacrifice, compassion, justice, etc. These virtues are considered to be praiseworthy, quite apart from their relation to our interests. They must find a place in the utilitarian system if its objective validity is not to be endangered.

This led to a distinction between purely selfish interests and other-regarding or social interests (or later, with Comte, altruistic ones). Love of one's neighbours has always played a part in British moral philosophy. Bacon and Locke had already begun to construct a harmony doctrine on this basis, and also Cumberland and Clarke. Shaftesbury elaborated the idea and made it the centre of his philosophy. Butler, Hutcheson, Hume, and Adam Smith took it over, each with a somewhat different emphasis.

The main thesis was that there is no real contradiction between social instincts and self-interest. To achieve supreme happiness, one must suppress, to some extent, the directly egoistic impulses in favour of the altruistic. It was assumed with naïve optimism that the point at which egoistic impulses become harmful to society coincides with the point at which they become harmful to the individual.

Altruistic feelings thus turn out to be also egoistic, irrespective of whether self-interest is considered to be their motive or not. It is prudent to be considerate and to love one's neighbours. If we examine our interests conscientiously, we find that they coincide with the public interest. If they are enlightened, they will tend to maximize social welfare. Once again there is the same optimistic faith that society is governed by the harmonious interplay of individual interests which must be given free scope. The reality of 'evil' could not, of course, be denied. But it was believed that the wicked did wrong either because they could not see their own true interest, or because legal barriers prevented the free play of their natural goodness.

This type of argument appealed to the English. Well versed in the classical literature, they could draw perhaps somewhat far-fetched analogies with Platonic and Socratic rationalism and with the Stoic doctrine of virtue. Religion was an even better ally. Christianity, like other religions, did not scorn utilitarian support. The Sermon on the Mount uses idealized utilitarian arguments. The threat of eternal punishment and the prospect of reward after death for good conduct make it a matter of self-interest to be good.

Although probably influenced by religious beliefs, British philosophers usually tried to prove their propositions without recourse to revelation or eternal retribution. The religious sanction was certainly of help; it provided a strong interest in doing good works. But it was also dangerous. Since the sanction was not empirically verifiable, moral conduct could not be determined scientifically. Any set of moral rules could, after all, be made irrefutable on utilitarian grounds by adding to them the religious sanction. Utilitarians tried to get round this difficulty by proposing a purely empirical, i.e. psychological, verification and trusted that the result would have the religious sanction. They thought that associationist psychology provided the empirical basis. When somebody has noticed repeatedly that his altruistic actions are advantageous to himself, he will tend to endow them with some value in their own right. Tradition, convention, and education will reinforce this tendency. Moreover, social convention strengthens the social impulses in a more direct manner. People obviously want others to behave virtuously towards them. Hence altruistic actions find approval in the eyes of one's fellow beings, which in itself is a source of pleasure and happiness to the agent. A certain amount of satisfaction is also derived from doing a good deed and avoiding the pains of conscience that follow wrong-doing.

The peculiarly utilitarian feature of these arguments was the attempt to establish the doctrine of harmony psychologically. At the same time, this attempt was dangerous, for it emphasized the distinction between egoistic and altruistic motives, thus threatening to contradict the psychological premises of utilitarianism.

The concept of altruism became the rock on which the utilitarian philosophy was wrecked. As soon as altruism was introduced into the discussion, one was tempted to see the criterion of moral conduct in the good will or in the virtuous feeling which prompts the good will. Utilitarianism was thus abandoned; for it stands and falls by the thesis that an action is good in virtue of its consequences, and not in virtue of the will which motivates it. But now the will was considered to be good because it springs from a moral feeling which in turn was explained, for example, in terms of sympathy for the good and ill that befalls others. It does not help if one adds that moral conduct will promote the general good. The result is no longer the criterion. Such moral optimism is not peculiar to utilitarianism. It is part of the general attitude to life of all well-meaning people. What characterizes utilitarianism is not this general belief in the social usefulness of morality, but the conviction that there is a particular method by which moral conduct can be deduced objectively from social utility.

The internal contradiction does not appear until the harmony of interests is questioned. Once again the desire for logical consistency tends to strengthen the doctrine of harmony. Given the assumption of harmony, the good will can also be defined as the will for the good of one's fellows, and it is still possible to combine both criteria of morality in the utilitarian framework: *ex hypothesi*, they cannot conflict with each other. This elucidates Hutcheson's otherwise curious distinction between material and formal goodness; materially, an action is good if it tends to increase general happiness, formally it is good if it springs from a good will. But as soon as any doubts arise about the harmony of interests—and convincing proof has never been advanced—the foundation of the utilitarian attempt to build a system of social ethics upon the fact of enlightened self-interest is shaken.

It is not surprising, therefore, that an opposition to the utilitarian moral philosophy arose in England and even more in Scotland. Where the break was incomplete, internal inconsistencies in the writings of individual authors bear witness to the same tendency. Much has been said about the lack of correspondence between Adam Smith's economics and his moral philosophy in his *Theory of Moral Sentiments*. German philosophers have even promoted him to a forerunner of Kant.

On the other hand, the same split gave rise to a younger and purer version of utilitarianism. As one would expect, the later utilitarians were particularly keen to prove the harmony of interests in order to preserve the objectivity of their criterion of morality. The theological utilitarians took refuge in a theological sanction which, as we have seen, though always open, is not without danger to the system. Although Bentham mentioned the theological sanction amongst others, he did not make much of it and after him it lost all importance. Yet, he did not provide a satisfactory substitute.

It is not easy to establish precisely Bentham's views on the doctrine of harmony. He held, in principle, that man could not be asked to strive for anything but his own happiness. At the same time his political aim was 'the greatest happiness of the greatest number'. It was then up to the utilitarian reformers to set sufficiently strong political, educational, legal, and religious sanctions to compel individuals to seek the general happiness.

In his attempt to create such sanctions, the social reformer must be guided by his concern for the public interest. But this makes sense only if a general harmony of interests is already presupposed. Only then can it be squared with Bentham's proposition that there are not different social valuations but only different degrees of insight. Bentham never stressed specifically the natural harmony of interests either in his doctrine of legislation or in his economics; but it is emphasized in his posthumously published *Deontology* which was compiled from manuscripts and edited by one of his pupils. There he said that 'vice may be defined as a miscalculation of chances'. If we assume that Bentham was consistent, the only purpose of the reformer's sanctions can be to *strengthen* an already existing private interest in moral action. Such reinforcement is certainly necessary since Bentham believed that people are both weak and ignorant. He did not seem to attempt an adequate proof of the doctrine of harmony. It is, however, not unfair to consider it as one of his premises and, moreover, as one of those despised 'higher principles'.

It should be added that only the crudest version of utilitarianism was incorporated in economic theory. Altruism has, on the whole, been dropped and the harmony of interests has become the central notion. It is conceived in terms of 'purely egoistic' and 'purely economic' interests and repeatedly throughout the nineteenth century economists tried to prove it, sometimes along new lines and surrounded by new qualifications.

The utilitarians were vexed by the problem of how different 'kinds' of wants should be treated in their computations. Tnis is, of course, an old problem and part of the eternal controversy between ethics and economics. It will be debated as long as economists pronounce on what is 'correct', i.e. as long as economics contains tacit moral precepts. Since Carlyle and Ruskin moralists and moral philosophers have attacked economics as 'amoral'. They did not see that the only justification for their attack on economics is that it is full of ethical implications, i.e. that it is *not* 'amoral'.

The utilitarian position in this question is quite clear. It follows from its premise of a homogeneous sum of utility that every valuation must enter into the calculation as a definite quantity. Already the early utilitarians had expressed, often quite drastically, the identity in kind and the mathematical commensurability of all wants. Thus Abraham Tucker held that satisfactions vary in degree but never in kind, whether we prefer to listen to good music, to look at something beautiful, to eat good food, to act virtuously or to get satisfaction from thinking. Bentham coined the famous phrase 'quantity of pleasure being equal push-pin is as good as poetry'. According to psychological ethics, there are no 'bad' motives. The only motive is the desire for happiness.

Yet, the idea that there are lower and higher pleasures is so old and deep-rooted and has enjoyed religious sanction for so long that the arithmetical method was accepted only after long arguments and with certain reservations. These reservations arose in the course of the discussion of the rôle of altruism. The question of differences in kind of different wants has alienated many potential followers from utilitarianism. This is not surprising since it is the standard objection to Epicurean philosophy.

It is interesting to see how J. S. Mill tries to get over this diffi-culty. His argument is fairly typical of utilitarian mentality. To begin with, he sides with the Epicureans, but with a slight reser-vation. He says that Epicureans had always valued the 'pleasures of the intellect, of the feelings and imagination, and of the moral sentiments' more highly than the pleasures 'of mere sensation'. But they had 'placed the superiority of mental over bodily pleasures chiefly in the greater permanency, safety, uncostliness, etc., of the former'. Mill agrees but adds that they had forgotten an important argument, which he calls 'the higher ground'.[11]

He goes on to argue that if all or almost all people prefer one of two pleasures, both of which they have experienced and have the capacity to experience, irrespective of any feeling of moral obliga-tion to prefer it, then this is the more desirable pleasure. Now it 'is an unquestionable fact that those who are equally acquainted with' both mental and bodily pleasures generally prefer the former.[12] He admits that temptation and habit may lead to divergencies from the 'correct' valuation,[13] two factors which we shall find again as 'distortions' in marginal utility theory.

Without further proof both factors are dismissed as unim-portant. If somebody who has experienced 'higher' pleasures should nevertheless happen to prefer 'lower' ones consistently, then, says Mill, this person must have lost his capacity to enjoy the former. He compares the capacity to enjoy nobler feelings with a 'very tender plant, easily killed, not only by hostile in-fluences, but by mere want of sustenance'.[14] The upshot of the discussion is that the utilitarian calculus must rely upon the judge-ment of those who are qualified by a knowledge of types of pleasure or, if they differ, upon the judgement of the majority (sic) among them.[15] Thus Mill tries to prove inductively and with a dubious appeal to democratic procedure that qualitatively 'higher' pleasures are also quantitatively greater. This must be the mean-ing of Mill's argument if it is to make sense, although his exposition is not altogether clear. Morality is again deduced from true self-interest. Mill sacrifices his intelligent doubts to the exigencies of his method. As Sidgwick pointed out, 'the distinctions of *quality* that Mill and others urge may still be admitted as grounds of preference, but only in so far as they can be resolved into distinctions of quantity'.[16]

We now come to the last and most serious difficulty. Let us suppose that the impossible is possible; that quantities of utility exist, that they can be computed and added to a social sum. The question then is: Why define the good will as that which aims at maximizing the amount of social utility? Why is this supposed to be the political optimum?

Neither Bentham nor Paley nor any of the other early utilitarians were much concerned with this question. The objectivity of utilitarian morality seemed to them obvious. They simply postulated a common psychological origin of actual and moral conduct. But this identity of 'is' and 'ought' rests, of course, on an *a priori* proposition. Empirical proof had to be abandoned exactly when it became of crucial importance.

J. S. Mill, with a keener eye for the epistemological difficulties, was more cautious. He remarked somewhere that 'questions of ultimate ends do not admit of proof, in the ordinary acceptation of the term'. This did not prevent him from speaking in other places like all other utilitarians of proofs in the ordinary sense, from calling utilitarian ethics a 'science', or from defending its objectivity against all other brands of philosophy.

It will be remembered that Mill argued that the only proof that anything is desirable is that people do actually desire it. Happiness is desirable because everyone desires it. If the happiness of each is desirable to him, the general happiness is desirable to all.[17]

Sidgwick criticized Mill on this point. He argued that 'there seems to be no *necessary* connexion between [Mill's] proposition and any ethical theory: but in so far as there is a natural tendency to pass from psychological to ethical Hedonism, the transition must be—at least primarily—to the egoistic phase of the latter. For clearly, from the fact (if it is a fact) that everyone actually does seek his own happiness we cannot conclude, as an immediate and obvious inference, that he ought to seek the happiness of other people.'[18] The whole doctrine of harmony is implied in this logical transition.

Sidgwick's own derivation of utilitarian ethics was much more cautious. He was clearly aware that an *a priori* postulate was required. He discovered a link between utilitarianism and intuitionism in the fact that utilitarianism is, in the last resort, based

on the principle 'which if known at all must be intuitively known
—that happiness is the only rational ultimate end of actions'.[19]
He tried to support this *a priori* principle with the claim that only
thus can we frame 'a coherent account of Ultimate Good' and
then, as a last resort, asked the question: 'If we are not to systematize human activities by taking Universal Happiness as their
common end, on what other principle are we to systematize
them?'[20]

This argument is convincing only if we suppose with Sidgwick
that such an ultimate moral principle of universal validity actually
exists, a principle which binds 'the unconnected and occasionally
conflicting principles of common moral reasoning into a complete
and harmonious system'.[21] Sidgwick's argument presupposes that
men's moral ideas can be systematized logically under one single
principle of synthesis and then be deduced from it. He assumed
that our moral ideas are logically consistent and that they can be
discovered by moral reasoning, although lack of reasoning power
may, of course, obscure matters.[22] Had Sidgwick been as sceptical
in this respect as he was in others, this road of deriving utilitarian
ethics would also have been closed to him.

What Sidgwick stated explicitly has, no doubt, been an implicit
assumption all the time. The utilitarian principle lent consistency
and objectivity to the countless and apparently conflicting moral
obligations. Bentham had argued against the school of natural law
that even they, if pressed, had recourse to utilitarian arguments.
J. S. Mill tells us in his *Autobiography* how, like a revelation, the
Benthamite principle gave unity to his conception of things, and
how it made his philosophy of life objective and systematic. 'The
"principle of utility" understood as Bentham understood it, . . . fell
exactly into its place as the key stone which held together the
detached and fragmentary component parts of my knowledge and
beliefs.'[23] This, of course, is the common aim of all moral
philosophers, however much they may otherwise differ: to discover
a deductive proof for all moral valuations.

We have traced the general outline of the arguments of utilitarian philosophy. They recur time and again in the development
of economic doctrines. The terminology changes, special assumptions are introduced for the treatment of special problems, but
there is always the same notion of measurable individual amounts

of utility which are later openly called 'values'. There is always the attempt to add up these subjective amounts of value into a social sum which is to be maximized. Usually, there is also the assumption of a social harmony of interests.

In this rough sketch of the ideological background we have tried to summarize certain criticisms of utilitarianism. In the following chapters we shall elaborate these arguments with reference to the relevant economic theorems.

Something remains to be said about the constructive contribution of the utilitarian method to economic theory. Frequently theories which turned out to be logically untenable have yet had historically a positive value, because they prepared the ground for genuine scientific progress. It is probable that the ideas of the interdependence of economic phenomena, of a virtual equilibrium, and of the rôle of the margin in price formation would not have been formulated so soon, had it not been for the illusion that economic inquiry can yield prescriptions for reform as well as descriptions of reality, and had it not been for the highly abstract fictions of utility and disutility curves, which only superficially seem to make the problem more concrete. The normative bias gave emotional drive to research. Hedonistic psychology, over-simplifying the issues, glossed over the countless complicating psychological factors and focused analysis on the ideas of the margin and of functional interdependence. Thus certain fallacies had possibly in their day a beneficial effect upon the development of scientific thought, though obviously only in fields where they were less relevant. This is, of course, no reason to refrain from criticizing these errors to-day. No historical justification makes the task of removing errors less important. There is no point in retaining the scaffolding after the house is built. We are in the fortunate position of being able to retain the best and reject all that is deficient in the work of our ancestors.

In order to appraise properly the significance of English utilitarianism for economic theory, we must also be grateful for the things it has spared us. Its predominance scotched the influence of other contemporary social philosophies. From this point of view, too, economic theory did well to come under utilitarian influence. A probable rival would have been the then current German social philosophy: romantic, organic, absolutist and yet no less imbued with notions of natural law. We believe that the individualistic utilitarian approach made possible a truer analysis of society than the mutually conflicting theories of the German political metaphysicians.

Utilitarians are never tempted to speculate too wildly about the essence of the state. It is for them simply the sum of its members and can therefore be neither absolute reason, nor an organism, nor a 'superorganism'. By defining social utility as the sum of individual utilities, they make it more difficult to fall into the trap of endowing a super-individual personification with a general will or a 'folk soul'. Since they base moral conduct on psychological data, they have no room for such 'duties towards the state' as the duty to pay taxes. In other theories this duty appears as an *a priori* category which is supposed to originate directly in membership of the state. For the same reason utilitarians are immune against other legal fictions. Legal institutions are for them primarily facts. When they justify them, they do not deduce them from *a priori* principles but try to show that they are useful.

One can get a certain idea of the horrors from which utilitarainism has preserved economic theory by looking at economic writings such as those of O. Spann, which sprang from German political philosophy. Even a scientifically respectable publication like Schanz's *Finanzarchiv* contains articles which might serve as warnings. Time and again economic problems are discussed on purely *a priori* legalistic and metaphysical grounds.

Yet, liberal utilitarian atomism and the more heterogeneous organic or legalistic German philosophy of the state are at heart akin. Both use in some form or other an objective political concept with respect to society as a whole, whether it be 'social welfare' or 'the will of the state', etc. This is their common metaphysical element. For the former it is only a mathematical sum, whereas for the latter it is a whole which is more than the sum of its parts. It depends upon the point of view and the point at issue whether the similarities or the differences of the two philosophies stand out.

If we stress the similarities, it appears that the utilitarian writers also tend to be forced into an untenable 'communistic fiction' about the unity of society. A typical example is the theory of economic liberalism. A dangerously ambiguous terminology facilitates the conceptual confusion. The theory of 'wealth' or 'welfare' or '*Volkswirtschaft*' becomes a theory of how a nation, guided by a common purpose, runs or ought to run its economic affairs. We shall discuss this problem in greater detail later. We mention it here in order to suggest that as soon as attempts are made to draw political conclusions, the individualistic philosophy leads to an abstract social fiction. Superficially, this may seem odd, but it is an inexorable consequence of the premise and the logic of utilitarian thought.

Chapter 3

THE CLASSICAL THEORY OF VALUE

Iɴ the Aristotelian system economics is a subdivision of politics, which again is a part of ethics or practical philosophy. Economics is distinguished from other branches of political science (a distinction which was not drawn sharply before the Physiocrats) not so much by its object of inquiry. Like politics, it is the study of social activity. The peculiar feature of economics is rather its method which is best brought out by its central concept. In the same way as the concept of 'right' and its correlative 'duty' have always occupied a central position in jurisprudence and theories of the state, the concept of 'value' has been of crucial importance in economics. The development of these two concepts shows interesting parallels.

These two concepts, and with them the two branches of knowledge, have been, throughout the history of thought, associated in a number of different ways. The differences depended upon the varying emphasis laid on each of the two concepts. In contrast to the Greeks, the Romans with their highly developed legal system neglected the concept of value and with it the economic method of treating social problems. The Schoolmen again showed more interest in economic problems. One might look upon the doctrines of the medieval church fathers and, later, the teachers of natural law, as attempts to combine the concepts of 'right' and of 'value' by deriving both from the same ultimate principles. The utilitarians continued this trend. Since Bentham, at any rate, the objective has been to subordinate 'right' and 'duty' to 'value'. This is the meaning of the principle that social utility should determine rights and duties.

Economics thus came to occupy a key position in the social sciences. It became its task to discover what was 'socially useful'. But economists had adopted the concept of 'law' from the philosophy of natural law. As long as 'natural law' concealed the peculiar ambiguity of the word 'natural', the same doctrine could contain both scientific descriptions and political prescriptions. But as a result of the empirical tendencies of utilitarianism and perhaps even more under the influence of the rapidly developing natural sciences, the concept of the law of nature came to mean more specifically scientific, empirical law. This was the beginning of the conflict between 'value' and 'law' in economics.

From the point of view of its ideological origins, political economy is a grandiose attempt to state in scientific terms what ought to be. Even to-day it is often said that it is the function of economics to discover how social welfare can be maximized. The concept of 'value' betrays the normative character of economics and it is the instrument for discovering the social 'ought'.

It is the tragedy of economic inquiry that the further we have advanced in our attempts to observe and explain social phenomena, the further away have we moved from our aim of defining the conditions for the maximization of social utility. As value theory has been developed and refined, it has become increasingly formal, empty, and tautological. To-day economists are beginning to abandon the attempt to determine welfare scientifically. They are gradually accepting the idea that 'value' had best be used in an ethically and politically neutral sense, denoting actual exchange relationships, or demand and supply prices, i.e. the prices which individuals in certain specified conditions are prepared to accept or to pay for goods and services.

Yet, this is not just an admission of defeat. While aiming at a fictitious goal, economists have developed a science of causal relations. Since Adam Smith and the Physiocrats, and in some fields even earlier, they have formulated in many instances correct propositions about actual events and their causal connections. Empirical findings have gradually accumulated and, while pursuing an impossible aim, economists have produced, almost incidentally, a body of scientific knowledge.

There has been general agreement on the fact that the concept of economic value indicates the normative ambition of economics. One may be tempted to smile at J. S. Mill's belief that all problems of value theory were settled for all time to come and that there was nothing about it that called for further explanation either by himself or another writer. But one should remember that he added: 'Almost every speculation respecting the economical interests of a society thus constituted [i.e. founded upon division of labour and exchange] implies some theory of Value: the smallest error on that subject infects with corresponding error all our other conclusions; and anything vague or misty in our conception of it creates confusion and uncertainty in everything else'.[1] As social philosopher and social reformer Mill had to believe in the absolute validity of his value theory, or he would have had to disown all he stood for. v. Wieser, more than any other neo-classical author, tried to provide a philosophical basis for his theory of value. He said: 'As a man's judgement about value, so, in the last resort, must be his judgement about economics. Value is the essence of things in economics. Its laws are to political economy what the law of gravity is to mechanics. Every great system of political economy, up till now, has formulated its own peculiar view of value as the ultimate foundation in theory of its applications to practical life; no new effort at reform can have laid an adequate foundation for these applications if it cannot support them on a new and more perfect theory of value.'[2]

Let us finally quote one of the most outstanding critics of the neo-classical theory of value. Cassel saw the main reason for the preoccupation of political economy with the theory of value in the fact that 'men urgently want to know more than what prices *are* actually paid . . . they want to know what prices *should* be paid, what is the *right* reward of the different services; in other words, they want to know the *value* of the different commodities and productive services'.[3]

Anybody who rejects value theory exposes himself to the criticism that he renounces the possibility of *judging* economic life, that he shears away the moral foundation of economics.[4] The unanimous agreement on the function of value theory in economics provides a good starting-point for a critical examination.

As we have seen, theories of economic value have existed long before the classical economists. We shall not discuss them in detail but a few words may be said about some of the traditional views that were handed down to the classics.

One meaning of the term 'economic value' referred to the amount of other goods against which a unit of one good could be exchanged. From the earliest days 'value' had been used in this empirical sense as something observable, as value in *exchange*. But 'value' has always also stood for something very different.

Exchange value seemed to be too fluctuating, too ephemeral, too arbitrary. The idea of a *normal* value arose. It is, of course, possible to derive it from observable value-in-exchange. Normal value can be defined either as some kind of average of exchange values at different times and places, or as that exchange value which would prevail in the absence of certain specified disturbances. These two definitions can be combined into one by the theory that, in the long run, normal value in the first sense is independent of random disturbances. These are still perfectly unobjectionable definitions of normal value. As long as we do not read something metaphysical into them, we are just dealing with averages of actual exchange values or with exchange values which would, hypothetically, prevail in certain specified conditions. But this is not the way people looked at the matter. There has always been a tendency to endow the real world with animistic properties and even to-day we are tempted to give quite a different meaning to the 'normal'.

We tend to look behind observable exchange ratios for some 'inherent' quality, something more real, of which exchange value is merely a reflection. We look for some criterion for the correctness or justice of actual exchange ratios. The notion of such an 'intrinsic value' appears in different formulations but they all aim at something other than exchange value, something universal and eternal which could provide a 'natural' starting-point, both for the explanation and the ethical evaluation of exchange value. Aristotle already had searched for such a universal standard to measure 'real' value as distinct from actual exchange ratios.

In earlier times, value was occasionally conceived as some intrinsic quality of commodities, a kind of force or even an immaterial substance. But when the writers attempted to explain the connection between this inherent quality and exchange value, they paid little attention to the naïve theory of force or substance. Nevertheless, this theory has remained latent and continues to influence arguments as a tacit assumption.

Others associate the idea of value in some way with 'human nature' by basing it on man's condition in society and on society's organized struggle against nature's niggardliness. There are two approaches: Some derive value from an abstract *usefulness* of objects or from man's estimation of their usefulness (value-in-use).

A commodity has economic value to the extent to which it is useful, or is held to be useful. Others again emphasize the *costs* (usually labour costs) incurred in producing the good. Costs, like utility, can be interpreted more or less psychologically. If the psychological aspect is stressed, value stands for the sweat and toil, the sacrifice and pain that have gone into the production of a commodity. Less psychologically, value is the labour which has, as it were, become part of the object, so that the commodities contain the labour which has produced them.

All these ideas of value can be found in various combinations and also together with other theories. They all are usually identified with the 'just' or 'right' price, the *justum pretium*. It is then a matter of political philosophy whether or not the *justum pretium* is believed to be manifested in the actually ruling or in the normal exchange ratios.

All these attempts to discover a deeper meaning of value behind actual exchange ratios are inspired by the quest for economic norms. Whether utility or costs are believed to determine value, what matters ultimately is a value which is the same for all, a *social* value. Strictly speaking, this is necessary in order to be able to identify value with *justum pretium*, which must be something objective and universal. *Justum pretium* itself is a social value. Social value is the valuation of 'society' and it must therefore express the utility or the sacrifice to society as a whole. In order to maintain this fiction, it is possible either to assume that all men are identical with respect to utility and labour costs; or one can work with average utility or average sacrifice which can be attached to the 'economic man' who is defined as an average or 'normal' individual. Alternatively, it is sometimes assumed that society, like an individual, sets its own valuations. Society is then conceived as an organism or a person which chooses, enjoys, sacrifices, works, etc. This organic view of society may be stated explicitly or it may be concealed behind references to the 'natural'.

These, roughly, are the most important notions of the 'natural', 'real', 'absolute', 'intrinsic', 'inherent', etc., value which were handed down to classical and neo-classical value theory. They all reappear in different combinations and with different emphases, except the primitive theory of force or substance.

·　　　·　　　·　　　·　　　·

Classical value theory consists, as it were, of two layers. The outer and visible layer is a theory of exchange value, and beneath there is a theory of real value.

Adam Smith distinguishes between value in use and value in exchange, but only in order to dismiss the former from the discussion, which he then confines to value in exchange. Ricardo and most of his followers adopt a similar line. But there are other authors who pay more attention to value in use, amongst them Say and the French writers, some Germans like Rau and Knies, to some extent Malthus, MacLeod, and certain other British writers outside the main classical tradition. For the classical writers utility is a necessary condition of the existence of exchange value, but the amount of exchange value is determined by quite different factors. Their real value theory, which is intended to explain exchange value, is a cost theory.

They introduce the theory of real value, however, somewhat surreptitiously. Both Adam Smith and Ricardo define value in the first place as exchange value. In the course of the explanation of exchange value, they smuggle in the theory of real value without a thorough discussion of its nature. Indeed, some people have studied the classics without noticing anything of their real value theory at all. But their peculiar theory of exchange value can only be understood in relation to their theory of real value. The latter has determined in important respects their exchange value theory and also their practical conclusions.

The logical procedure now would be to begin with a discussion of the theory of real value as the basis, and then to go on to the theory of exchange value, which is built upon this basis. But just because real value theory is incomplete and partly implicit can it not be stated fully until certain aspects of the theory of exchange value have been elucidated. This we shall now do. We shall be concerned primarily with Ricardo, partly because his presentation is more consistent than Adam Smith's or Malthus's, partly because his influence on later writers was greater.

The main thesis of the theory of exchange value is the proposition that goods are exchanged in ratios which correspond to the amount of labour-time expended on them. Exchange value is determined by labour costs, where costs mean labour expended, not wages paid to workers. The part played by labour is stated in various ways: Labour costs 'determine', 'regulate', 'cause', 'measure', 'indicate', exchange value, they are its 'source', or 'origin'. The idea is simply that a good which requires twice as much labour as another, should cost twice as much in a normal exchange transaction.

We shall now briefly enumerate the unrealistic assumptions which are required if this theory is to hold. Ricardo's genius is revealed in the precision with which he states these assumptions.

In the first place Ricardo must assume that there is only one homogeneous factor of production. Yet, he, like Adam Smith and many others, assumes three factors, labour, capital, and land. This division, which was to play such an important part in economics, was, of course, merely a simplified model of the contemporary social stratification. But it is incompatible with the labour cost theory. Ricardo therefore has recourse to additional unrealistic assumptions in order to maintain the assumption of homogeneity.

To begin with, *labour* itself must be assumed to be completely homogeneous. If there are differences, they must be capable of being reduced to quantitative differences. There must be an independently given scale of values by which different types of labour can be made commensurable. This whole aspect of price formation is left unexplained. Where he deals with the different kinds of labour in the first chapter of his *Principles*, he says little more than that supply and demand determine their exchange values—a commonplace which explains nothing. It is, after all, one of the merits of the classical economists to have seen that one had to go behind this phrase of supply and demand and had to discover the causes which determine them. At the same time Ricardo contends, without giving reasons, that the scale of relative values by which different types of labour can be compared does not change through time, i.e. that it is itself independent of price formation.[5]

Next, *capital* must be assumed to play no part in determining exchange values. It will be remembered that Ricardo has therefore to assume fixed proportions of capital and labour in all branches of production. This assumption is criticized, above all by Malthus.[6] Ricardo admits frankly its weakness, but cannot abandon it without wrecking his whole theory.[7]

Land, finally, has to be excluded from the theory of exchange value and relegated to a special theory of the price of land, viz., the theory of rent. To the assumption of homogeneous labour corresponds, in the theory of rent, the assumption that soil is only used for the production of a single product, corn. Land and rent are excluded from the theory of costs and exchange value by the assumption that the exchange value of corn is determined at the margin of cultivation where no rent is paid.

These obviously unrealistic assumptions are motivated by the desire to explain exchange value in terms of labour cost. But although the labour cost theory dominates the manner in which the whole problem is stated and involves a quite arbitrary model, its application is strictly limited. It is used directly only to explain the exchange values of commodities and, moreover, not of all, but only of reproducible commodities.[8]

Ricardo considers that the primary task of political economy is to explain the prices of the three productive factors, labour, capital, and land, and thus the distribution of income. Yet his theory of costs is entirely irrelevant to this problem, for it merely states that the prices of goods are determined by their physical production costs in terms of labour. The theory of production costs plays a purely negative part in his treatment of income distribution. It forces him to certain highly artificial devices which would otherwise be unnecessary. Had he treated the problem of income distribution in the same way as the other problems which were not amenable to his labour cost theory, i.e. had he just referred to the law of supply and demand and left it at that, his whole theory could be rejected, not just as an oversimplification, but as empty and meaningless. For all he says about the value of produced goods is that *if* we assume a homogeneous factor (labour), such goods will be exchanged in the ratio of the required amounts of labour. This does not get us very far.

But in his theory of distribution Ricardo does not simply refer to the law of supply and demand. In spite of the fetters imposed by his theory of labour costs, his ingenious power of reasoning breaks through to an analysis of the causes of demand and supply of productive factors and hence of the forces which determine distribution. He makes use of the rudimentary analysis of Adam Smith's theory of 'natural price' (= wages + profit + rent), and Malthus's theory of rent and population. In Ricardo's detailed analysis of distribution, which remains his greatest achievement, his theory of costs is quite unimportant and appears only occasionally as an irritating intrusion.

This is not the place to discuss Ricardo's theory of distribution.

He analyses the functional interdependence between quantities and relative prices of the three productive factors. The determining causes are the amount of land available, its position and fertility, the existing stock of capital,[9] the number of workers,[10] and the state of technological knowledge. From a modern point of view only demand is missing. Consumers' demand, too, determines factor prices indirectly. But this would obviously play a smaller part if one assumes with Ricardo only three homogeneous factors of production, two of which, moreover, labour and capital, have to be combined in fixed proportions. Thus shifts in demand from one of these two to the other are *ex hypothesi* excluded. The neglect of demand as one of the forces which determine distribution illustrates again the manner in which Ricardo is hampered in his distribution theory by his cost principle. But apart from this deficiency, he succeeds in clarifying the relationship between wages, profit and rent, and in his oversimplified analysis of long-period changes he is able to construct a theory of economic development.

An examination of Ricardo's theory raises the question, Why does he commit himself to the proposition that the exchange ratios of commodities are determined by their labour costs? As we have seen, Ricardo is forced to his fantastic premises by this proposition. He must have been aware that they are wildly unrealistic and are bound to reduce the scientific value of his theory. The careful way in which he discusses them also shows that he knows that they follow from his initial thesis.

This is even more puzzling if we remember that his analysis derives no advantage from his labour cost theory. It forces him to assumptions which turn the theory into a truism. At the same time, many of his explanations are based on quite different considerations. Why build upon a premise which leads to endless difficulties without yielding any gains?

How much easier would it have been to interpret costs of production as costs in terms of money, or in terms of some commodity unit! Ricardo, following Adam Smith, could then have defined equilibrium as the equality of cost (the component parts being wages, profit, and rent) and price. It would then have become an obvious condition of equilibrium that the factors of production should be combined for every commodity in such a way as to minimize costs. Almost all his excessively abstract assumptions would have become redundant. With the assumption of varying factor proportions and given productive conditions he could have developed a more elegant, more consistent, and more realistic theory. One might even speculate how near he might have come to a general marginal productivity theory through an extension of the marginal principle which he had applied to land.

Such reflections are, of course, quite unhistorical.[11] One is not free to choose one's presuppositions. Before we can answer the question why Ricardo started from a premise which complicated rather than simplified his task, we must examine more thoroughly the classical theory of value. Let us look more closely into that complex of metaphysical ideas about a real or absolute value on which the theory of exchange value is based. These ideas are vague, self-contradictory, and difficult to pin down precisely. But they all refer to an intrinsic and essential 'value' which is also, in some higher sense, 'real', 'necessary', and 'enduring', in contrast to the accidental, ephemeral, value in exchange or price. It is therefore also taken to stand for what is 'right', 'just', and what ought to be.

Our analysis of the classical theory of exchange value has thus led us back to its implicit theory of real value. The classical theory of exchange value would appear quite arbitrary and incomprehensible if our explanation stopped short at this stage.

Ricardo's labour cost theory rests on the conviction that the labour which is 'embodied in' or 'bestowed on' or 'transferred into' commodities constitutes their real value. Ricardo stresses repeatedly that the theoretical significance of this proposition is that labour—or a commodity the production of which requires always the same amount of labour irrespective of technical development—represents an 'invariable measure of value'. He justifies the necessity for such a measure with the old metaphysical proposition that the yardstick which is used to measure something must itself be invariable, or else an observed change might be ascribed to change either in the yardstick or in the object measured.

Let us for the moment ignore the question why embodied labour should represent real value and therefore the invariable measure of value. Let us ask what precisely is meant by an 'invariable' measure of value. Clearly, a measure of value measures value at *different points of time*. Ricardo uses the concepts 'measure of value' and 'real value' exclusively for the purpose of dealing with the question as to how much prices have risen or fallen 'in reality'. This shows that he is no longer concerned with exchange value, although he and all other classical writers before and after him define 'value' initially as 'exchange value', and introduce 'real value' only gradually, without a clear logical transition. Exchange value, like price, must refer to a definite point in time or it must be an average referring to several exchange ratios over a period of time.

Ricardo and others who endeavour to measure the value of one commodity at two different points of time, try to establish a type of value, although exchange relations do not exist and are not even conceivable. Bailey, in his brilliant criticism of Ricardo's value theory, points out that it is impossible to speak of the 'value' of one commodity at different times in the same sense as we speak of the 'value' of two commodities at the same time. All that we can do is to compare the exchange ratios in which one commodity stands at each period to some other commodity.[12] In order to be able to say something about the relation of the value of the first commodity in the first period to its value in the second period, the value of the second commodity, which is the standard of value, must be assumed not to have changed between the two periods. This is the classical argument which leads to the assumption of an invariable measure of absolute value.[13]

Even when the classical writers examined only *ratios* of real values, they presupposed an absolute real value in terms of which both magnitudes of the ratio are expressed. An invariable measure of value implies an absolute, intrinsic value. This entirely unempirical fiction underlies the whole classical system and pervades even its otherwise sound arguments. De Quincey, who, in a few elegant essays, also tried his versatile mind at economics, took, on the whole, Ricardo's side against Malthus. But he too said, though only incidentally, that an invariable measure, an *ens rationis*, is inconceivable, and compared it with the ideas of perpetual motion and the squaring of the circle.[14]

The next question is, Why did Ricardo and his followers choose *labour* as the origin of real value? Why should the ideal and invariable measure of value be a commodity which embodies always the same amount of labour?

Ricardo did not provide a satisfactory answer to this question.

It is true that he, like Adam Smith, referred to an early state of society in which labour was the dominant factor of production.[15] But such historical allusions, quite common in arguments of the natural law type, are not convincing. They are usually bad history and are really intended to describe ideal types rather than historical facts. The supposedly higher reality of an ideal masquerades as an event of the past. For those, incidentally, who are still not convinced of the normative character of real value theory this type of derivation should provide additional evidence. The contention that in a primitive economy labour was the only factor of production and that it has remained the most important one merely shifts the question. Why should the real value of a commodity be determined by the factors used to produce it, irrespective of whether labour is the only one or not?

Ricardo's position, which came to dominate classical economics, seems even odder when we remember that alternative concepts of real value were available. Adam Smith had given *two* definitions of real value: first, labour used up in the production of a commodity (which is identical with Ricardo's), and second, the quantity of labour which a commodity can command in the market. No doubt Adam Smith had aimed initially at the first concept. But in his theory of the natural price which consists of wages, profit, and rent, he approached the second definition. Some of the subtlest criticisms in Ricardo's *Principles* were directed against this ambiguity of 'embodied' and 'commanded' labour.[16] Ricardo was certainly right when he said that the two definitions are incompatible. But the question remains, Why did he retain any, and why the first?

Malthus preferred the second definition of real value, although he was not altogether consistent. His 'absolute' or 'natural' value is the amount of labour which a commodity commands. Starting from his law that population always grows to the limits of subsistence, he can also assume that the exchange value of labour, measured in terms of the means of subsistence, is always equivalent to the value of labour itself, which is accepted as the standard. Thus Malthus concludes that the only satisfactory definition of real value is 'the power of an object to command the necessaries and conveniences of life'.[17] Shortly before, Malthus says:

'What we want further [i.e. apart from price in terms of money] is some estimate of a kind which may be denominated real value in exchange [i.e. exchange value expressed in units of the standard measure of real value] implying the quantity of the necessaries and conveniences of life which those wages, incomes, or commodities will enable the possessor of them to command.'[18]

This concept of real value has nothing to do with costs or sacrifices, but shows a renewed attempt to base value on usefulness. Starting from the idea that the real value of a commodity is its exchange value in terms of labour, already Adam Smith, though less rigorously, had arrived at the thesis that the real value of labour itself consists in the quantity of means of subsistence which is used to pay for it ultimately.

To put it into modern terms: Malthus says that the internal value of money would be constant if its purchasing power over means of subsistence were constant, i.e. if a cost of living index were kept unchanged. Ricardo, on the other hand, says that the value of money is constant as long as it contains a constant amount of labour, i.e. if the same amount of labour is used for its production. Ricardo explains carefully that its exchange value, either in terms of labour or in terms of means of subsistence or traded goods generally, can, at the same time, change for a number of reasons, such as technical development, growth of population or capital, etc.

Malthus's concept of real value is much less dangerous than Ricardo's. Ricardo's concept forces him to his untenable artificial assumptions without being of any analytical use. Malthus's concept is equally metaphysical and therefore redundant for economic analysis, but it does not require the same set of assumptions. This remains true whether real exchange values are calculated in terms of the command of commodities over labour or in terms of their command over means of subsistence. For Malthus the problem of price formation is therefore independent of his concept of real value. The acceptance of his definition means no more than the decision to measure all exchange values in terms of one commodity, viz., labour or means of subsistence. They must, in any case, be expressed in terms of some commodity or group of commodities. Modern theory also measures exchange values in terms of some commodity, the choice of which is left open.

Obviously this does not mean that the Malthusian definition of real value is therefore sound or even less false. But, unlike Ricardo's, it does not necessarily infect the analysis of exchange values or relative prices. Of course, all intertemporal value comparisons which go beyond observed exchange ratios and are based on the idea of an absolute intrinsic value are impossible for empirical analysis. Intertemporal comparisons of values are possible only in relation to a definite point of view, i.e. with respect to a certain commodity or group of commodities. This point of view cannot be discovered by observation or by theoretical speculation. It is entirely a matter of convenience, however much the interests of an individual or a class may suggest that it is inherent in the nature of things. A study of modern literature of monetary and index number theory shows that this fact has not yet been fully realized by all.

Socialists have debated whether workers in the ideal state of society ought to be paid according to 'merit', i.e. according to what they produce, or according to 'needs', or 'according to working hours'. This discussion reflects both logically and historically the conflict between Adam Smith's two theories of labour value and it is interesting to see that it is the starting-point of the discussions of the pre-Marxist British Socialists.

We now return to the question, Why did Ricardo define real value as the amount of labour expended on commodities? It cannot be because there were no alternative definitions, or because he did not know them. His criticism of Adam Smith's second concept of real value and his controversy with Malthus, who tried to reintroduce it, remove any doubt on this point.

Ricardo never attempts to give a reason for his choice of concept. His criticism of Adam Smith is merely that *if* by real value is meant the work expended on commodities, then it cannot be defined as the command of the commodities over labour in the market. This is correct but the argument can be reversed. If Adam Smith chooses the second definition, he must abandon the first. Ricardo *presupposes* that his own definition of real value is correct and thus presupposes what he should prove, if he wants to prove more than that Adam Smith's discussion of real value is somewhat confused.

The same is true of the controversy between Ricardo and Malthus. Both point out very skilfully the difficulties and fallacies in the argument of the other but when it comes to substantiating their own view, both evade the issue with vague and irrelevant banalities.

Similarly, a careful examination of Ricardo's positive pre-sentation of real value and the invariable measure in his *Principles* shows that he continually begs the question. The hypothetical commodity which contains always a constant amount of labour has, according to him, a constant value and serves as a measure of value just because it contains a constant amount of labour. He then tests a number of actual commodities for their suitability to serve as such a measure of value. But he rejects them all on the ground that one cannot be certain that their production would actually in all conditions require the same amount of labour. Again, his lengthy discussion of the difference between 'values' and 'riches' is one long string of tautologies. Bailey pointed out that Ricardo simply says that what a million men produce always costs the labour of a million men.[19] Ricardo maintains that *value* remains constant, whether the men produce more or less, but by value he means simply amount of labour.

It is not enough to show that Ricardo's reasoning is circular. This merely suggests that he took his assumptions to be self-evident. Why did he (and Adam Smith before him) believe so firmly in the self-evidence of his definition of real value in spite of criticism which he highly respected? This criticism came not only from Malthus but also from J. B. Say, who could never quite accept that real value is governed by cost of production, rather than utility. Even Bentham, who otherwise accepted the Ricardian system, occasionally reproached him for confusing value and costs, instead of defining value in terms of utility, which would have been more natural for a utilitarian.

The solution of this puzzle may be found in the natural law notion that property has its natural justification in the labour bestowed on an object. Hobbes had introduced this idea into British political philosophy and Locke had developed and elaborated it, especially in his second treatise *Of Civil Government*.[20] It then became generally accepted by British political philosophers. Its roots, of course, go further back. In contrast to the notion that property is based on *occupatio*, or simply on taking possession, one tried to find a justification which is more acceptable to the con-science of the common man. Generally, *occupatio* was retained as a natural title to property but was applied only to ownerless goods. For these it was justified by the 'tacit consent' of others, and the argument was often strengthened by the historical or analytical assumption of a social contract.[21] Otherwise and in principle, work was considered to be the title to property.

This justification of property is contradictory on its own assumptions, partly because *occupatio* must be retained as a just title to property. But further contradictions arise when one attempts to express the value of time through interest on capital. The value of time would have to be separated and subtracted from the direct value of work.

In its purest form, the theory demands laissez-faire, for it implies the view of the 'sacred' right of man to the fruits of his work. Where interest on capital, itself a result of laissez-faire, interferes with the direct connection between work and property, the choice between two alternatives arises: *either* one maintains, consistently, the natural law view and thus arrives at the metaphysical radicalism of the theoretical socialists; *or* one maintains, inconsistently, the principle of laissez-faire in conditions in which there is no longer a direct connection between work and product. To support this latter view, arguments are used which justify laissez-faire only in conditions in which such a direct connection between work and product is assumed to exist. Some, indeed, like Locke, stress that work creates *the greater portion* of the value of all goods. But unless it determines the whole, the natural law argument breaks down.

The second alternative leads to the conservative liberalism of the classical school. The most fatal internal criticism of their laissez-faire doctrine is therefore that it contradicts its basic belief that labour is the source of value and property. They get into trouble as soon as they admit that changing technical conditions, such as changes in the quantities of productive factors, or in technical knowledge, may cause a change in the relative share of workers in the total produce. From the point of view of the legal ground of value and property, viz., labour bestowed, these changes are quite irrelevant. Yet, these changes do, in conditions of laissez-faire, determine the value of labour and the income of the workers. We shall have to say more about this conflict between the conservative liberalism and the radical value theory of the classics. We may note here that it goes back to the theory of property of the school of natural law. This theory was the starting-point both of the labour theory of value and of the doctrine of economic liberalism.

Let us now disregard these contradictions and examine the substance of the theory that labour justifies property. Locke argued that even if all other objects were common property, 'yet every man has a property in his own person: this nobody has any right to but himself. The labour of his body, and the work of his hands, we may say, are properly his. Whatsoever then he removes out of the state that nature hath provided, and left it in, he hath mixed his labour with, and joined to it something that is his own, and thereby makes it his property. It being by him removed from the common state nature hath placed it in, it hath by this labour something annexed to it, that excludes the common right of other men. For this labour being the unquestionable property of the labourer, no man but he can have a right to what that is once joined to. . . .'[22]

At the root of this theory is a definite idea about man's place in nature. Man alone is alive, nature is dead; human work alone creates values, nature is passive. Man alone is *cause*, as Rodbertus said later, whilst external nature is only a set of *conditions*. Human work is the only active cause which is capable of creating value. This is also the origin of the concept 'productive factor'. It is not surprising that the classics recognized only *one* productive factor, viz., labour. The same metaphysical analogies that were used to establish natural rights were also used to expound the idea of natural or real value. It is an example of the previously mentioned attempt of the philosophy of natural law to derive both rights and value from the same ultimate principles.

There can be no doubt that such notions of property and value underlay Adam Smith's proposition that labour is the only real source of value and hence its only correct measure. Many a passage from his *Wealth of Nations* would otherwise be inexplicable. He spoke of 'the property which every man has in his own labour, as it is the original foundation of all other property, so it is the most sacred and inviolable', etc. Only such ideas as these can explain why Adam Smith had to draw for a justification of his labour-cost principle on an ideal state of nature in which there was neither accumulated capital nor private property in land, and why he rarely missed a chance to make a caustic remark about landlords and others who 'love to reap where they never sowed'.

Various allusions to the 'sacred rights of property', the 'inviolable right of natural liberty', or to 'human rights' indicate clearly whence Adam Smith took his premises for his postulate of liberty. The natural system of property in which everyone enjoys the fruit of his own labour, requires perfect liberty. Only then is property 'sacred'. But his laissez-faire theory was applied to the existing society and it therefore clashed with his labour theory of value.[23] It was used as a justification of the 'natural price', which includes rent and profit as well as wages. The same logical slip accounts for Adam Smith's second definition of value, i.e. 'commanded labour', which he advanced in addition to the labour cost theory ('labour bestowed'). It is not surprising that this second concept is analytically less harmful. As we have noted in our discussion of the Physiocrats, a conservative view of property is less damaging to scientific analysis than a revolutionary.

Adam Smith did not see the obvious contradiction between his premise and conclusion. He evaded the issue lest his whole system of rationalization collapsed. But his remarks against landlords and capitalists are symptomatic for the conflict in his construction, which he must have felt unconsciously.

Ricardo's value theory was derived from the same ideas of natural law. Although he carefully avoided detailed discussion of his philosophical presuppositions, his terminology does not make sense without them. He spoke of labour as the 'original source' or 'foundation' of value. Any possible doubts about Ricardo's philosophical leanings disappear when we remember James Mill's influence. He was largely responsible for Ricardo's philosophical views. In his *Government* he reproduced faithfully the whole gamut of natural law arguments about labour costs and property, referring back to Locke. Is there any other way of accounting for Ricardo's labour theory of value? It is no more than an unsupported hypothesis which leads to insuperable difficulties without being of any analytical use.

The classics already had given the concept of 'labour' a psychological connotation. Although Hobbes's conception of law and society rested, as we have seen in the last chapter, on a sensory psychology, in the course of a long chain of arguments in support of the natural system of property the psychological point of view was lost. Property was no longer connected with the pain caused by the effort of producing the object. At least, pain was not supposed to be the ground for the claim to the product of one's labour. Locke

G

too used psychological arguments occasionally but not about property. The view that labour is the source of property has nothing to do with pain and sacrifice but follows from the idea of labour as a natural property of the worker and as the cause and creator of value. But the general trend of English utilitarian philosophy was towards a more psychological interpretation of labour and of the metaphysical justification of property. Economic theory expresses most consistently this aspect of the philosophic trend, as so many others.

The real cost of getting something is 'the toil and trouble of acquiring it', according to Adam Smith.[24] The classics maintained repeatedly that labour should be understood as the trouble caused by effort. This seemed so obvious to them that they used expressions like 'trouble', 'sacrifice', 'pain', 'exertion', 'inconvenience', synonymously with 'labour'. Real value became the obverse of the disutility of work. Mill said explicitly in the beginning of his *Principles* that labour must be interpreted psychologically.[25]

If labour is interpreted as psychological disutility, if labour is the foundation of real value and its invariable measure, and if this measure consists of invariable units of disutility, then the disutility per unit of labour must be the same for everybody and at all times.[26] This was a tacit assumption of the classical theory. Only rarely was it stated explicitly.[27] Yet, the classics were bound to make it, because they identified labour with disutility. They derived the value of commodities from the labour used up in their production and this labour was taken as the measure of value in time.

The psychological idea of labour value was always linked with a metaphysical conception of man's place in nature. 'Man' was always used in the singular. By this grammatical device, the tricky problem of interpersonal comparisons of sacrifice was avoided. Cairnes, for example, was apt to dwell with some satisfaction on the polarity of 'man' and 'nature'.[28] Such reflections did not flow from a pompous desire for philosophizing. They followed from fundamental philosophical premises.

We also come across the proposition that labour cost or sacrifice does not refer to a *single* individual but to the *average* sacrifice of a class.[29] But once inequality of sacrifice is admitted, it is difficult to maintain a labour theory of the classical type. First, sacrifices would have to be commensurable, and second, they would have to be nearly the same per unit of labour so that deviations from the average are negligible. This idea of an average should probably be considered as just another formulation of Adam Smith's thesis of the equality of sacrifice.

Having treated labour as a psychological sacrifice, the classics could now do the same with capital. Adam Smith and Ricardo already appear to have aimed at this. The classical theory distinguished between only three factors of production of which land was considered not to require an explanation in terms of sacrifice. Throughout the classical period and even later the exchange value of the produce of land was supposed to be determined at the margin of cultivation where the productivity of land is zero. Thus rent does not enter into price. Although rent does not determine price, price determines rent which is a residual after other factors of production have received their share. But capital presented greater difficulties. Ricardo had to make the assumption of fixed proportionality of capital and labour, knowing well how unrealistic it was. Malthus's criticism displayed the weakness of this assumption even more clearly. Ricardo wrote repeatedly in his letters that this is one of the most unsatisfactory points in his value theory and he hinted at his intention to include in a revised edition, as Malthus had suggested, profit on capital amongst production costs. Ricardo never carried out this intention, probably because, masterly logician that he was, he saw that it would have knocked the bottom out of his analysis.

Why not co-ordinate the two factors of production under the common denominator 'disutility'? Senior attempted this. In his view capital is related to profit as labour is to wages. Profit is the reward for the subjective sacrifice of abstaining from present consumption. Having thus found a common ground for both capital and labour, he could explain the prices of both by their scarcity which also explains the prices of monopoly goods. He was the first of the forerunners of modern equilibrium theory, stressing scarcity[30] as one of the value-determining components and, more than other classical writers, the importance of demand and utility as the other component.

The analogy between saving and labour on the ground that both involve sacrifices was, however, dangerous for the classical argument. If it were worked out, a common unit of sacrifice would be required and some indication of how sacrifices vary as an individual varies the amount of labour or saving supplied. This would lead to psychological marginalism on the cost side, combined with a theory of social value. But in spite of rudimentary ideas, especially in Senior, the classical writers never advanced to a theory of marginal social sacrifice. They only mentioned occasionally that sacrifices may be, to some extent, different for different individuals. Although they did not discuss the problem in detail, they seemed to think on the whole of some kind of average sacrifice. In any case, they confined the thesis that subjective sacrifices render labour and saving commensurable to discussions of general principles, and based their theory of exchange value proper on an unqualified labour value hypothesis.

But the theory of abstinence completed the old idea, inherited from the philosophy of natural law and utilitarianism, that costs are entirely psychological sacrifices, man's tribute to nature. If capital is included, the laissez-faire postulate makes better sense. Senior's whole theory of abstinence is coloured by a tacit assumption of economic harmony. One of the driving forces in the development of theory is this desire to reconcile the conflict between what we have seen are two divergent postulates of liberty.

Later classical writers took over Senior's concept of subjective real costs without elaborating it, probably because they felt the difficulty of reconciling it with the basic hypothesis of labour cost. But the marginal utility theorists took up Bentham's felicific calculus, introduced psychological units and developed a theory of utility as a diminishing, and of sacrifice as an increasing, function of the quantity of the commodity. They rejected the emphasis which the classical theory of value placed on costs. At first, their opposition to the classical writers induced them to overstress the pleasure side in the calculus. But their successors took a more balanced view and incorporated the classical ideas, especially Senior's extension of the psychological interpretation of costs from labour to capital.

Sidgwick, Pierson, and Marshall were the main exponents of the new emphasis on real costs. Thus Marshall defined real costs as the social sum of 'efforts and sacrifices'.[31] It is, of course, impossible to compute such a sum scientifically. The notion is a social value concept. Although it would probably have puzzled the early philosophers of natural law, it is, if our argument is sound, the latest variant of their ideas about work, property, and value.

·   ·   ·   ·   ·

Shortly before his death Ricardo wrote to Malthus, his old friend and disputant: 'My complaint against you is that you claim to have given us an accurate measure of value, and I object to your claim, not that I have succeeded and you have failed, but that we have both failed. . . . In answering you I am really using those weapons . . . which are I confess equally applicable to your measure and to mine, I mean the argument of the non-existence of any measure of absolute value.'[32] Ricardo never doubted the existence of an absolute value, only the possibility of measuring it. If Ricardo distrusted his theory of value, he found comfort in the knowledge that his theory of income distribution did not stand or fall with it. He wrote to McCulloch: 'After all, the great questions of Rent, Wages, and Profits must be explained by the proportions in which the whole produce is divided between landlords, capitalists, and labourers, and which *are not essentially connected with the doctrine of value.*'[33]

Perhaps there is no better proof of Ricardo's genius than these two judgements on his own theory. He had to write economic theory without academic training, without even that general education which was then common to the English upper class. Although his writings are unsystematical and often obscure, their logic is penetrating. They represent the greatest single advance in economic theory. And in the end he saw clearly where the defects of his work lay and where its lasting merits.

Unfortunately, Ricardo had over-credulous pupils. McCulloch and, as far as value theory is concerned, James Mill selected just the metaphysical elements for their systems and propaganda. In his letters, Ricardo tried continually to make his pupils sceptical, particularly on value theory, but without success. After his death his *Principles* became a gospel. Bailey's ingenious criticism was almost completely ignored; it was too fundamental. Malthus's less lucid objections were, indeed, taken up, but only in order to be rejected. De Quincey went so far as to suggest that Malthus had been moved by envy. Ricardo's theory became classical. It was expounded from academic platforms, compiled in big tomes, and promulgated in popular pamphlets. It penetrated into journalism and politics and shaped public opinion.

Later, the classical theory was attacked by the historical school and by the earlier marginal utility theorists. But a new vogue of Ricardianism followed, inaugurated by Sidgwick, and carried on by Marshall. Particularly the latter's credulity drove him to new extremes. Whereas the earlier circle of disciples had clung rigidly to the master's doctrine, Marshall interpreted Ricardo and read views into him which Ricardo had never held nor could have held. It is Cannan's merit to have protested against this well-meaning historical falsification. Even although Cannan's own arguments are not always to the point, he is right in objecting to the Cambridge apologists who believed that Ricardo had meant, in the beginning of the century, what Marshall said at its close. As Cannan pointed out, Marshall obscured Ricardo's arguments. This is all the more regrettable as Ricardo is difficult enough to understand without this added complication.

One point which emerges from our analysis of the classical exchange value and real value theory is that Marx's theory of surplus value is not the result of a 'gross misunderstanding'. This opinion is widespread amongst its critics who fail to see the importance of real value theory in the classical system. They tend to focus their attention on the theory of exchange value, neglect its foundations, and ignore the discussions of the invariable measure and of value relations in time. Marx was right in saying that his surplus value theory follows from the classical theory of real value, admittedly with additions from other sources. Moreover, Marx was not the first to draw radical conclusions from it. All pre-Marxist British socialists derived their arguments from Adam Smith and later from Ricardo.

Economists did not welcome these inevitable conclusions. 'Bourgeois political economy', to use Marx's term, had harboured since Adam Smith an internal conflict between the conservative postulate of liberty, presented as a scientific conclusion, and the revolutionary theory of real value, a theory which implies a revolutionary postulate of liberty. The revolutionary real value theory is preserved as a premise in the conservative postulate. Marx exposed this conflict by pursuing the premise to its logical conclusion. He thus touched upon a sore point of economic theory and, probably for this reason, caused so much irritation amongst economists. They often tried not so much to prove him wrong, which would not have been too difficult, as to show that he was an utter fool, a bungler, misguided by those despised German philosophers. They felt it impertinent of him to dare tamper with classical theory.

It is not difficult to explain how the socialists arrived at their conclusions. The classical theory of value leads inevitably to a rationalist radicalism, if not necessarily in Marx's formulation, at any rate in that direction. For the historian of thought the real puzzle is why the classics did *not* draw these radical conclusions. We shall return to this problem in Chapter 5 after a discussion of the neo-classical theory of marginal utility.

Chapter 4

THE NEO-CLASSICAL THEORY OF VALUE

W E have seen in the last chapter that the classical theory of value had its origin in the natural law doctrine that labour is the legal ground of property. This view had originally little to do with a psychological interpretation. No attempt was made to derive the right of the worker to the product of his labour from the fact that labour was irksome and a subjective sacrifice.

Later classical writers, under utilitarian influence, showed a more psychological bent. In the first place, they stressed 'utility' as a necessary condition of value. A thing must be useful in order to be produced at all. Since the classical theory explains value differently, the emphasis on usefulness as a general condition of value does not shake the natural law argument.

The labour cost theory was psychologically interpreted in another way too. Labour and production costs in general were identified with subjective sacrifice. Effort has a negative utility. This psychological interpretation of the central concept of classical theory prepared the ground for Senior's treatment of saving as analogous to labour. Both saving and labour involve sacrifices. This notion developed gradually into Pierson's and Marshall's definitions of real costs as the sum of different people's sacrifices of work and abstinence.

But the endeavour of the classical writers to interpret the labour value theory psychologically led to a dead end. It did not go beyond general and rather vague reflections and some terminological changes. In fact their theory of exchange value rested on a concept of labour which ruled out a psychological interpretation. The marginal utility school was right when it called the classical theory of value 'objective', i.e. non-psychological. The hedonistic trimmings of classical theory show merely a desire to conform to the utilitarian philosophy. Not until later did utilitarianism exert its full influence upon economic theory.

The classical writers never arrived at a psychological interpretation because they did not analyse in detail the sacrifice involved in labour. It is somewhat puzzling that they should not have done this. Bentham's quantitative approach to pleasure and pain could have provided the psychological 'thermometer'. His felicific calculus, both for individuals and society, would have furnished a suitable methodological frame. After Bentham and Ricardo there was even a personal union between utilitarianism and political economy. James and John Stuart Mill were the main exponents of both utilitarian philosophy and Ricardian economics. It was not for want of stimulus that the theory remained nonpsychological.

It is difficult to say whether this was due to Ricardo's overwhelming authority. Moreover, his immediate successors, for all their merits, were not very original thinkers. These facts are, of course, mutually dependent. The development which economic theory might be expected to have taken in the beginning of the nineteenth century did not occur until the end of the century. Not until German critics had shaken Ricardian theory, was a hedonistic interpretation of economic value attempted. Those who had anticipated the concept of marginal utility in earlier days had been obstinately ignored.

Meanwhile, scientific thought in other fields had moved on. From the period of the later classics onwards, economic theory has been out of step with the general advance of ideas. Marginal utility theory attempted to give a hedonistic interpretation of value at a time when psychologists were abandoning hedonism in favour of a more realistic analysis. The new psychological approach led, on the one hand, to an experimental psychology on the lines of the natural sciences, and on the other, to an introspective analysis. The latter, in contrast to the introspections of hedonism, treated critically the phenomena which the older school had accepted uncritically. It tried to analyse, rather than accept, conscious intellectual notions and rationalizations. It rejected the hedonistic attempt to press all explanations into empty formulae which left no room for empirical research. The theory of psychological associations was abandoned and soon it was no more than a doctrinal relic. Marginal utility theory indicates clearly the lack of contact between economics and psychology. At the same time, the theory made it possible to formulate a more closely reasoned moral system of utilitarianism, unfortunately at a time when a philosopher of Sidgwick's calibre, the last and perhaps most penetrating utilitarian, almost despaired of his task.[1]

The fact that the development was thus artificially retarded also affected the way in which value theory was eventually psychologically interpreted. If our argument is correct, a psychological interpretation might have been expected in the beginning of the century. The premises for it were there; it would have fitted into the general philosophy of the classics and it would have followed from some of the rudimentary analysis in their writings. After having been held up for half a century by the post-classical predilection for a systematizing interpretation of the masters, the final discovery of psychological marginalism seemed much more like a revolution. This would not have been so, had it occurred a few decades earlier as a natural development of the psychological arguments of the classics. Not only in politics do reactions sometimes make for revolutions.

If a hedonistic theory of value had been formulated earlier and developed more gradually, it would probably have been at first a theory of marginal *sacrifice*. As it was, the new theory of value was one of marginal *utility* instead. In protest against the classical theory which explained value exclusively in terms of cost, the new theory overemphasized utility. It is not surprising that this tendency was particularly strong in Jevons, the English representative of the new school. He had more direct contact with classical theory than the Continental marginal utility theorists.

The overemphasis of the positive aspect of the pleasure-pain calculus, which is still noticeable in modern formulations, goes back to the beginning of the marginal revolution. This is not the place to discuss the controversy between the subjective theory of cost and the theory of utility. It can be considered as settled, in principle, by Marshall's dictum about the two blades of a pair of scissors. Nevertheless, later writers still lapse occasionally into an overemphasis of the utility side.

We shall also have to ignore many other aspects of the subjective theory of value. There is a good deal of terminological ambiguity and some confusion about the relations between its fundamental concepts. Pleasure, pain, want, satisfaction of wants, marginal utility, total utility, subjective value, etc., are used in different senses by different authors. Much has been written about these ambiguities, especially in Germany. They need not detain us here. For a criticism which goes to the heart of the theory, they are irrelevant. We shall be concerned only with those controversies which are sufficiently important, or which are particularly relevant to our problem. One of these is the dispute between marginal utility theory proper and its modern behaviouristic interpretation (*Wahlhandlungstheorie*).

Neo-classical, like classical, value theory falls into two parts, an exchange value and a pure value theory. We found that the classical theory of exchange value is closely related to its theory of real value. The conclusions of the latter provide the basis for the former. We therefore started in the last chapter with an outline of exchange value theory and then examined its foundation in the theory of real value.

Similarly in the neo-classical theory, the pure theory—the 'real value' theory, as it were, although the term is no longer used—is intended to be the basis of the theory of exchange value and of price formation. It is presented in order to give a profounder explanation of economic phenomena. Yet we shall find that the marginal utility theory of exchange value is logically completely independent of the pure value theory.

This is one of the reasons why marginal utility theory was such an important advance. Its subjective definition of value resembles the definitions of Adam Smith and Malthus in one point: It is less fatal to theoretical analysis than Ricardo's. This does not, of course, mean that it is therefore sound. It was the merit of marginal utility theory to liberate price theory from those unrealistic assumptions to which Ricardo's labour cost principle had forced it. But the same objective could have been equally well achieved with Malthus's concept of real value, or even better with Bailey's rejection of any concept of real value, not to speak of Cournot who had formulated important parts of modern theory in 1830 without a theory of pure value.[2] He simply treated demand as a function of price, $D = f(P)$. Jevons, who recognized Cournot as one of the most ingenious forerunners of modern theory, praised him generously for this discovery. But his reproaches are also significant. Cournot had started from the observable fact that there are systematic relations between the prices and the production and consumption of commodities, but, Jevons complained, he never endeavoured to penetrate to an 'ultimate theory' of the nature of utility and value.[3] Thus on Jevons's view, Cournot's theory lacks the psychological and metaphysical insight which the subjective theory of value sets out to provide.

Marginal utility theory succeeded in freeing the analysis of price formation from the abstractions of the labour cost theory. Subjectively, all factors of production and all commodities are put on an equal footing. Without assumptions about different types of factors, about fixed productive coefficients, and without limiting arbitrarily the field of application, it attempts to explain uniformly the causal sequence of economic phenomena by a general application of the idea of the margin, which the classics had used only in their theory of rent. The new theory studies the way in which supply and demand depend upon price. This relationship can be studied statistically. The theory presupposes continuity of demand and supply functions but it does not presuppose the concept of utility. With certain simplifying assumptions about equilibrium, it can present a model of general relationships between supply, demand, and price of consumption goods, intermediate commodities, and productive factors. Until the assumptions are dropped and until the supply and demand functions are filled with empirical content, these models are, of course, only a set of questions and hypotheses for inductive research. Nothing need be assumed about pleasure and pain, utility and sacrifice or subjective value.

We shall not criticize the neo-classical theory of exchange value. As we have seen, its connection with pure value theory is historical, not logical. To-day it is a widely accepted tool of economic analysis.

When we say that there is no logical connection between exchange value theory and pure value theory, this is, of course, only true after the two have been logically separated. In the literature they are often confused. It has always been the desire of marginal utility theorists to weave value arguments into their explanation of price formation in order to justify the claim that pure value theory is indispensable.

It is one of Jevons's merits to have searched conscientiously for the forerunners of his theory. Like Edgeworth later, he was primarily concerned with stressing its hedonistic ancestry. He tried to show that it is a consistent application of the Benthamite calculus.

Jevons defined political economy as the analysis of the mechanics of pleasure and pain. Pleasure and pain dominate everything, hence also economic activity. Since this chapter is concerned with the possibility of constructing social value judgements on the foundations provided by the marginal utility theory, this orientation makes Jevons's theory a good starting-point. The Austrians never advanced to a general equilibrium analysis. The Lausanne school, which went further in this respect than even Jevons and his followers, was never very explicit about its psychological and metaphysical value premises. As we shall see, this does not, of course, mean that it did without them. Jevons was simply more explicit and consistent in this respect, and that is why his theory provides the best starting-point.

Jevons, and most marginal utility theorists after him, begin with a criticism of Adam Smith's distinction between value in use (utility) and value in exchange, and his comment that goods with a high value in use may have a low value in exchange and vice versa.[4] It is often overlooked that Adam Smith's treatment had already been criticized by classical writers, above all by De Quincey in his *Logic of Political Economy*. J. S. Mill summarized the criticism by saying that exchange value may be less than value in use, but never more.[5] In typical classical fashion he regarded utility as a necessary condition of exchange value and believed therefore that utility can be above but not below exchange value.

Now marginal utility theory links exchange value with utility by distinguishing between total and marginal utility. Total utility is the utility of the total number of units of a good at the disposal of a person, marginal utility is the utility of the 'last unit', i.e. the utility derived from an additional small increment of the same good, or the sacrifice involved in reducing the total by a small amount. Adam Smith's mistake was to think only of total utility when he said, for example, that water has a high and diamonds have a low utility. Marginal utility, however, must, in equilibrium, be equal to the price of the good or, more precisely, to the marginal utility of the amount of money or whatever else is exchanged for the good. If, for an individual, the marginal utility of a commodity were greater than this, he would buy more of it until its marginal utility had fallen to the level of equality. The marginal utility derived from a commodity falls with an increase in the quantity consumed; hence a greater 'degree of satiation' and, eventually, equilibrium, would be reached. If, on the other hand, marginal utility were less than exchange value, the individual would trade the commodity in exchange for other commodities until its marginal utility is equal to the marginal utility of the objects received in exchange for it.

In equilibrium, i.e. when the individual has acquired just that amount of every commodity which he wants, given their prices and his income, the marginal utilities of all commodities are proportional to their exchange values. From the point of view of money income this means that the utility yielded by the last penny is the same for every commodity on which income is spent. Otherwise it would be profitable to plan a different layout of income, thereby increasing the total utility derived from it; a suitable rearrangement of expenditure would add more to utility in certain lines than it would subtract from it in others. A similar argument can be used for the negative side of the pleasure-pain calculus. A worker works, a capitalist saves, up to the point at which a small additional sacrifice causes pain just greater than the pleasure of the corresponding reward.

The subjective theory of value is built upon this simple hedonistic argument. It is an attempt to use psychological introspection to go behind the observed behaviour of demand, supply, and price. The exponents of this theory are not content to observe and to register regularities which, in many cases, had been discovered before. They want to give them a hedonistic interpretation: every relationship between demand, supply, and price is derived from a more fundamental relationship between pleasure, pain, and the means of satisfying wants. These relationships are represented as graphs which register total utility (i.e. pleasure surplus) or total disutility (i.e. pain surplus) against amounts of commodities or productive services. Marginal utility or marginal disutility are the first derivatives of these functions.

In fact, things are, of course, much more complicated. The utility of a good or service does not depend only on the amount of the good or service in question but also on the amounts of other goods and services. Utility may also depend directly on price, as in goods wanted for ostentatious display. They are demanded because they are expensive. Moreover, a hedonistic calculus which ignores time is bound to be unsatisfactory. Economic behaviour takes place in time and this complicates the idea of 'satiation'. But none of those difficulties is fatal. They can generally be overcome by resorting to the appropriate mathematical techniques.

A more serious difficulty arises from the assumption of the continuity of utility and disutility functions. There is hardly a marginalist who doubts that these functions could be shown to be continuous, if only the commodities were infinitely divisible. But the point is rarely discussed. All marginalists do, however, make qualifications with regard to the imperfect divisibility of commodities when it comes to applying the theory. But this objection to the theory is not too serious. The assumption of the continuity of the psychological functions, on the other hand, is more fundamental. It is never proved and appears to contradict the findings of empirical psychology. We shall, however, refrain from criticizing it here because we shall attack an even more fundamental aspect of the theory.

Occasionally marginal utility theory is criticized on the ground that it requires a direct comparison of the utilities and disutilities of different individuals. This objection may be misleading. All the more distinguished exponents of the theory have emphasized that they do not assume the possibility of such comparisons. Many have dismissed them as meaningless.[6] They retain the hedonistic *individual* calculus but reject utilitarian comparisons and computations and the *social* calculus. At this point economic theory parts company with utilitarian philosophy. It aims at a positive psychological analysis and does not as such intend to be rationalistic political metaphysics.

In view of the close historical affinity of economics to utilitarianism, however, much becomes comprehensible which might otherwise be obscure. There is first the fact that neither Jevons nor other marginalists ever attempted to criticize utilitarianism. Curiously enough they do not seem to have noticed that they deny the premises of the social calculus. Moreover, almost without exception they soon violate their own declaration to refrain from interpersonal comparisons. Jevons speaks, in the paragraph following immediately upon the one quoted in footnote 6, of 'average' or 'aggregate' psychological functions and has no scruples in assuming such functions for whole groups of persons and for whole nations. Not only does he assume that motivations of a group of persons can be represented analogously to individual reactions, but also that the shape of the functions will be the same.

Economic laws, i.e. propositions about the form of these functions, which apply to individuals are supposed to apply also to groups. Such assumptions are not even false, they are meaningless.

Although the distinction between hedonism and utilitarianism is maintained in the subjective theory of value, which is intended to form the basis for the theory of price formation, every practical, i.e. political, application of the theory implies interpersonal comparisons of utilities and sacrifices. This vacillation between, on the one hand, the attempt to limit the theory to positive statements and, on the other hand, the transgression of these limits, makes subjective value theory so peculiarly elusive.

The inconsistency between psychological premises and metaphysical deductions is quite understandable from our point of view. The subjective theory of value, like other theories with a normative intention, makes it appear possible to deduce, by logical process, rational political principles from its analysis of social phenomena. The argument of this book is that such a deduction must involve a fallacy somewhere; some link must be omitted in the chain of reasoning from positive analysis to normative conclusions. In this case, the fallacy is the assumption of interpersonal comparisons of feelings. Analysis is based on incomparability, conclusions on comparability. The theorist is often incapable of seeing the fallacy. It is latent in his approach to the whole problem for he sets out with the aim to arrive at certain conclusions which are precluded by his premises. Jevons is one outstanding example but there are many others. These economists are scientific in their positive analysis. They introduce carefully the necessary qualifications, and firmly believe that their political conclusions are rational because 'built' on scientific analysis.

It is significant that value theory applied the hedonistic calculus only to single individuals. Thus an adequate theory of price formation could be developed, in spite of a poor psychological basis and a metaphysical objective. The theory of value which formed the foundation of the theory of price formation is purely individualist, even although it is intended to be only a step towards a doctrine of social value.

We shall next examine the individualist theory of value although such an analysis is not an essential part of our argument. From our point of view individualist value theory is harmless as it stands. It is impossible to make political recommendations without computing the valuations of different individuals. Whenever the utilities of different people are computed, the result can be criticized with the arguments used by the subjective value theorists themselves, irrespective of whether their theory is sound or not. Nevertheless, it may be of interest to look more closely at those quantities which are held to be incomparable in principle, yet compared in practice. But the reader who is interested only in the main thread of the argument can omit this section and continue at page 100.

The most common objection to the subjective theory of value is that utility and disutility are not quantities, or at any rate that they cannot be measured. This objection to the mathematical operations of the marginalists does, no doubt, touch the core of the problem. Yet, probably no marginalist has ever considered himself defeated by it.

This is not surprising. It is the classical argument against utilitarianism and especially against the Benthamite felicific calculus. The marginalists would hardly have dared to come into the open had they not considered themselves to be well equipped to meet this attack. Jevons, for example, discussed it at length in his *Theory of Political Economy*, and Edgeworth's *Mathematical Psychics* is largely concerned with this problem. Their arguments in defence of measurability enter, with only slight variations, into the whole literature on the subject. Therefore it is best to begin with an examination of these replies to the attack. If the intuition of the critics, who return time and again to their attack on measurability, is sound, the discussion of these counter-arguments must lead us to the central weaknesses of the system.

Unfortunately they are not very clearly thought out, or at least not very clearly expressed. A frequent reply, which goes back to Bentham, is this: It may be true that we cannot apply the calculus in any given instance. There are no ways of observing amounts of pleasure or pain. But, in order to get some order into the picture, we must think in some such categories and must at least try to guess roughly how these quantities vary in different conditions. It is admitted that the theory of value is highly 'theoretical' and that its 'practical' application is possible only within wide margins of error.

This argument sounds plausible. Let us note at this stage that

H

it *presupposes* a hedonistic psychology, i.e. it presupposes that amounts of pleasure and pain actually exist.[7] The objection to the theory is met with the reply that the difficulties of precise measurement do not prove that the psychological quantities do not exist. The marginalists then try to prove that there actually are such things. They almost always fall back on Senior's and J. S. Mill's methodological views on economics as a science, which we discussed in the first chapter. Thus Jevons believed that there are certain ultimate laws of economics which can easily be grasped intuitively: 'that every person will choose the greater apparent good; that human wants are more or less quickly satiated; that prolonged labour becomes more and more painful, are a few of the simple inductions on which we can proceed to reason deductively with great confidence. From these axioms we can deduce the laws of supply and demand. . . . The final agreement of our inferences with *a posteriori* observations ratifies our method.'[8]

The idea that utility and disutility are, in principle, though not in practice, measurable, is thus based on certain psychological generalizations which were believed to be somehow verifiable. It is therefore curious that the marginalists generally do not believe that utility and disutility can ever be measured directly. Jevons said that he does not believe that 'direct' measurement in terms of 'units of pleasure' is practicable. What matters, he argued, are not absolute but relative magnitudes because they alone determine behaviour.[9] We shall find that Jevons nevertheless suggested methods of measuring utility and disutility and it is therefore difficult to see what he meant when he spoke of 'units of pleasure' and denied the possibility of 'direct measurement'.

As far as I know no clear answer to this question has been given anywhere. We must therefore try to derive an answer from the general historical and logical premises of the theory, at the risk of misinterpreting it. It would appear that we are faced with another form of the assumption that *interpersonal* comparisons of utility and disutility are not necessary for the theory. But the concepts of utility and disutility which the marginalists took over from the utilitarians were intended for interpersonal comparisons. The marginalists never really abandoned the idea of social summations, even although they could not give a theoretical foundation to their intentions. For reasons into which we cannot go here, an extension of the meaning of utility and disutility to apply to society would not have been possible without the assumption of an invariable measure, an *ens rationis*, which was also the idea behind Ricardo's insistence on measuring value in quantities of embodied labour.

Jevons must also have been thinking of such a metaphysical unit of value when he rejected the possibility of directly measuring pain or pleasure. This becomes clear from his discussion of indirect measurement which presupposes that people in fact do compare quantitatively the pain and pleasure of different courses of action. If we want to compare only, and not to measure, we do not need units, said Jevons. He must therefore think of 'measure' in relation to an absolute standard, for otherwise there would be no opposition between 'measure directly' and 'compare'. But for him 'compare' must have meant what one usually means by 'measure'.[10] For Jevons individual choice is the expression of a preceding quantitative comparison of individual sensations of pleasure and pain which are, in principle, measurable and commensurable.

All measuring is comparing. A 'direct' or absolute measure is inconceivable. To measure is always to register the relation of the sizes of two things which are, in some respect, similar. When therefore Jevons and others rejected 'direct measurement' as impracticable, they merely formulated the main argument against their own practice of adding up subjective values to *social sums*. But they did not meet the criticism which denies *intra*-personal measurability of utility and disutility, i.e. comparisons for one individual and at one moment in time.

We have already said that the marginalists also suggest methods for determining the hedonistic quantities. Their argument is this: Whenever motives conflict we decide on that line of action which promises the greatest amount of pleasure. For the subjective theory of value it is sufficient to assume that individuals act in the belief that a certain advantage is either greater or smaller than another, or equal to it. Mathematical analysis is considered to be possible even if empirical data are not available. Sometimes it is also pointed out that comparisons of pleasure and pain sensations of very different magnitudes are rarely required by the theory. Thus Jevons argued that comparisons are made only at the critical points where pleasures are virtually equal. The analysis is concerned with the neighbourhood of the margins, i.e. with positions near the equilibrium.[11]

If this is correct, there is certainly no lack of data for the construction of pleasure and pain functions. According to Jevons every book-keeper collects such data. We can measure the subjective marginal utility of a commodity for an individual by the price which he is prepared to pay for it, or more precisely by the utility which he would have derived from the expenditure of the same amount of money on some other commodity. As Cassel has stressed, the utility of a commodity is measured by the utility which corresponds to its price or exchange value in actual or hypothetical conditions. Indeed, once the idea of a 'direct' or absolute measure is abandoned, no other interpretation is meaningful.

The argument which has just been summarized rests on the important assumption that the hedonistic interpretation of human behaviour is true. If it is, the subjective theory of value is not rendered false or redundant merely because it uses supply, demand, and price to determine these concepts quantitatively. For a criticism of subjective value theory it is not sufficient to say that hedonistic quantities are not measurable. They are measurable if we grant the psychological premises, since these premises already imply measurability. It can hardly be denied that the subjective theory of value is true if hedonistic psychology is true.

Now marginal utility theorists proper—we shall consider the more modern behaviourist interpretation (*Wahlhandlungstheorie*) later—make an important reservation. Action is said to be a direct result of the hedonistic calculus only if it is *rational*. The whole psychological theory applies only to the economic man who is *defined* as a man who assesses pleasure and pain effects (note that their existence is thereby implied) at their *true* value and who always chooses that line of action which maximizes his net pleasure.

Now this is the fundamental flaw of hedonistic theory. It presents an elaborate mechanistic system in which men are guided by sensations of pleasure and pain, which they associate with various courses of action, always maximizing net pleasure. The theory is claimed to be correct in the sense that anybody who acts in accordance with it acts as the theory claims he does.

This is, of course, circular reasoning. The subjective theory of value is empty, not because it cannot define its terms quantitatively, but because it uses an abstract, admittedly unrealistic, assumption which already contains all its conclusions.

·   ·   ·   ·   ·

Even if the objection of circularity were decisive, the subjective theory of value could not be dismissed so simply. If it is empty, how can it be false? Yet, psychologists have maintained, apparently with some justification, that it is false.

The error lies in mistaking the mechanistic model for a true generalization of actual behaviour. One does not build models into the blue. They are intended to elucidate some aspect of reality. In spite of many exceptions, the hedonistic model is thought to apply, by and large, to human behaviour. Ordinary people are believed to behave rather like economic men. Neo-classical theory in this respect bears clearly the mark of the rationalist philosophy of utilitarianism and classical economic theory.

The economic man is turned, more or less explicitly, into the 'statistical type'. But this is a dangerous assumption. The initial assumption is that human behaviour is not completely 'rational'. Besides 'rational motives'—pleasure and pain—there are supposed to be 'irrational impulses'. But the theory never says what 'irrational impulses' are. A clear indication of their nature would also define 'rational motives' by relating them to actual behaviour which admittedly comprises both types. The contention that the rational man is also the average man, that the so-called economic motives dominate actual conduct, should, logically, lead the marginal utility theorists to a clear definition of the difference between 'rational' and 'irrational' impulses. But they have never been able to show what precisely this difference is. This is not surprising in view of the fact that they have never been in touch with empirical psychology.

When it came to stating the distinction between actual and economic behaviour, they have always had recourse to those forces which, according to utilitarian philosophy, prevent men from seeking their own and the general happiness: habit, temptation, ignorance, stupidity. Modern writers use psychological terms which do not fit well into this company, e.g. suggestion, conditioned behaviour, instinctive or symbolic actions, etc. It is not unfair to say that the marginalists have never succeeded in drawing a clear distinction between real people and economic man. They defined the behaviour of the latter clearly but went on to claim vaguely that their abstraction is a fairly accurate picture of actual behaviour.

In expositions of the marginal utility theory it is always said that the theory is based on empirical observation. What sort of observation? The idea that we weigh utilities and sacrifices against each other and seek to maximize net utility is derived from introspection. If we pay any attention to our mental processes, we do, no doubt, rationalize them in some way. We always try to invent good reasons after the event. But modern psychology attempts to show that we ought to look behind the rationalizations of this introspective pseudo-knowledge and that we ought to discover their causes. Rationalization is not an explanation but becomes itself a phenomenon which has to be explained. Only marginal utility theorists go on accepting it as genuine psychological insight.

For the general shape of utility and disutility curves the neoclassical writers adduce other evidence, besides uncritical introspection. Every grocer knows that demand tends to fall when the price of a commodity is raised and other things remain equal. But when these writers then draw conclusions about the shape of the marginal utility curve from this observed relationship between demand and price, they presuppose the whole system of hedonistic psychology. They attempt to *explain* observations by *interpreting* them in a particular manner.

Efforts have been made to support the theory with the aid of the results of certain psychological experiments, e.g. the Weber-Fechner law. This would nowadays be regarded as a dangerous analogy. Again, it presupposes the hedonistic interpretation. One has also tried to look for confirmation in physiological investigations of fatigue. But the results of time and motion studies are certainly not encouraging to the plotting of marginal sacrifice curves. And again, interpretation would have to precede explanation. It is always the initial tacit assumption of the hedonistic interpretation of mental acts which vitiates the reasoning and makes it circular. Because the hedonistic scheme is taken to be self-evident, and because this scheme relates human action to sense experience, non-sensory psychological explanations are excluded. This is good English empiricism.

The bias appears most clearly in the type of empirical data which the marginal utility theorists attempt to collect in order to verify their theory. There is a sentence in Wicksell which expresses admirably the faith which inspired economic thought and particularly subjective value theory during the nineteenth century:

'Perhaps some day the physiologists [*sic!*] will succeed in isolating and evaluating [*sic!*] the various human needs for bodily warmth, nourishment, variety, recreation, stimulation, ornament, harmony [!], etc., and thereby lay a really rational foundation for the theory of consumption.'[12]

In view of its materialistic and rationalistic bias it is not surprising that the theory comes continually into conflict with modern psychology. All modern psychologists are agreed that the popular type of introspective rationalism to which hedonism tries to give a learned appearance is indefensible.

The unquestioning faith of the marginalists in rationalistic hedonism as a substantially correct account of human behaviour, and their blindness to its difficulties, become most glaring in their unhappy choice of examples: boys swapping apples and nuts, horse-dealers in the market, Robinson Crusoe shipwrecked on an island where he must adjust himself to a situation without any social relations. One wonders what insight and wisdom an analysis of such situations could yield. A modern psychologist who wanted to refute hedonism could probably choose no better examples to show how absurd the notion of rational motivation is. The illustrations, like the theory which they illustrate, can hardly be said to be the result of observation. If ever there was an armchair theory, this is it.

There remains one last problem. The application of a theory of 'rational behaviour' to actual behaviour which contains 'irrational motives' should require, as we have argued, some indication of what 'rational' and 'irrational' motives are. Now we have seen that the marginal utility theorists have never clarified the difference. Their comments on actual behaviour bear the stamp of the naïvest version of popular psychology. But let us assume for the sake of the argument that they succeeded in drawing a clear distinction. Their next step is to identify 'rational behaviour' with *normal* behaviour. We are asked to believe that the economic man is also the 'average man', for only then can the theory be applied to the world. Now the question arises: How do we know that 'irrational' deviations are distributed in such a way as to cancel out? May there not be a systematic bias? To my knowledge this question has never been answered.

It is now generally recognized that psychological phenomena are interrelated and tend to be cumulative, so that it is quite impossible that 'irrational impulses' should show a normal frequency distribution. We have therefore no reason to expect that the average type of behaviour would approximate rational behaviour if we aggregate a sufficiently large number of cases. One might just as well expect that the force of gravity alone determines the curve and speed of descent of pieces of paper which are thrown out of a particular window. The direction of the wind in a particular area is not a random influence. (Even this analogy holds only on the unjustified assumption that 'rational' and other motives have been defined with the same precision as the force of gravity and other influences which determine the descent.)

The answer to the previous question, How can the theory be both empty and false? is, therefore, this: The proposition that rational action is also normal action renders the theory false. The theory applies a model to real life which cannot fit it. It is interesting to note that the same theory, in its explanation of the rate of interest, presupposes systematically 'irrational' behaviour of the 'normal' person.

The practical results of the subjective theory of value are not particularly impressive either. It neither conveys knowledge of facts, nor does it solve practical problems. It is an abstract, barren construction of great complexity for the uninitiated. It is one of those systems so common in the social sciences, which yield only pseudo-knowledge. An abstract theory of price formation without a theory of value does not even pretend to describe empirical facts: it is primarily concerned with formulating questions.

We shall have to say more about the application of pure value theory to political problems later. Such application presupposes in addition the dubious computation of social utility. Its failure may simply be due to this impossible attempt. But subjective value theory is of little help even where no social computation is required. We have mentioned the question of the length of the working day. Are we any wiser for plotting disutility against working hours? Such attempts are at best an inadequately substantiated *interpretation* of the relation between supply and price, etc. These relations are first forced into generalizations in order to make them amenable to a particular interpretation.

Another instance is the treatment of saving. Its theoretical explanations have always had a moralizing tendency. Bacon used the fact that pleasures near in time appear more urgent than distant ones as an example of the detrimental influence of emotion and imagination on reason. A rational man, apparently, would distribute his pleasures evenly over his lifetime. Bentham introduced time as a dimension of pleasure and pain, without very clearly stating his meaning. He was soon criticized and Sidgwick returned to the old proposition that the timing of a pleasure can influence its *rational* valuation only through the greater uncertainty of more distant pleasures.[13] The notion that a rational man distributes his pleasures evenly over his lifetime is taken over by the subjective theory of value with suitable qualifications about changes in the capacity to enjoy as one grows older, increasing risk of death, and the fact of a positive rate of interest which itself is supposed to be partly the result of 'irrationality'. Often the whole question is avoided, but when the subjective theory of value has anything to say about the important psychological phenomenon of saving, it is a dubious and complicated theory of how a rational man ought to save, coupled with the admission that man is not rational but improvident. Psychological studies and statistical inquiries in this field would, of course, break new ground but they would have little use for marginal utility theory.

We cannot dismiss the subjective theory of value simply by saying that it cannot be reduced to quantitative terms. It can if the hedonistic explanation of human behaviour is correct. Nor can it be dismissed as a circular argument which contains all its conclusions in its assumptions about the economic man, for it claims that these assumptions are realistic. The question is whether the claim of marginal utility theory to be an accurate explanation of human behaviour is justified.

We are not attempting an exhaustive refutation of hedonism. Nor is there any reason to go into a detailed psychological discussion, because the marginalists themselves, with certain exceptions, are retreating from rationalistic hedonism. The behaviourist interpretation of choice (*Wahlhandlungstheorie*) which is symptomatic for this retreat, is more easily criticized than the old-fashioned psychological interpretation. The new fashion is to abandon the hedonistic stronghold, viz., the contention that the theory is a psychological explanation of human behaviour. It is an attempt to construct a subjective theory of value without psychological content. Such an attempt is bound to lead to empty mathematical scholasticism. Logical procedure never yields more than what is fed into it.

It is by no means a new development. Bentham already—not to speak of earlier authors—tends sometimes to identify the net sum of pleasure with the impulse of choice and to regard choice or volition as the totality of all causes that lead to action. Later associationists, especially Bain, tend also to turn hedonism into a truism. J. S. Mill and Sidgwick are inclined to do the same. The early marginal utility theorists seem uncertain in this respect. Sometimes they define rational action as an ideal which is never fully realized because of conflicting impulses; at other times they identify the balance of pleasure with choice or will, which embraces all motives.[14] The difference is this: In the first case we are concerned with independent, psychologically defined concepts of pleasure and pain; in the second, these concepts are defined in terms of the resulting choice and action and can therefore not be used to explain behaviour.

When the hedonistic terminology ceases to be convenient, there is a tendency to abandon it. But it is hardly surprising that the new terms stand for the same hedonistic ideas. Future generations of economists, who will probably have little sympathy for the hedonistic approach, will be amused by the terminological quibbles of the last decades.

Marshall, who was certainly no iconoclast, replaced in later editions of his *Principles* the word 'pleasure' by 'satisfaction'. But no significant change of content has resulted from this change of terms. Yet, it is significant as an indication of coming developments. Marshall wanted to suggest that he is discussing not the behaviour of an abstract economic man, but of ordinary people. Most other subjective value theorists try to give the same impression. Even Böhm-Bawerk rejected, with the thoroughness that characterizes all his writings, any hedonistic interpretation of marginal utility theory in later editions.[15] He also pointed to various anticipations of this point of view in his earlier writings. He indeed went on using such terms as 'well-being', 'increase in well-being', 'pleasure', 'pain', 'utility', 'disutility', 'discomfort', etc., but they were not meant to have any hedonistic connotations. But his professed rejection of hedonism is not very convincing in view of the fact that his analysis of subjective value is the purest and most rationalistic hedonism.[16] He felt that hedonism was no longer quite up to date and he could not resist paying lip service to the current fashion.

The same retreat from hedonism is apparent in Pareto's coinage of the term *ophélimité*. It was so important to him to differentiate his analysis from hedonistic associations that he went to the length of inventing a new monstrosity. Yet, the concept was obviously used to express hedonistic ideas.[17] This tendency is characteristic of the entire Lausanne school. Walras himself tried hard to eradicate hedonism.

When hedonism is abandoned, utility, subjective value, satisfaction, pleasure and pain, etc., must be defined in terms of observable choice (*Wahlhandeln*). This is done by Irving Fisher. But he, unlike, for example, Cournot and Cassel, does not try to give up the subjective theory of value. He abstains from psychology and yet retains a purely formal, behaviourist utility and value theory.

But why retain psychological concepts without psychological content? What is the purpose of an analysis which is intended to prop up the theory of price and which, apart from small improvements and terminological changes, is identical with the old theory? Marginal utility theory proper had at least an objective; it purported to be a psychological explanation of price formation. But what is the point of the new theory of choice which claims to be non-psychological?

I am not saying that one should not elaborate and reformulate the simple relationships between supply, demand, and price. Such reformulations are useful. With their aid empirical data can be subjected to clear questions (e.g. demand elasticities, etc.). But they must be made with a purpose in view. The comprehensive modern non-hedonistic value analysis seems to have been constructed in order to replace marginal utility theory. The latter was intended to provide a psychological explanation of price formation. When hedonism became discredited psychological explanation generally suffered a loss of reputation. But the flaw in the marginal utility theory was not that it endeavoured to explain economic phenomena psychologically, but that hedonism could not explain them. The new school tries to salvage the hedonistic model by stripping it of its psychological content. Its concepts are formal and 'purely economic'. But its theoretical model is not likely to provide a very happy formulation of the specifically psychological problems of economics, for in so far as it formulates them at all, it does so hedonistically.

Of course, economics requires as its foundation a psychological explanation of the causes of supply, demand, and price. It is probable that the most important future advances will be made in this direction. But such psychological inquiries must be of a very different type from those of hedonism and subjective value theory (including the behaviourist interpretation). Much can be learned from detailed statistical inquiries, although they must, in the first place, be interpreted empirically in terms of 'stimulus' and 'response', not 'want' and 'sacrifice'. We must overcome our old hedonistic prejudices. Social psychology and sociology may yield even more rewarding results. It will probably prove impossible to arrive at an elegant, logically coherent, psychological system, similar to that of subjective value theory. Particularly now, when psychologists are divided into numerous schools and are highly specialized, it seems hardly possible that formal coherence should ever be achieved. It is even less likely that this problem, which in itself is almost insoluble, should be solved by economists. They can never be more than amateurs in a science whose empirical material is growing rapidly.

This is perhaps why our endeavours to systematize must be confined to the framework of supply, demand, and price, although it is always rewarding in a study of special topics to keep in touch with neighbouring sciences, particularly psychology. Moreover, it is doubtful whether it is possible, even within the narrow framework of the theory of price formation, to construct a coherent system which is relevant to the explanation of reality.

It is unfortunate that the subjective value theorists have given the theory of price formation a bad reputation. Social psychologists, sociologists, historians, institutional lawyers, and statisticians tend, in discussions, to dismiss the whole theory of exchange value with arguments which apply only to pure value theory. If we want to retain the theory of price formation as an integral part of positive economics, if only as a method of formulating relevant and empirically answerable questions, it would be best to abandon completely the pure theory of value.

The subjective theory of value starts with the assumption that interpersonal comparisons of pleasure and pain are impossible.

This assumption bars the way to speculations about social value. But only few authors have been able to adhere to their resolutions consistently.

We have mentioned Jevons's lapse from the principle of non-comparability in connection with his fictitious average. He develops this idea in his doctrine of 'trading bodies'. Not only individuals, but also collective bodies are considered to be economic subjects, e.g. all members of a trade in a country, all inhabitants of a country, of a continent, etc.[18] These 'trading bodies' are regarded as buyers and sellers of certain objects, as subjects of the process of exchange. This is all right as long as we are concerned only with supply and demand. Quantities of the same commodities can, of course, be added, and the total quantities exchanged between the trading bodies can be computed. But Jevons's analysis runs in terms of pleasure and pain and he works with such odd magnitudes as the utility and disutility of the collective subject. He applies the individual pleasure-pain calculus to the social bodies. The same argument is used to demonstrate the laissez-faire doctrine. There it represents the subjective interpretation of the 'communistic fiction'. It also inspires the doctrine of the 'national economy' (*Volkswirtschaft*) as a system guided by a purpose.

Marshall rightly criticizes Jevons on this point.[19] But he is guilty of the same fallacy when he speaks of 'real costs'. He takes this concept from the classics and defines it as the sum of disutilities. Marshall uses occasionally the assumption that a unit of money has the same subjective utility for all. He admits that this is an unrealistic assumption. But it is only meaningful if the existence of an objective measure of value is presupposed. Pigou elaborates and applies Marshall's method. What has come to be known as welfare economics has become one of the links between science and politics. Marshall's doctrine of consumers' surplus and Pigou's concept of the social net product are specific applications of Marshall's method. Both authors admit, of course, difficulties and even logical impossibilities, but that does not prevent them from doing the impossible: it cannot be done, but here it is!

The general philosophical elaboration of marginal utility theory has been carried out by the theory of welfare economics and, above all, in v. Wieser's and J. B. Clark's theories of social value, as well as in the earlier German theory of 'social use-value' (*gesellschaftlicher Gebrauchswert*). To-day subjective value theory also provides the material for that web of metaphysical doctrines which forms the general part of the theory of public finance. In short, every modern formulation of the old doctrines of economic policy is based on the marginal utility theory.

One might expect that the anti-hedonistic proponents of the positivist, behaviourist interpretation refrain from social value theories. But this is not true. Although Pareto says that inter-personal comparisons are 'strictly speaking' impossible, he concludes, after drawing some dubious analogies with the theory of colours, that common sense sanctions approximate comparisons.[20]

Irving Fisher defines more strictly than any other author volition in terms of behaviour, and utility in terms of volition, and rejects any association with the 'old utilitarian "calculus of pleasure and pain" of Bentham and his school'.[21] Nevertheless, he never loses his faith that the utilities of different individuals are capable of being measured and compared. In a recently published essay he even suggests a practical method of measuring statistically these magnitudes. For our inquiry it is interesting to note what it is that he wants to measure. He says explicitly that it is 'purely psychic magnitudes', 'wants', 'desires', 'the valuation of a dollar', etc.

Under the heading 'Comparability of Wants of Different People'[22] he raises the general question of principle. He affirms that comparisons are possible but the only important argument he advances is that we make them all the time 'in actual practical human life. Academically we may have philosophic doubts as to bridging the gulf between mind and mind. . . . But somehow we do bridge those gulfs. Human intercourse largely consists in so doing even if we cannot tell how we do it.'[23]

This argument goes to the heart of the matter and one wishes one could agree. But let us pause to see what Fisher is saying and what the acceptance of what he calls his 'assumption' implies. He wants to divest statistical economics of its empiricism by adding a 'rational' element. This rational element has nothing to do with observation, is clearly opposed to the rest of his philosophy but is sanctioned by 'common sense'. He offers a method of measuring what he calls the subjective value of a dollar. He admits that it is only rough and ready but believes that it can in principle be applied to all people. If it is possible in principle, the method can be improved later.

Utilitarianism failed just because an interpersonal measure of hedonistic quantities and hence their computation and maximization is impossible. Fisher claims to have solved this problem. It is true that he is careful to avoid hedonistic terms, but his innovations express substantially the old hedonistic meaning. Otherwise his whole argument would be meaningless and pointless.

If Fisher is right, all social problems could be solved rationally. He himself points to those nearest to his heart but the same would have to be true, in principle, for all. He would not have answered merely a question of detail; he would have solved the crucial problem: What is rational policy? This solution would be the result of a set of abstract and largely incomprehensible 'assumptions', derived from the interpretation of observations of the direction of demand, the level of income, and prices. Does this make sense?

Let us now turn to the practical side. Fisher appeals to our practical interests and deep-rooted dislike of purely academic criticisms. Of course, Fisher is right: we do compare utilities daily. Every political conviction presupposes such a social estimate. But we do it by using our judgement, at best a well-informed judgement based on a correct understanding of the facts, but it remains fundamentally a moral judgement. It expresses what we think should be done in a situation, according to our ideals or according to our desires. The weighting of different people's desires and needs itself involves a new valuation. Now Fisher wants to replace this moral value judgement, indeed all political valuations, by empirical statements of facts which can, in principle, be gathered from official statistics. This is the practical implication of his proposal.

We have confined ourselves to Irving Fisher's most recent proposal because his treatment is lucid, because he sees the implications of his premises, and because he works out a practical method. Others are content with more general reflections. But since this is a matter of principle, our criticism applies with the same force to looser statements about the possibility of social utility calculations. In other words, the criticism cannot be escaped by dismissing Fisher's argument as a mathematical 'exaggeration'. He does not exaggerate, he is consistent. Of course, doctrines which are so general as never to face the problem of interpersonal comparisons of utility, while yet contending their possibility, are proof against criticism. They are void of content.

Chapter 5

ECONOMIC LIBERALISM

EVER since the days of the Physiocrats liberty has been of the essence of economic speculation. It is the thread that links the diverse political doctrines which have been woven into the fabric of economic theory. It has been proclaimed with varying degrees of emphasis. Whereas earlier writers postulated complete non-intervention, to-day the postulate of liberty is surrounded by a long list of qualifications. Nevertheless it has always been there and it determines at least the manner in which problems are approached and expounded. Thus the idea of free competition, for example, has been surprisingly tough. The fact that it has always been an assumption in the analysis of price formation has, of course, contributed to its survival. But analytical *ideal types* turn all too easily into political *ideals*. The principle of liberty has the same philosophical roots as economic theory as a whole. It thrives in the same environment of expanding capitalism. By 'liberalism' we shall mean in the following discussion this general, chameleon-like conception, including its vague, emotive associations with a certain way of life and its overtones which make for its highly adaptable and tough tradition.

Even the severest critics of liberalism find it difficult to free themselves from its fascination. Often they raise only one more or less ingenious objection to the liberal doctrine without touching its core. Veblen is a case in point. According to the liberal theory entrepreneurs earn profit because they combine productive factors in the most 'economic' manner. By seeking profit for themselves, they also increase the efficiency of the productive system. According to Veblen, however, entrepreneurs may also earn profit by thwarting production. They can do this in virtue of certain institutional devices. In a sense, Veblen's theory is, of course, diametrically opposed to liberal theory. Yet, his premises are the same: he, too, thinks of an ideal economy which would maximize production if there were no interventions, although 'interventions' in his model may be caused by entrepreneurs. Veblen's criticism is of the kind which can easily be understood by a liberal economist. It is merely a question of deciding what is an 'intervention' and what is 'free' or 'natural'. His criticism does not reject the general presuppositions of liberal theory. A liberal can remain inside the boundaries of his theory when he tries to refute Veblen.

We shall say more later about theoretical socialism. Its value theory can be traced back, via classical economics, to the natural law theories of property. Like these theories, it is, granted the assumptions of its ideal type, a revolutionary brand of liberalism at heart. In several countries the labour movement has never been very closely wedded to any theory. It has become 'middle class' as a result of higher living standards, of its growing importance, and of familiarity with the exercise of power. Its views are often not very different from those of ordinary liberals, except on certain specific issues. On questions of tariffs and monetary policy and of the organization of production and trade some labour politicians have acted as convinced and enthusiastic liberals. There is more basic agreement between the two apparently so divergent ideologies than might appear at first sight.

Finally, there are the conservative interventionists. Inasmuch as they have ever formulated a coherent theory, which, in more recent times, has mainly taken the form of protectionism, they usually acknowledge initially that the liberal doctrine is correct 'in the abstract' and 'in principle'. At a later stage in the argument they introduce qualifications, intended to take account of actual conditions. In these cases they believe that exceptions from the general rule are warranted.

So much for those who are usually considered to be the deadliest opponents of liberalism. Liberalism is, of course, even more deeply rooted in orthodox economics. It is therefore not surprising that we have already come across it in various connections. We have seen how the Physiocrats took it to be a postulate of reason. We have argued that their conservatism in matters of property accounts for the fact that their analysis of the 'natural' state came to influence economics decisively, and that all the many other contemporary utopian and more revolutionary 'natural systems' were ignored. The 'natural' state on which the Physiocrats focused their

I

attention was sufficiently like the actual state to make their analysis relevant.

We have seen that utilitarians believed in the doctrine of social harmony and that they were almost compelled to it in order to resolve two difficulties: first, the difficulty of estimating and computing individual utilities; second, the difficulty of basing both actual and moral action on pleasure and pain as empirical facts. The only way to solve both problems is to assume a harmony of interests. Since the days of the classics, political economy has developed in the intellectual climate of utilitarianism.

We have noted that the classical theory of exchange is based on the metaphysical principle of labour value. This, in turn, we have traced back to the natural law notion that property is sanctioned by labour. These notions, to which later the classics gave a psychological façade, contain already a liberal theory. Only in the absence of compulsion and external interference does property in the natural state meet the requirements of natural law. The theory is then applied to actual conditions. But since in actual conditions there are other titles to property besides labour, a conflict arises between two brands of liberalism: one advocates non-interference under actual conditions, the other propagates liberty for the natural state only, but interference with the actual state in order to restore the natural.

This conflict of two liberal theories pervades the work of Adam Smith. It is apparent in the contrast of his two key concepts: labour value (= amount of labour employed) and natural price (= wages plus profit plus rent). It also determines the method of his proof: his arguments for liberty are developed on the assumption of the natural state, but he uses them as if they could be applied to actual conditions. The postulate of liberty is more to him than a mere theory; it is a beneficent law of nature. It promulgates a sacred right of man, it carries out the intentions of Providence. Therefore men may hamper or distort its workings, but can never put it out of action. Adam Smith attacks the mercantilists for their interventions but at the same time shows how ineffective their interferences were. By and large, the principle of liberty carries the day. One gets the impression that smuggling is God's way of removing the obstructions of foolish politicians who want to upset His wise and liberal reign with tariffs and prohibitions.

A sunny optimism radiates from Smith's writing. He had no keen sense for social disharmonies, for interest conflicts. Whenever he does discuss such conflicts, he appears as a benevolent humanitarian, taking the side of the poor and oppressed. But he did not go beyond a few bitter reproaches against the wealthy. On the whole, it is true to say that he was blind to social conflicts. The world is for him harmonious. Enlightened self-interest ultimately increases social happiness. We must remember that Adam Smith had neither a pessimistic population theory nor a clear theory of rent. But one could also argue the other way: that he never developed these points clearly because his belief in harmony was too deep-seated.

Adam Smith wrote, of course, in an early phase of the industrial revolution and, above all, before the French revolution. Communication of ideas across the Channel was then more lively than ever. Old prejudices were subjected to fierce criticism; liberalism was in the air and man was believed to be good at heart. It was fashionable to be humanitarian and benevolent towards the lower orders and to be sarcastic about wealth and power. Therefore nobody objected to Adam Smith's occasional venomous remarks about landlords and capitalists. On the contrary, there was strong appeal in a subtle, critical utopianism particularly if seasoned with an occasional reference to liberty. The British claimed, with a certain pride, the new ideals as their own. The French Enlightenment had, to a large extent, followed in the steps of the early British philosophers. The common debt to Locke was a unifying bond.

The industrial revolution gathered momentum. Adam Smith's ideas spread and were admired. They were quoted in political debates; his influence extended to legislation. Then came the French revolution. At first it was hailed with enthusiasm by all enlightened and by some unenlightened men. The welcome was reinforced by patriotism: at last the most advanced Continental country had decided to follow Britain's glorious example of parliamentary government. But soon the French revolution took a nasty turn. Democracy was followed by terror and terror by reactionary dictatorship.

The zeal for reform began to abate. Fifteen years after its publication the admiration for Adam Smith, or at least for some of his arguments, declined. This was true of the majority of Britain's intelligentsia, but a minority pursued another path all the more tenaciously. If our argument is correct, two very different types of liberalism can be derived from Adam Smith. This view is confirmed by later developments. Classical political economy develops the conservative brand of liberalism, socialism the revolutionary. The growth of political tension makes it impossible for the two to remain under the same roof.

At the same time events proved catastrophic for the vague optimism and the faith in harmony. In the course of the fifty years after the publication of Adam Smith's book industrialization and the resulting social problems, the French revolution, and the Napoleonic Wars with their economic repercussions, shook the world and shattered the faith in harmony. Malthus published his theory of population in 1797 and developed it into his theory of rent in 1815. On the basis of Adam Smith's general ideas Ricardo combined these two 'laws' in his theory of distribution. Thus economic speculation took a pessimistic turn. Conflicts of interests between the three classes were now stressed. Rent is an income which landlords reap without work or merit. The interests of landlords, according to Ricardo, are directly opposed to the interests of the other classes. With the growth of population rent rises automatically, means of subsistence become dearer, and the share of the other classes in the social product falls. But there is also conflict between the two other classes. The share of profit cannot rise without a reduction in the share of wages and vice versa. This, roughly, is Ricardo's gloomy view of the social aspect of economic development.[1]

Yet Ricardo adhered to the labour theory of value. Indeed, his formulation of real value came nearer to the prototype of the philosophy of natural law than Adam Smith's. Adam Smith had used two concepts, one of which was less revolutionary. Ricardo's views on the invariable measure of value prove the metaphysical content of his labour theory of value. As we have seen, the problem is not how did the socialists reach their revolutionary conclusions, but rather how did the classics reach their conservative conclusions.

Utilitarian philosophy itself contains strong revolutionary elements. It is radical because it treats rich and poor alike for the purpose of the social pleasure calculus. Utilitarians had inherited the radical principle of equality from the eighteenth-century philosophers. Previously it had by no means been taken for granted that the working classes were a proper subject for enjoying social welfare.

Bentham attempted to prove that a more equal distribution of income would increase total utility. His argument is the same as that which was later elaborated by the marginal utility theorists, though they use it with reference to individual commodities in the first place. As a person's income rises, the utility which he derives from an additional unit of money falls. He will satisfy his most important wants first. Gradually, as his income rises further, he will meet less important wants. Given total social income, total utility is maximized if income is distributed equally.[2] Bentham qualifies this in several respects about which we shall say more. At this point I only want to stress the revolutionary character of the argument.

James Mill combined social maximization of utility with the principle of labour value, particularly in an essay which we have already mentioned, in which he developed this argument systematically.[3] He there discussed the economic conditions in a state in which 'nature' does not provide enough resources to satisfy all wants. Government should aim, on the one hand, at that distribution of scarce resources which maximizes total utility, and at the same time everyone should receive what corresponds to his labour contribution. Both objectives are supposed to coincide and Locke's authority is invoked. Mill tried to reconcile the utilitarian principle of happiness with the natural law principle of property. This reconciliation is not very satisfactory from the utilitarian point of view. Capacities to work and capacities to enjoy happiness are clearly not equally distributed. But this difficulty does not detract from the revolutionary implications of the utilitarian maxim.

The classical conservative solution of the conflict between the two types of liberalism is therefore all the more surprising. The conflict was glaring. It had been exposed by the theories which Ricardo combined in his distribution theory. He certainly did not fail to stress interest clashes. Moreover, he chose the revolutionary concept of real value. The two philosophical influences on economic theory, natural law and utilitarianism, were at heart revolutionary doctrines. Philosophical radicalism had been presented, particularly to Ricardo, not only by Bentham but above all by his friend and counsellor James Mill.

In order to get a more proper perspective of classical liberalism let us trace the development of socialist ideas from Adam Smith. Marx was certainly not the first to draw socialist conclusions from the premises of the classics. All British socialists at the end of the eighteenth and the beginning of the nineteenth century claimed Adam Smith as their master. Historians have not done full justice to them. Godwin alone is occasionally mentioned and then only as a hopeless utopian visionary whose approach to population problems is unfavourably contrasted with Malthus's solid achievements. Yet, Malthus's law of population was by no means original and had been developed by the very writers whom he attacked. His merit lies in the greater completeness of his more rigorous treatment and his illustrations and, of course, in his political conclusions which differed from those of his predecessors. The British socialists had also developed a relatively clear and well-thought-out system of economic policy and had raised important and still relevant questions, particularly in their criticism of the classics. Unfortunately, we can only touch upon a few characteristic features.

Their common starting-point is the classical labour theory of value, which they, like Ricardo, take from Adam Smith. The theory states that in society as it is the workers do not receive the whole product of their labour. The real value of wages (= the cost of production of labour in terms of labour) is less than the real value of the products (= the labour embodied in them). Rent and profit on capital intervene. The socialists do no more than draw explicitly the conclusion which is already contained in the metaphysical idea of real value. Only that social order is right and natural in which the workers receive the full product of their labour. Capital, as Adam Smith had said, is power over the labour of others which bestows property on some. They might have said profit on capital is an illegitimate 'exploitation' if they had used the term which was to have such powerful effects through Marx's propaganda.

The labour value principle was only one of the starting-points of the British socialists; the other was the utilitarian principle. Supreme objective is the maximization of social utility. As Bentham had shown, total utility could be increased by a more equal income distribution. Every penny which landlords and capitalists keep from the poor reduces the utility of the latter much more than it increases the utility of the former. Ideally, everyone ought to receive a share of the social product which is proportional to his needs.

The two principles certainly do not tally. The product of labour has nothing to do with needs. Usually the two are expounded separately and then connected by a short cut, as by James Mill. But, compared with the conditions which prevailed at that time, the difference between the two ideals was negligible for all practical purposes and of only academic significance.

After this digression it will have become clearer why the socialist ideal is presented as a liberal theory. Liberty is all-important but, it must be noted, liberty in the natural state. The bad ruling conditions have been brought about just because men have departed from liberty. There is little revolutionary force in the writings of those British socialists. They never make clear how exactly the ideal should be brought about. This, apparently, was of little interest to them. The practical and dynamic question of how to get there is not raised before Marx introduces the idea of the class struggle. It distinguishes him, as he himself stresses, from the early 'utopian socialists'. But since he, like other political system builders, sets out to be 'scientific', he has to mobilize a whole mystical philosophy of history.

Yet, the criticism advanced by the pre-Marxist British socialists went to the core of conservative classical liberalism. As we shall see, their critique continued to affect the development of conservative liberalism. Time and again it is used to develop arguments against the superficial interpretation from which liberalism suffers in the hands of harmony theorists.

In order to understand this criticism we must go back to what was said at the beginning of Chapter 2 about Bentham's view on rights and duties in jurisprudence and on legal institutions in general. We have seen that these views may be described as pragmatic institutionalist or functionalist. Rights and duties are purely fictitious concepts. If applied to a given institutional set-up, they refer to certain probable pleasure and pain effects which result from certain lines of action. There are no legal institutions which are natural merely because they are actual. They must be judged by their efficiency to produce utility and can be defended only if they contribute to its social maximization. In this respect particularly are the early British socialists faithful disciples of

Bentham. They invoke his authority whenever they draw practical conclusions from his doctrine.

They draw their revolutionary premise straight from natural law and utilitarianism. They go on to ask what caused the deviation of the actual state from the ideal state, in which everyone received the fruits of his labour, or alternatively, a share in the social product which is proportional to his needs. Their answer is that the departure was caused by certain legal institutions, property, inheritance, etc. Therefore these institutions cannot be defended. Property is legitimate only if it is a trust held in the interest of society. Godwin and Thompson already used this phrase which found wide appeal.

We are not here concerned with the specific value premises of the socialists. They were right when they pointed out that classical liberals accepted as natural the existing institutions, particularly the distribution of property. Their acceptance was usually tacit. But the crucial issue in any problem of economic policy of such far-reaching implications as classical liberalism is the justification of the prevailing legal institutions. To take them for granted is to beg the whole question. The socialists regarded them as unjustified. In the light of their institutional criticism it is clear that the problem cannot simply be eliminated by assuming that the state should protect only life and property, and for the rest let things alone. Such an assumption is ambiguous and arbitrary. It is debatable *what* property should be protected, and *to what extent*. According to the answer given to this question, liberalism can assume very different forms. Unless one approves of the whole system of property distribution, including changes which are the 'natural' consequences of the exchange process, one does not arrive at the conclusions of classical liberalism.

To have pointed this out is the most important theoretical contribution of the pre-Marxist socialists. Often it was sensed only vaguely. It was most clearly expressed by Thompson in his book on income distribution, published in 1824,[4] and by Hodgskin.[5] Through J. S. Mill the socialist argument has influenced British political economy and through Marx the historical school in Germany. It reappears in modern American institutionalism. Yet, as a rule, the development is not traced further back than Marx, and not always even as far back as that.

.   .   .   .   .

So much for the background of classical liberalism, which was the conservative version of Adam Smith's doctrine of harmony. Next we shall examine its content. It is convenient to introduce at this point a distinction which plays an important part in later discussions between *production*, including exchange and distribution of goods, and *income distribution*. This distinction goes back to the early classics, although they did not emphasize it in this connection. Indeed, they had good reason to gloss over it. Their argument in proof of liberalism applies only to the sphere of production, but they use it tacitly as if it applied to both spheres. With this distinction in mind, the later development of classical liberalism can be much better understood.

Looking at classical theory as a whole, the division into the two spheres is not unnatural. It can be traced back to Adam Smith who, in this respect especially, was under the influence of the Physiocrats. For Ricardo the separation of production from income distribution is fundamental. As we have seen in Chapter 3, he has an altogether different explanation of price formation for the two spheres. The idea underlying this distinction is that labour and the natural factors of production yield a social product, a fund of goods, or a *national income* which is then distributed amongst the various classes. Each side of the process is believed to be amenable to independent treatment because it is determined by a different set of causes. Let us, for the moment, accept this argument.

The classics are more successful in their proof of the liberal doctrine for the sphere of production. This part of their argument is, with certain qualifications, still widely accepted. In the preceding analysis we have not done full justice to Adam Smith. In advocating liberalism for production he uses a sounder argument, in addition to pointing to the natural harmony and the sacred principle of liberty, viz., the *principle of the division of labour*. It is taken over by Ricardo and his followers without alterations.[6]

The theory of the division of labour is based on the labour cost principle which we have seen is of fundamental importance for classical price theory. Costs mean costs of production, measured in labour units. As we shall see, difficulties arise if values are not measured in 'embodied' or 'necessary' labour. In the theory of international trade, where the free trade postulate was most thoroughly discussed, the tendency has persisted into modern times to measure all costs in terms of a single factor of production.

Bastable calls it 'productive power'. He thus tries to anticipate the criticism that the attempt to measure in terms of labour units neglects other elements of cost.[7] He certainly recognizes the existence of the problem, but it is difficult to believe that it can be solved by a simple change of words.

The classical postulate of liberty in the production sphere is taken over, after a change of terms, by modern theory. There are two problems: first, whether the general assumption that the formation of price can be separated analytically into two processes, production and income distribution, is justified; second, whether a uniform measure of value, be it units of labour or productive power, or anything else, can be used. We shall postpone the discussion of these questions until later.

Classical liberalism also claimed to be valid for distribution. Now there have been repeated attempts to show that neither Adam Smith nor Ricardo believed in laissez-faire, a term which has in the course of time acquired a bad flavour. These attempts are usually made by neo-classical authors who try to defend the classics on all fronts. Such attempts are well-meant but misconceived and dangerous. We are not yet sufficiently free from dogmatism to be able to dispense with an honest and thorough criticism of the masters. The proposition that the classics did not advocate laissez-faire presumably means—it is rarely clearly expressed—that they intended to confine liberal doctrine to the sphere of production and to exclude it from the sphere of distribution. Now it is true that both Adam Smith and Ricardo admitted certain exceptions to laissez-faire, usually on grounds of what they called practical considerations. The exceptions do not refer to distribution but to production and exchange. Some of those exceptions are incompatible with their fundamental views, e.g. when Adam Smith approved of a legal limit to the rate of interest. Bentham refuted Smith on this point[8] with Smith's own arguments and it is said that Smith, after having read Bentham's book, agreed with him. Although Ricardo's theoretical work was largely a rationalization of his practical political convictions, in his *Principles* he concentrated on theoretical exposition and drew political conclusions only occasionally and incidentally. Yet there is a good deal of evidence that he intended to apply laissez-faire also to distribution.[9]

It is remarkable that a separate proof of laissez-faire for the sphere of distribution was never offered. The expression 'natural' which is often used in this connection is no more than a natural law cliché which could equally well be applied to any other political recommendation. It is a standard phrase which was introduced into economics by the Physiocrats and Adam Smith and which has been used ever since, whenever, on any political question, anybody tried to maintain anything without proof. On the ethical premises of classical theory very different principles should have appeared natural. The principle of labour value, which is implied in the proof of the doctrine of liberty in the sphere of production, ought to have led to different conclusions for the sphere of distribution.

It appears that the classics intended their proof for production and exchange to apply also to distribution. They never stated this explicitly but some evidence is provided by the fact that they never mentioned this otherwise so fundamental distinction in their discussion of economic liberty.

The same device of neglecting the distributional aspect is used by modern economists whenever they advocate unrestricted laissez-faire on grounds which have been proved only for the sphere of production. It is an instance of what we have called the 'communistic fiction'. Adam Smith, following an old tradition, compared the state with the family and thus implied that a unified purpose directs the economic system. In discussions of internal policies 'society' and 'social needs' are popular expressions; internationally, the interests of 'country A' and 'country B', 'England' and 'Portugal', or 'trading bodies' in Jevons's terminology. Interest conflicts, which Ricardo had stressed, have been forgotten altogether. A tacit political value premise underlies the use of such concepts in arguments. By using the fiction of a purpose where there is only causal sequence, value judgements are smuggled into the arguments.

It will be remembered that the subject of political economy was 'man's struggle against nature'. This innocent-looking singular conceals a host of theoretical difficulties.

There must, however, be better reasons for Ricardo's extension of laissez-faire to distribution. It is not likely that such a scrupulous thinker should have been so easily satisfied with arguments which contradict both his real value theory and the political tendencies of natural law and utilitarian philosophy and which, moreover, had been criticized by contemporary socialists. Their criticism may not have always been lucid, but it was, on the whole, sound. In any case, it is not enough to dismiss Ricardo's argument as untenable; the psychological problem of its motivation remains. This is not a matter of logic but of psychology. We shall not attempt such an examination here but shall only sketch briefly the emotive content of Ricardo's 'reasons', i.e. his rationalization of the psychological 'causes'.

The general mood which pervades Ricardo's writings is very different from Adam Smith's, even where their political recommendations happen to coincide. Adam Smith was an optimistic and confident humanitarian, who trusted in reason and harmony. Ricardo's liberalism, on the other hand, strikes a fatalistic note. On questions of 'pure production policy' Ricardo too could grow glowingly enthusiastic, but when he discusses social questions gloom descends. His laissez-faire views on distribution appear to express a deep-rooted sense of helplessness.

It has often been suggested that Ricardo's fatalism is a Jewish characteristic. A similar explanation has been advanced for Marx, especially by those who were concerned with his conception of history and his theory of catastrophe. Ricardo and Marx have been regarded as exponents of oriental fatalism. If this interpretation is true, both great thinkers would seem to have something in common, even in their political conclusions which, on the face of it, seem diametrically opposed. But since there appear to be as many different types of intelligence among the highly gifted race to which both belong, as among men in general, this factor cannot explain much. Even if there is anything in this interpretation, it would have to be supported by much more psychological evidence. Just because political economy so often rationalizes political attitudes, it is best understood as the reflection of social conditions by a human personality. Ricardo was, in many ways, a curious man, and because of his enormous influence a psychological analysis would be worth while. Although this is not the place for such an attempt, one should not overlook that part of the explanation which may have to be sought in Ricardo's enigmatic personality. He did not believe that it is possible to improve the lot of the poor. This is most apparent in his chapter on wages, especially in his discussion of the English poor laws. His argument rests on Malthus's law of population. Malthus and

Ricardo did not fail to point out that ambitions for higher living standards, say as a result of better education, could alter the whole situation. But in most of their theoretical arguments they used what they took to be an empirically verified assumption, viz., that there is an equilibrium level of wages which is determined by the cost of production of the means of subsistence. The standard of living of workers in terms of the real goods and services which their wages can buy was regarded as constant. Higher wages, more generous poor relief, or any other 'artificial' interference aimed at increasing the share of the poor, can only result in a higher reproduction rate. Capital formation is reduced because profit is reduced. The reduction of profit is aggravated by the increased share which goes to landlords, for the population increase forces up rent. Wages, in terms of means of subsistence, soon return to their original level. Thus any intervention aimed at an increase in the standard of living of the workers is doomed to failure because of their natural urge to procreate. The poor would always stay poor, only the rich would be less rich.

This is not the place to discuss Malthusian population theory. The law itself is old, although its pessimistic conclusions are rather new.[10] Malthus's *Essay on Population* was written as a polemic against the radical optimism of the Godwin type. At the turn of the century and shortly after, a reactionary wave swept over Europe. It penetrated almost all spheres of social activity. Malthusian theory and the conclusions derived from it were part of this movement. In politics it took the form of the Holy Alliance and a return to monarchy; in jurisprudence of historicism; in literature and philosophy of the romantic movement. This general reaction is a fascinating and still partly neglected problem of social history. Apparently there is a close connection with the development of the French revolution. In economics the reaction was expressed by Malthusianism which, in turn, steered economics into more conservative channels.

Let us look at the part played by utilitarianism in this change of mood. As we have seen, utilitarianism had inherited a strong revolutionary tendency from the philosophy of natural law. Bentham had actually proved the desirability of equal income distribution. Nevertheless, on questions of property he was conservative. Like the English middle class, he had been shocked by the development of the French revolution. There can be no doubt that his fight against the principles of natural law was inspired by a correct appreciation of their connection with the French revolution. The case for an egalitarian income distribution was invalidated by the greater advantage of stability of property. Security of property must come before everything else. Even Marshall spoke of Bentham's almost superstitious reverence 'for the existing institutions of private property'.[11] This is an odd fate for a radical philosopher whose greatest achievement was his fierce criticism of natural law and of its avowed prerogative to sanction certain institutions because they are natural.

Yet, utilitarianism was a revolutionary doctrine not only in theory but also in practice. The Benthamites are known as 'philosophic radicals'. And they were radical in all respects, except in their views on property. They were anti-Church and came to be considered as enemies of religion. They fought for humanitarian legal reforms, especially of criminal law. They advocated teaching reforms. They were, though not always consistently, critical of colonial imperialism, and they propagated limitation of armament. Their demands for freedom of speech and of meetings, for women's rights, etc., were certainly radical for their days. Their reform interest extended to almost every social sphere. Property alone was sacrosanct.

Now political economy deals with those problems with respect to which the philosophic radicals were revolutionary only in theory, but conservative in practice. This is also part of the explanation why the utilitarians, who were originally a small sect and unpopular for their atheistic views, came to wield such an enormous influence so soon. People thought, then as now, that their economic views at least were sound, and that, after all, was considered to be the most important point.

Utilitarianism soon underwent a change. James Mill and other disciples of Bentham held, as we shall see, somewhat more radical views about property than their teacher. J. S. Mill's generation went even further. The wave of reaction had subsided and there was a return to radical ideas. The utilitarians, whose system contained a revolutionary legacy from the eighteenth century, were the forerunners of this new development.

At the time of Ricardo the utilitarian attitude to property was conservative in practice, in spite of theoretical declarations in favour of equality. Bentham's case rested primarily on 'security'

and Ricardo's on the law of natural wages which was derived
from Malthus's law of population. What did the opponents of
reaction, the socialists, reply to these two arguments? They had a
certain weakness for the security argument. They disliked revolutionary means to further their ideals. They preferred to rely on
peaceful evolution in the course of which people would be gradually convinced of the advantages of socialism. But they reacted
violently against Malthusianism. Socialists have always feared it
as a powerful conservative weapon. Their replies were not altogether convincing. Occasionally they took up the admission of
the Malthusians that all depends on the customary standard of
living of the workers. They suggested that to accept this standard
as given is superficial; that the argument begs the crucial question and that the conclusion is implied in the premise. Godwin and
Thompson seem to have believed, although they never expressed
it very clearly, that the urge to reproduce would be weakened if
the standard of living of workers could be substantially raised and
their share in the national income increased. Thompson even pre-
dicted a stationary population. By and large they anticipated the
views of later socialists, that the 'iron law of wages' is only true
in a 'bourgeois society' in which the masses are kept poor and
ignorant.

The socialists were fortunate in their predictions. Higher living
standards were accompanied by lower reproduction rates. It is
frequently said that Malthus and Ricardo were at least right for
their own times. Even this is doubtful, for the problem was not
how did the masses behave then, but how would they behave in
the long run if their standard were raised substantially.

But whether Ricardo was right or wrong, we are concerned here
with what he actually believed. There are several indications that
Ricardo regarded the lot of the workers as regrettable but inevitable.
Social utility, or at any rate a substantial part of it, was believed
to be represented by the values which go to the propertied classes.
In the short run one might increase social utility by taking from
the rich and giving to the poor. But in the long run the poor
would sink back to their lower standard and the situation as a
whole would be worse, for the rich would now be somewhat
poorer.

Even if this argument were correct, the laissez-faire conclusion
would not follow. A utilitarian ought to advocate protectionist

measures to increase the wealth of the rich. There is no reason why one should stop at laissez-faire. That would merely stabilize an arbitrary *status quo* distribution, including those changes which are latent in it. If, for example, tariffs were imposed on agricultural products, the share of rent in the national income would be increased, and the share of wages reduced. Wage rates, in terms of means of subsistence, would fall in the short run. But in the long run they would rise again to the old level as a result of a lower reproduction rate. One could elaborate the argument further by adding certain, to Ricardo quite acceptable, assumptions about the elasticity of supply of saving, pressure on profit, etc. One would find that such duties, without lowering wage rates, would raise rent by more than they would reduce profit. Thus tariffs could be justified with utilitarian arguments. If it is objected that the hardships of adjustment in the transition would hit workers hard, one could quote the classical reply to the analogous problem of the abolition of poor relief; reform should be introduced gradually, and in times of prosperity, when workers could otherwise have afforded to reproduce more rapidly; in any case, population was growing.

It may be objected that Ricardo did not accept the utilitarian premises. This is hardly true, but even if it were, it would not make his liberalism more conclusive. Whatever his initial value premises, there is no reason why he should arrive at laissez-faire conclusions. He would have had to make specific assumptions about the concrete economic situation, and also highly artificial, to Ricardo quite alien, value premises. Even then he would have had to prove first that those concrete conditions actually prevailed, even if we assume that he suppressed all his value premises. Nor can it be replied that the line of argument suggested in the previous paragraph would have been too far-fetched; on the contrary, it would have been entirely in accordance with Ricardo's method of reasoning.

Although Malthus had protectionist sympathies, he never used this particular argument against Ricardo's liberalism, except for a few incidental remarks.[12] Later protectionists, however, made use of Malthus's law of population as an argument for a tariff on wheat. This argument was not advanced more frequently and earlier because Malthus's views on population were decried by the Tories as godless and revolutionary. This rejection is one of the oddest blunders in the history of politics. Never has economic theory produced an argument more favourable to conservative policy.

Our hypothetical argument in favour of protection throws some light on the question, How did Ricardo, from his law of wages, arrive at a fatalistic laissez-faire? His reasoning is not clear. He must have had a hunch that the argument would probably lead to protection in favour of the rich. On the other side he wanted to protect the poor, partly for reasons of personal sympathy, partly under the influence of the revolutionary implications of the labour theory and utilitarianism. The principle of laissez-faire is, as it were, the resultant of those two opposite forces. How this comes about cannot be explained theoretically, for it is not a matter of logic. It also allowed Ricardo to fall in with the tradition of harmony and thus with Adam Smith whose system he considered as the basis of his own. Yet he could not reconcile himself altogether to the result and avoided a detailed analysis of the question.

After Ricardo, liberalism divided into two branches. Ricardo's two disciples, McCulloch and James Mill, were men of very different stamp. McCulloch was a peculiar, but amongst economists not unfamiliar, type: a compiler of historical and statistical material, admired for his encyclopaedic learning, but as a theorist doctrinaire and superficial. He gave Ricardian theory an optimistic slant; class interests seem to conflict but they are fundamentally in harmony. For McCulloch laissez-faire becomes once again the explicit foundation of the whole of economic theory, not, as for Ricardo, the vague, not too strongly emphasized, conclusion. McCulloch can be considered as the first of the so-called harmony theorists. Slight deviations on some practical questions (poor law, etc.) do not impair his thoroughly optimistic liberalism. Followers of the harmony doctrine are Bastiat in France and in America Carey, who nevertheless managed to be a protectionist. French political economy was thus strongly influenced in the direction of the harmony doctrine. This may be one of the reasons for its relative barrenness. But a similar line of development was followed in most countries. It was least pronounced in Germany where the climate created by the historical school and rising nationalism was less favourable to a belief in harmony.

The whole development is characterized by a relapse to natural

K

law arguments of a very primitive type.[13] Liberalism was presented as a system of natural forces. Though these presentations are often formally ingenious, the 'proofs' never amount to more than the proposition that an act of exchange always benefits both trading partners. The place of a proof is often taken by such emotive terms as 'natural', 'economical', 'equilibrium', etc., which suggest the required conclusions to the reader. Hence this type of liberalism lends itself particularly well to popular exposition. Unfortunately, the other brand of liberalism, of which we shall say more presently, also tends to take this simplified version when it is popularized. That is why students of economics often go away with strange ideas of natural economic laws according to which productive factors and capital always flow into the uses in which they are most needed, everyone earns the income he deserves, wages settle down to a natural level, and all is generally for the best. The dogma often incorporates certain outmoded nineteenth-century ideas, e.g. that 'evolution' as such always puts a premium on what is valuable, or that in the struggle for survival the 'fittest' always win. A whole philosophy has been built on such doctrines, and sociology is still full of them. This type of liberalism is popular because it is simple and because its metaphysical premises have wide appeal. It quietens ethical doubts about economic processes and it makes a sustained effort of thinking about social problems unnecessary. These are qualities which make for popularity. We shall not examine this popular brand of laissez-faire further. Whatever is true of the second, more cautious, version is true *a fortiori* of this superficial variant.

The second version goes back to James Mill, a man of very different calibre to McCulloch. As a philosopher, he was not only well read but he had really mastered his problems. He was the first to give a coherent exposition of the psychology of associations. His work on India also testifies to his familiarity with empirical research, even although its organization reveals weaknesses in the scientific method which he had developed on the basis of his philosophy. In contrast to McCulloch and the later harmony theorists he did not deny that interests clash. His account of the situation of the workers in capitalist society is well known. The capitalist 'owns' his workers like the slave-owner. The only difference is 'in the mode of purchasing'.[14] One must, of course, remember that neither trade unions nor social legislation had as yet substantially improved the position of the workers at that time.

James Mill already was inclined to take up some of the more revolutionary convictions which became current after the great reaction. He mentioned tentatively taxation of the increase in land values and certain inheritance reforms. He did not develop these ideas beyond a few casual remarks because he believed blindly in the iron law of wages. But he, like Malthus and Ricardo, knew and stressed that its assumptions limit its validity. James Mill's liberalism was roughly similar to Ricardo's. The tentative revolutionary beginnings mentioned above, which are significant for later developments, were more in the nature of hints at theoretical possibilities than practical proposals.

J. S. Mill continued this trend. Perhaps it is easiest to understand his attitude towards liberalism if we consider the influences to which he was exposed. This is not difficult, for he enumerated them at length in his *Autobiography*.

Mill reflected the crisis of the classical school. He tried to resolve the conflict between the two opposed versions of liberalism which, since the days of Adam Smith, classical theory had harboured. As an eclectic, he attempted to rebuild the system by piling up conflicting fragments. The crisis was also felt in other fields. He made concessions over the wages fund theory. According to Cairnes these are quite unnecessary. Although utilitarianism was in his blood, he was responsive to the growing criticism, particularly when it was emotionally inspired, as, for instance, the attacks on its materialistic and inhuman aspects. We have seen in Chapter 2 how he tried to defend the utilitarian reply to the question of 'higher' and 'lower' pleasures, but he threw in a few arguments which made it a little more acceptable to humanitarian sentiment.

Mill was also a disciple of the British socialists whose institutionalist criticism of the classics he had studied conscientiously. He was not well acquainted with German socialist thought but knew the French utopians, Saint-Simon, Fourier, Louis Blanc, etc., who had much more in common with their British counterparts. His knowledge and understanding of German philosophy was relatively small. But Comte's influence was considerable. Though he did not allow himself to be convinced by Comte's criticism of economic method, he learned from him a good deal. He lived at a time when neo-Malthusianism and social developments made the 'iron law of wages' look less obvious and begin to lose authority. We have seen how crucially important this law had been for the faith of the early Ricardians.

Finally, there is J. S. Mill's personality—a logician with a strong sentimental streak. This accounts for his cautiously formulated speculations about social policy, which he tried to base on economic liberalism. The great merit of his *Principles* is the introduction of historical and sociological views into the discussion of economics. As a result, his analysis rests on a much broader basis and economics is discussed in more humane terms than in any previous work of a similar type. Its weakness is its lack of logical consistency. Mill's premises conflict with his conclusions, and both his premises and his conclusions are self-contradictory. This is the inevitable outcome of his attempt to force institutionalist criticism into the liberal doctrine, without accepting fully the implications. Without being prepared to abandon his basic principles, he yet wants to incorporate all justified modifications.

We have discussed above the institutionalist criticism which Mill took over from the pre-Marxist socialists. Only a few remarks need be added here. Like the British socialists, Mill was not willing to give up the principle of liberty. He discussed it repeatedly and his argument was unmistakably based on natural law, especially in his discussion of rent, inheritance, and taxation.

Now an essential part of liberty is the right of free contract. But economic necessity may force a man to make a contract which binds him for a long time or which conflicts in some other way with his liberty. The reason for this is his poverty; and he is poor as a result of the ruling distribution of property. Here Mill used the socialist-institutionalist objection to laissez-faire as the defence of true liberty, as against merely formal liberty.

Mill tried to make out that this is just a more comprehensive view. What is the basis of free contract or of freedom in general? Even in the most ideal institutional setting, society cannot be disinterested in what the individual does. Sometimes he benefits, sometimes he harms 'society as a whole' through his actions. Thus the principle of liberty may conflict with the utilitarian maxim. Mill discussed this problem at length in his essay *On Liberty*. But his solution follows the old natural law tradition: everyone should be free to act as he likes as long as he does not harm anybody else. There are, of course, borderline cases. Thus Mill wanted to restrict prostitution as socially harmful, but not alcoholism which he wanted to be judged more as a private concern, to be left to social sanction. But in economics nothing is merely a matter of private concern. One of the fundamental tenets of economics is that all phenomena are interconnected. As a result of marginal interrelationships and of the cumulative effects of individual actions, lines of conduct may have politically relevant repercussions, although they appear to concern only the individual. Thus Mill's proof breaks down already at this initial point of principle. Sidgwick also criticized Mill's principle of liberty with utilitarian arguments along similar lines.

Collective bodies present another problem. Freedom of contract includes freedom to join a union or a corporation. But this will affect the price structure. Since the days of Adam Smith and until late in the nineteenth century the views of economists on collective bargaining of workers had been ambiguous and inconsistent. They approved of it partly because they sympathized with the weak, partly because they believed in principle in freedom of contract. On the other hand, their predilection for 'free competition' induced them to propagate certain restrictions on freedom of contract. Mill offered no clear way out of this dilemma.

Mill's treatment of a special problem of this kind is interesting. Suppose workers could get the same, or almost the same, wages for nine hours' work which they get for ten hours'. It is not certain, he argued, that a shortening of the working day, which would be clearly to the advantage of the workers, could be brought about under free competition. Either the workers must act collectively or the state must enact social legislation.[15] Followed to its logical conclusions, this type of argument would require far-reaching modifications of the doctrine of free competition. It amounts to a social defence of monopolistic action.

Mill favoured all social reforms which he believed to be reconcilable with his deep-rooted attachment to free competition. His views are best illustrated by the following declaration. He said that he sympathized with many ideals of the socialists and even that the time was ripe to try them out—one must remember what sort of socialists he was concerned with—but he repudiated all their attacks on free competition: 'I utterly dissent from the most conspicuous and vehement part of their teaching, their declamations against competition. . . . They forget that wherever competition is not, monopoly is; and that monopoly, in all its forms, is the taxation of the industrious for the support of indolence, if not plunder.'[16]

Free competition is the alpha and omega. He never doubted that it is beneficial 'in principle'. Like many of his contemporaries and utopian forerunners, Mill favoured guild socialism because its associations are 'voluntary', and because they could, if sufficiently insignificant, be part of the process of price formation under free competition. Free competition and individualism formed the religion of Mill's childhood. However much he desired, later, a more social form of organization, it had to be one which is capable of being part of an individualistic society. This was Mill's insoluble dilemma.

Now Mill tried to make his curious blend of orthodox liberalism and desire for social reform look like a consistent system. It is hardly surprising that he made use for this purpose of a sharp distinction between the sphere of production and the sphere of distribution. We have seen that this distinction is fundamental for the whole classical system and we have criticized its use by Ricardo and James Mill. According to Senior the laws of production and exchange were universally valid, whereas the laws of distribution depended upon the institutions of different countries. The distinction became, as it were, a concrete formulation of the difference between theoretical and practical economics. J. S. Mill stressed even more strongly that the laws of production—always including exchange—are 'physical truths', whereas distribution may be determined entirely by arbitrary institutional factors.[17]

Mill asserted dogmatically that in the process of production and exchange the principle of economic liberty rules as a natural law. Interference can only wreck the work of nature and reduce welfare. But Mill also used the institutionalist argument that welfare can be increased by distributional reforms. In the field of production free competition must remain the law. Social evils are not the result of deficiencies in the process of production and exchange. They are entirely due to faulty distribution. It is typical of Mill the eclectic that he emphasized this distinction and yet occasionally made practical recommendations which entail changes in production and exchange.

Later in this chapter we shall examine the application of laissez-faire to production and exchange. The same liberal policies, without substantial improvements, are advocated in the most recent versions of economic theory.

The crisis of liberalism, which Mill illustrates well, is still unresolved. Mill became the founder of a school of liberal eclectics with sympathies for social reform. British welfare economics, in both the Cambridge version and the Sidgwick-Cannan version which has dominated until recently the London School of Economics, shows the same contradictions. The great treatises on welfare economics by Sidgwick, Marshall, Pigou, and Cannan are largely vain attempts to put into a system arguments which, by their nature, cannot be systematized.[18]

Pigou, the most consciously eclectic of the school, proceeds from a discussion of 'general welfare', which is a social sum of utilities, to 'economic welfare'. The latter's connection with the former is somewhat obscure, but it seems to be that aspect of general welfare which can be 'measured'. It is also defined on utilitarian lines. Now economic welfare depends upon two factors, 'national income' and its 'distribution'. Next Pigou examines national income in the light of the question whether the 'social marginal net products' (a metaphysical concept) are equal everywhere and whether they coincide with the 'individual marginal net products'. Pigou's procedure is fundamentally the same as that of the qualified version of liberalism. He, too, raises the question whether income is distributed equally or unequally in the manner of Bentham's principle, which, however, he modifies in several respects. By interpreting given situations along these lines, we can discover how we ought to act.

The whole school of thought shows an admirable endeavour to point out all kinds of difficulties except, of course, those which are so deeply rooted in their method that they are not aware of them. There are many assumptions of which it is frankly admitted that they are unrealistic. But the decisive question is never raised. The assumptions of an argument, whether they are true or merely imagined, must be logically conceivable. Sometimes, in order to make an assumption conceivable, additional assumptions are required of which the same must be true. The whole set of necessary assumptions must be conceivable. It has been suggested that if one tried to construct a consistent system from Marshall's footnotes and reservations, one would arrive at something very different from the Marshallian system. But it seems to me that if the job were done critically, one would not arrive at any system at all.

It cannot be denied that a good deal of ingenious reasoning has gone into the metaphysical speculations of British welfare economics. They also contain much valuable empirical insight and a good deal of common sense. British welfare economics forms now the most impressive and most unified body of thought in economic science. Yet, I cannot help thinking—and I am not alone in this—that British economics, and particularly pure theory, has not lived up to its proud tradition during the last two generations. Analysis has suffered as a result of the normative approach to economic problems. Laissez-faire liberalism, with all its reservations and qualifications, is probably the cause of this normative bias. Economic theory and social policy are treated as a unified science. Wicksell once said that outstanding talents stand above their own method; they cannot help making intelligent contributions, however impossible their questions and however false their reasoning. But this is true only up to a point and it becomes less true the more eclectic the contributions are.

As before, British political economy exercised again a considerable influence. In Germany, theoretical problems have been somewhat neglected until recently. In Austria, economics has never had direct political aims in spite of the close connection of the Austrian marginal utility theory with utilitarian philosophy. The Austrians were preoccupied with value theory and never elaborated a detailed theory of welfare economics. The same is true of the Lausanne school. The Americans criticize British neo-classicism from various points of view. Nevertheless they remain under its influence. Their criticism does not go to the heart of the matter. Although they object to certain arguments and certain aspects of the definition of welfare, they accept the welfare concept as such. Their acceptance of the neo-classical position, though often only implicit or even denied, is obvious and results only in more muddled formulations of the same type of assumptions as those of neo-classical theory. Americans seem to find it especially difficult to rid themselves of these ideas. They are firmly convinced that there is a 'scientific' solution to every problem.

Yet, the most promising beginnings of an advance in economic theory are to be found in America, although they are perhaps not searching and thorough enough to solve the problems of principle with which we are here concerned. A hundred years of theory have shown that it is not enough to declare solemnly that we must be strictly scientific, that we must confine ourselves to the examination of what *is* and refrain from propositions about what *ought to be*. It is, after all, part of the problem to discover what it is that *is*, and to what extent social values can be said to exist. Moreover, values remain values, however much we disguise them in technical euphemisms, whether the terminology is pragmatic, institutionalist or behaviourist, and however vehemently we repudiate hedonism, natural law, and utilitarianism.[19]

We shall not embark on a detailed discussion of the circular arguments used in the predominantly eclectic period after Mill. Nothing new would emerge for the purpose of our inquiry, although it would be an interesting undertaking to pursue our criticism through the various branches of modern economic discussion of specific problems. It would be interesting because of the difficulty of even discovering the presence of the liberal doctrine in arguments which contain it only implicitly and without the author's consciousness of it. The conclusions of such arguments can never be more reliable than the weakest of their premises.

For the purpose of criticizing the central doctrine we shall use the construction which expresses the least vulnerable position of liberalism. If we can show that this position is untenable, we have also disposed of all more superficial versions.

J. S. Mill, following suggestions in the writings of James Mill and Ricardo, believed that the desirability of liberalism could be proved at least for the sphere of *production* and *exchange*. In other words, *national income* is maximized in a free economy, even although its *distribution* could be improved by political interference. This would be a very valuable proposition, if it were true. With proper attention being paid to distributional effects, it would be an important guide to policy. Or alternatively, distributional effects may be sufficiently small to be negligible.

'There is no rule of morals', said Jevons, 'to forbid our making two blades of grass grow instead of one, if, by the wise expenditure of labour, we can do so.'[20] 'Customs duties may be requisite as a means of raising revenue, but the time is past when any economist should give the slightest countenance to their employment for manipulating trade, or for interfering with the natural tendency of exchange to increase utility.'[21] Nobody would say this without qualifications to-day. Distributional effects are taken into account in the calculation of social utility. J. S. Mill had stressed that suitable interference with free competition could improve the income distribution. Sidgwick, Carver, and others applied the argument especially to foreign trade.

Conscientious writers do not even say that national income is always maximized under free competition. They say only that it would be the case 'in principle', i.e. on certain additional abstract assumptions. 'Rational' behaviour is one of these assumptions. All careful expositions introduce this reservation. If people act irrationally, say because of 'unhealthy' advertising or 'unfair' competition, free competition would have to be restored through intervention. We shall, for the moment, disregard this type of reservations.

The proof of the theorem is simple. If everyone is free to act as he wishes, he will buy what he wants most in the cheapest, and sell what he wants least in the dearest market. On Adam Smith's principle of the division of labour, national income or social product is thus maximized. The proof, which can, of course, be elaborated, is substantially that of the classics. It differs from the latter only in that it contains some additional abstract assumptions and in an explicit reservation about distributional effects.

Is it possible to separate two spheres of price formation in this fashion and to treat each in isolation? For a single individual it makes sense to separate receipts from expenditure, income from outlay. The way in which he distributes his income to meet his own and his family's various needs, i.e. his expenditure, does not determine the size of his income. His demand for goods has a sufficiently small influence on the derived demand for the productive factors which he supplies for it to be neglected. The same is not true for society as a whole. Now nobody denies that there is a connection between the size of the national income and its distribution. But the problem is supposed to be soluble in two stages: first the effects of an intervention upon the size of the national income are studied and then the effects upon its distribution.

This separation has important consequences. In the first place, since there are two elements, both must always be considered in any practical problem. The value premise must always refer to the desirability of various *combinations* of both elements. This does not necessarily mean that the separation is not legitimate. It might well prove analytically useful.

The second consequence is more serious. Since the result of any intervention must be judged by both criteria, the concept 'national income' which constitutes one, must mean something which is politically significant. It would be in line with the utilitarian assumptions to define the national income subjectively as a social sum of individual utilities. We have shown that this sum cannot be calculated. Let us assume then that the national income is defined objectively as the total physical product of a society. Nevertheless, the size of the national income must be defined in a manner which is relevant to political value judgements.

Moreover, together with distribution, it must constitute *the* object which is politically evaluated. This must be true irrespective of what specific value premises are chosen, unless these premises are derived from the theorem of laissez-faire itself. The latter procedure would, however, beg the whole question. This is all the more serious as the concept 'distribution of national income' is defined as the distribution of 'the national income' on the above definition. If 'national income' has not been defined as that which, besides distribution, is politically relevant in all conditions, then the concept 'distribution of national income' is politically equally irrelevant. A concept which is inadequate in the first case is also inadequate in the second. National income must be *measured* by a yardstick which is correct independent of political valuations.

Against this it has been said that for the limited purpose of establishing the theorem of laissez-faire no measure of the national income is required if one is concerned neither with its distribution nor with its composition but merely with the proposition that it is maximized under free competition. Edgeworth pointed out that in a problem of maximization we need not think in terms of definite quantities. The maximum can be defined by the change of sign of the first derivative.[22] But this makes sense only if the national income is conceived as a homogeneous whole. In fact it consists of a collection of heterogeneous goods and services. Intervention with free competition or laissez-faire, as the case may be, necessarily results in a change of the various component parts which form the whole. In order to be able to speak of a heterogeneous whole as a quantity which can be said to be greater or equal to another whole which consists of a different collection of goods, these goods must be rendered commensurable. Every good must be given a value in terms of the same unit and the unit must be relevant to its evaluation. Only then can the two aggregates be compared, for there is no presumption that laissez-faire would increase *all* items of the national income.

To be relevant for the liberal argument, the unit of the yard-stick by which national income and its component parts are measured must be such that their significance is properly weighted for *any* set of political value premises. If the theorem is to be of interest to any particular person, the yardstick must be capable of measuring the significance of the national income from the point of view of the political valuations of that person. If the theorem is to be scientific, i.e. universally valid, not only this particular person but *anybody* must be capable of being the subject of these valuations. Since the income distribution will also be affected by an intervention, the yardstick must be correct, independent of the income distribution.

Quite apart from the problem of practical application, in order to make the theorem meaningful the heterogeneous components of the national income must be properly weighted and thus be made commensurable. But practical application is, of course, the only justification of the theorem: it is certainly not required for an *analysis* of price formation. Its only function is to serve as an 'objective' statement in a *political* argument. Nobody would want to maintain that national income is maximized under laissez-faire irrespective of the relative significance, i.e. the weights attached to its component parts. It is also clear that the unit of measurement cannot be derived from the theorem itself for that would again be circular.

We conclude that the theorem presupposes a social unit of value which measures what is relevant from any conceivable set of political valuations. Such a unit does not exist and cannot exist. We cannot go into a detailed discussion of index number theory here. Suffice it to say that such a measure is impossible *in principle*, not just because of statistical difficulties. The latter would not affect the logical criticism.

The existence of this problem has always been vaguely felt. Definitions of the unit of measurement are therefore obscure when they are given at all: e.g. 'valuation by the free market', 'social valuation', etc. They express the idea of society as a subject of valuations, the familiar 'communistic fiction' and the idea of an exchange between Man (not men!) and Nature. These expressions indicate that the laissez-faire theorem must logically refer to national income as a sum of welfare, in the subjective sense, not as a sum of physical goods and services, in the objective sense. The latter is an objective sum of quantities with a clear meaning. The weighting system is required in order to add the components of the physical total product into a social sum which is the measure of the psychic income of society. Neither this psychic total nor the weighting system can be conceived as independent of income distribution. The whole construction is metaphysical.

The attempt to make the theory objective by the device of abstracting from income distribution, with the intention to isolate all the subjective factors in the latter, must, therefore, fail. Whenever there is an increase in some items and a decrease in others we face the index number problem. The index number problem does not arise because we are dealing with figures, but because we attempt to treat something as a homogeneous quantity whose heterogeneous composition changes in different situations.

There is no such thing as an ideal index which is theoretically correct, independent of the point of view from which the weights are determined. The indices which we calculate for the analysis of concrete economic developments are for this reason always subject to a margin of error or uncertainty which corresponds to divergencies of applicable points of view or valuations. A determination of the size of this margin can only be carried out by empirical study of the possible conflicting interests on an issue.

Let us suppose, for the sake of argument, that in the theory of economic liberalism we are thinking of national income indices of the type which we are using in empirical studies. In a general and abstract argument of this type we would have no means to define this index properly. But we would know that, like all other indices, it could be applied only within a margin of uncertainty, the size of which we could never discover. But what does the existence of a margin of error mean? It is surely a serious objection to a theory which claims to establish that national income is decreased by certain economic interferences with free competition. These effects would often be relatively small and would rarely run in one direction only. It is the now familiar difficulty: How can one arrive at definite conclusions without definite premises?

There is an even more important reason why an argument couched in general terms will remain nonsensical and why the *size* of the difference in national income *must* be discussed in connection with any particular intervention. Let us assume that our criticism has been entirely false and that it can be shown that national income is maximized under laissez-faire, irrespective of political value positions. Even then this would only be true on certain abstract assumptions. If the theory is to have any practical significance, one must be able to determine *by how much* national income would be reduced by some particular intervention in order to be able to discuss next the actual importance, in a particular case, of the assumptions made. We should have to know this also in order to weigh the arguments for laissez-faire against the arguments for intervention on grounds of its distributional results.

It is thus essential to know something about the order of magnitude of the change in national income, whether it is 5 per cent, or 0·5 per cent, or perhaps only 0·005 per cent. If we have no idea of the approximate order of magnitude of a change, the principle of laissez-faire, even if otherwise sound, tells us no more than that political intervention is only justified if it has desirable results. For this, no theory is needed. Quantitative precision is all the more important as, for a number of reasons, the 'social productivity curve' which the theory postulates would, on its own assumptions, have to be rather flat in the neighbourhood of the critical positions.

We shall mention only very briefly the assumptions and reservations of the laissez-faire postulate. They are treated more or less exhaustively in the literature. First there is the whole problem of rational behaviour dealt with in Chapter 4. Then there is the special question already treated by J. S. Mill: individuals have an interest to act according to certain rules but only if others obey the same rules. This raises problems of social and fiscal policy which cannot be discussed on the basis of laissez-faire.

Then there is the difficulty raised by statics versus dynamics. Laissez-faire is only supposed to be valid on the assumption of *ceteris paribus*. Yet every intervention is a dynamic event, designed to alter a development. The majority of protectionist reservations which the liberals concede freely are exceptions to the assumption of static conditions. There is a host of such exceptions and they can easily be increased by adding all kinds of dynamic considerations. All economic development is essentially dynamic.

Finally there is the assumption of free competition. The point at issue is an interference with free competition. In reality, free competition neither exists nor has ever existed. It cannot even be clearly conceived, for freedom of contract presupposes rules and regulations about the conditions under which contracts are to be made. These rules and regulations substantially affect price formation. They cannot be purely abstract rules. They must determine not only to what extent, but in what sense and with what effects competition is free. In practice the problem is always to assess the effects of a certain measure in a system of highly organized competition, which has very little in common with the liberal assumption. Generally, it is not even possible to decide whether a particular measure would bring us nearer to, or take us further away from, the purely fictitious state of free competition. Suppose there is complete monopolization in the labour and commodity markets of a country, with the exception of a single industry in which there is still a certain amount of competition. A protective tariff for this industry, or a subsidy, or monopolistic regulation or socialization could then be advocated on liberal grounds.

The theory is also incomplete. Its implied calculations are carried out in terms of positive magnitudes with the result of a sum of goods and services enjoyed. But a proper calculation would require the inclusion of negative magnitudes of things given up and services rendered, as well as the 'distribution' of these negative items. But work rendered and its distribution are assumed to be constant in the liberal analysis. This tricky assumption is unnecessary. In principle, a more inclusive theory would be no more or less conclusive than the narrower version. But if 'sacrifices' had been included as negative items, the difficulty of finding a common yardstick would have become too obvious; they are therefore omitted. As we have noticed before, this lop-sidedness is also connected with the opposition of the early marginalists to the classical value theory of costs. Utilitarians think in terms of means and ends; but they do not neglect the disutility of means (= costs) in their calculus. This is certainly not altogether satisfactory, but the argument becomes even more unrealistic if disutilities are excluded altogether.

In economics consumption is the sole end of production. This is a stock phrase of all the textbooks since Adam Smith. In other words: Man works in order to live. This is a possible philosophy of life. As long as work and the other real cost items are included in the valuation, this view is, at least formally, fairly complete. But the liberal argument assumes these items to be constant and pays attention only to the positive side. Fortunately, there are many people who live in order to work, who consume in order to produce, if we like to use those terms. Most people who are reasonably well off derive more satisfaction in their capacity as producers than as consumers. Indeed, many would define the social ideal as a state in which as many people as possible can live in this way. Now some of the most important economic interventions are aimed at the conditions in which production is carried on, and not directly at the results of production and their distribution.

We are interested not only in the technical aspects of production, not only in how owners of productive factors dispose of them, but also in what kind of production it is, quite apart from the exchange value of the products; we are interested in how people work and in their welfare as producers. There is more to this than health measures, regulations for the prevention of accidents, etc. Some, for instance, are disturbed by the decline of agriculture. If one asked them, as Wicksell did, whether they cared more for the acres than for the people who should live on what these acres could produce, one may discover all sorts of connections between the two which cannot easily be fitted into a scheme of costs and income. Views on these sociological aspects of production will, of course, differ according to one's political and moral convictions. The important thing in this connection is to remember that it is a matter of political valuations. Men's interest in production is not confined to its products and their distribution.

To this kind of objection the liberal may reply: Certainly, this brings out one of the most important assumptions of the theory and also a limitation of its validity. Economic life can be judged by other, perhaps higher, criteria but we confine ourselves to the 'economic aspect'.

The meaning of this and other admissions is somewhat obscure and the obscurity is connected with the underlying normative attitude. Social life and human valuations are forced into a logical scheme which finds its fullest expression in harmony models. Early socialist critics already pointed out the circularity of such arguments. In reply, the liberals make a general reservation for distributional effects in order to salvage liberalism for the sphere of production and exchange. List and other protectionists criticize its application to the sphere of production by raising dynamic objections. The liberals add new reservations but retain the model. It is discovered and increasingly stressed that people do not behave rationally. Once again, more points are conceded. Modern socialists agitate for a radical reorganization of all production, which does not aim only at the expropriation of rent, interest, and profit—the reservation about income distribution could look after that—but at a planned economy. In so far as they propagate social policies, these are also largely directed at changes in production. New reservations about 'non-economic' factors, 'higher points of view', etc., are introduced by the liberal apologists. Meanwhile industry and trade have organized themselves and their markets on a grand scale. Liberals respond by underlining more strongly their abstract assumptions.

Abstract assumptions may be excellent tools of theoretical analysis. It is difficult, however, to see what rôle they can play as a basis for a postulate of practical policy, or rather, it is impossible to see what such a postulate can then mean. Liberalism would be immortal, in spite of all its unrealistic assumptions, if it were logically tenable. But it is not. It sets out to isolate an 'economic' factor in political life and to measure it with a social yardstick, which is, however, inconceivable. Its only significance is that it gives a scientific appearance to an individualist, anti-interventionist prejudice.

This does not exhaust the whole set of its abstract assumptions and reservations but we shall leave it at that. We have tried to show that the theory is not only untenable as an abstraction, but also cut off by its assumptions from any connection with the real world.

Liberals have, however, always had two further strings to their bow. Bentham begins his *Defence of Usury* by asserting that the onus of proof always rests on those who advocate intervention.[23] This statement, which is repeated throughout the whole laissez-faire literature, presupposes, of course, that the theorem is correct *in some sense.* Otherwise there is no reason why the burden of proof should be distributed in such an unfair manner. Even if we grant this for the sake of the argument there is still a difficulty. Just because there are in the real world many deviations from free competition, is it difficult to decide whether any particular intervention would bring the fictional state of free competition nearer or remove it further. Hence the onus of proof cannot rest on the person who advocates intervention simply because it is an intervention.

Finally it is said that even if liberalism is theoretically untenable, it is still the safest *practical* guide. This has been the argument of last resort already before, but particularly since Cairnes, who, however, had the reservations in mind rather than a fundamental weakness of the principle itself. But if its basic theoretical idea is meaningless, this proposition is no more than an expression of a political prejudice. Cairnes himself qualifies it at once by saying that this practical guide must never stand in the way of carefully considered proposals for social and industrial reform.[24] In more recent times the argument of the 'practical' value of liberalism has also often been used. If it is to be more than sheer political prejudice, it must mean that persons who want to change social conditions through interventions have, generally, no clear understanding of economic and social problems. Such a sweeping condemnation is hardly convincing.

Historically, liberal economic theorists, no doubt, have had to fight all sorts of false popular notions. This struggle inspired them and helped to convince them that they were right, even if at times they must have felt uneasy about the proofs of their theory. There is something like a hierarchy of errors, although one would be hard put to it to say what precisely this means. An argument could hardly be worse than unrealistic in its premises and fallacious in its deductions. Yet, liberalism was useful educationally. It refuted crude and false ideas and popularized at least certain elementary economic notions.

The question remains whether it was the most effective instrument of education. We shall not discuss this question here. It seems, however, that in the long run error cannot, with impunity, be fought by error. One must also remember that it was not the most scrupulous version of the theory which was most apt to be used for popular education. For even if a skilful analyst were able to keep numerous reservations in mind, one cannot expect that these reservations should survive the type of popular propaganda which the liberals have practised since the days of the classics. The decisive argument against liberalism as an instrument of education is, of course, that it is redundant. It is simplest to fight errors as such, without replacing them by new errors. The only weakness of this method is that men, on the whole, do not want to be taught to think straight; they prefer to be told what they should believe.

Chapter 6

'SOCIAL HOUSEKEEPING' AND SOCIAL VALUE

THE idea of economy as a kind of social housekeeping inspires not only the theory of free trade but all other doctrines of economic policy. Its terminological presentation undergoes more changes than other metaphysical ideas in economics. Frequently, it is only implicit. We have already come across it in various connections and continue our criticism of the idea of a 'social household', which is the subject of social valuation, at this stage because liberalism seems to be the most suitable starting-point. Our discussion of liberalism has given us some idea of the kind of political assumptions that underlie the notion of social housekeeping and its criticism can therefore be briefer without loss of clarity.

The notion that society, like the head of a family, keeps house for its members, is deeply rooted in economic terminology. In German *Volkswirtschaftslehre* suggests to the unsophisticated that there is a collective subject of economic activity, viz., 'all citizens of the nation', with a common purpose and common values. In English, 'political economy' or 'economics' have gradually lost all clear associations with what they literally mean, but 'theory of wealth' or 'theory of welfare' express similar ideas.

In earlier times, the notion of a national or state economy as a unified household was more appropriate. In an absolute monarchy it described something real: 'l'état c'est moi'. The cameralists treated economic activity from the point of view of a collective purpose. Their test for the desirability of economic policies was the interest of the ruling prince. They did, however, usually assume that the prince has not only 'fiscal interests', but cares genuinely for the welfare of his people. His interest in public welfare was not considered to clash with his fiscal interest but rather to be part of it. The prince, representing the ruling house, had nothing to gain from killing the goose that laid the golden eggs.

However, this autocratic view of society, which left its mark on the concept of political economy, gradually lost ground. The great natural law philosophers, who had endeavoured to prove the necessity of absolute monarchy, but who had not been content with just calling it natural, had already been forced to widen the concept of the subject from whose point of view social activity was ultimately to be judged. It was, in the last resort, always the people. The absolute power of the ruler was considered to be a necessary condition for the enjoyment of the natural state by the people. The maintenance of internal peace was used as the main argument for the naturalness and necessity of this type of society. This shift of emphasis was aided by the traditions of Roman and Germanic law. Several other developments helped to create the conditions favourable to the growth of a political philosophy which no longer considered absolute monarchy as the only natural form of government: the growing wealth and power of the middle classes, the development towards democracy in England, and in many countries the revolutionary tendency of thought before the French revolution, were amongst them.

This interesting and very complex development of thought in the theory of the state has a bearing on our problem. As soon as the idea of the prince as the sole subject of political theory is abandoned, the problem arises how to make the multitude into a unified subject of valuations. The very attempt to study society 'from the economic point of view' makes it necessary to assume such a unified subject and to determine it scientifically in order to derive the general interest or the general welfare.

This requirement was admirably met by utilitarianism. Its social calculus provided just the right unifying concept, viz., social utility. Quite consistently the utilitarians also used their social calculus to prove democracy. Parliament became a kind of social agency for the application of the pleasure calculus.

The attack of the economists on mercantilism was therefore not directed against its fundamental concept of a national economy with national interests. On the contrary, the critics adopted it. What they tried to prove is that mercantilism misconceived the methods by which those interests should be pursued.

It may be worth remembering that the concept 'national economy' was somewhat differently interpreted by the two chief opponents of mercantilism. The Physiocrats had a more organic conception of society. Thus Quesnay, a physician by profession, looked upon society as a sick organism which had long been exposed to destructive parasites and quacks. The liberalism of the Physiocrats resembled the therapeutic theory of nature healers.

Adam Smith did not doubt the healing powers of nature but he made little use of the organic analogy, and his followers even less. It is, incidentally, odd that the nation whose social and cultural life comes nearest to an organic development has, with the exception of Spencer, so little use for this analogy. On the other hand, it has always played an important part in the philosophies of nations which, either because they did not care for it, or because they could not attain it, never had much 'organic' continuity in their development.

Adam Smith incorporated the concept of a purposive economy into the system of individualism. Disregarding such side-lines as the German historical school, it has remained in the centre of economic theory ever since. Society, for the British individualists, is the sum of individuals. For any organic theory, on the other hand, the whole is more than the sum of the parts.

Political economy is also called the science of 'wealth'. The term suggests material prosperity. According to Senior and J. S. Mill economics is confined to the study of the 'material' or 'lower' wants of men. Later, 'wealth' is often replaced by 'economic welfare', 'social welfare' or just 'welfare'. But the meaning does not change, except for a more psychological interpretation under utilitarian influence. We have discussed this change in the two chapters on the development of the theory of value.

It is typical of British thought that these important concepts are hardly ever properly discussed. One generation hands them on to the next. Terms are changed when it seems convenient, but their meaning is never questioned, just as nobody would question the authority of the 'common sense' which sanctions these concepts. British economists always appeal to 'common sense', or, to specify the authority, to the 'man in the street', who, it is true, possesses a good deal of common sense in Britain. In more technical arguments this appeal is not always possible although even there it is often attempted. This appeal to common sense is most successful when problems are stated and their premises formulated. As a rule, arguments which aim at establishing fundamental concepts are presented in a way which is palatable to an average man with some practical experience. The proof usually begins with an apparently obvious proposition which, however, already contains all conclusions. There are certainly worse criteria for sound reasoning than British common sense. But one should not forget that the man in the street may be firmly convinced of all sorts of things which are completely false. In a sense, all science and even more all philosophy is a struggle to defeat false notions cherished by common sense.

British political economy has always been conservative and eclectic in the choice of its basic concepts. This has been a source of its strength. Research generally suffers if there is too much originality in problems of principle, as for instance in Germany. The peculiar method of the British eclectics is this common-sense attitude. Instead of directing at the difficult problems of principle a searching analysis which might disrupt the basic structure of their arguments, they conceal these problems behind a word screen. They then shift the analysis to problems of detail which can be fitted into the traditional metaphysical framework. Comfort is taken from the reflection that we all agree in principle and that everybody knows what we are talking about, although it may not always be easy to put it precisely. The attitude to interpersonal comparisons of utility is a good illustration. 'We all do it daily.'

For a consistent utilitarian, there should be no difficulty about the meaning of 'social economy' and 'social welfare'. A satisfactory definition can be derived with the aid of the social pleasure calculus. Sidgwick and Edgeworth, the last and most penetrating utilitarians, and next to Jevons the most brilliant English neo-classicists, dedicated much painstaking and illuminating discussion to this problem. But by and large, the assumptions of welfare economics, though fundamental and all-pervasive in British economics, are tacit rather than explicit.

What is meant by a social economy whose function is social housekeeping? In the first place, it implies or suggests an analogy between the individual who runs his own or his family household[1] and society. Adam Smith and James Mill elaborated this analogy explicitly. After J. S. Mill's criticism, and with the wider recognition of the distinction between practical and theoretical political economy, the analogy was generally less emphasized.

Nevertheless, it remained in the background. We have practically unlimited wants but only limited means to satisfy them: therefore we must economize. This is the elementary empirical proposition on which the whole structure of economics is built. To economize means to meet given wants with the minimum sacrifice and to meet the maximum wants with a given sacrifice. This thought is elaborated, later, into the theory of hedonistic equilibrium in which marginal utilities and marginal disutilities are proportional to exchange values and individual net utility is therefore maximized.

The same is said to be true for society: means to satisfy wants are limited, not indeed absolutely, but their increase requires additional efforts. The wants of men are unlimited and can be satisfied only incompletely. Therefore society must economize. How this is done is the subject matter of political economy.

What is gained by this analogy? Its proponents would claim that it enables us to view the whole economic process coherently. Chaos is transformed into cosmos. Price formation is no longer the result of the play of blind forces but expresses the manner in which society economizes its scarce resources. An otherwise meaningless causal sequence is thus endowed with a purpose. Economic phenomena fall into two groups: some are obstacles to the efficient pursuit of ends, others have positive functions. Amongst the obstacles there are inertia and frictions, e.g. immobility of labour.

On certain abstract assumptions such as free competition, etc., all economic phenomena fulfil certain functions. Especially prices are of crucial importance for social housekeeping. They stimulate the supply of goods and hence of productive factors. They also induce the factors of production to produce the type of goods and the quantities which consumers want. A price rise of a good, for example, attracts factors into its line of production and thus brings about an increase in the amount produced just sufficient to meet the demand. The fact that through the price mechanism factors are directed into the right channels enables consumers to determine production. At the same time, price rises have the function of choking off demand where there are shortages, which again is part of the task of social housekeeping. Since prices thus regulate both demand and supply, an equilibrium position is reached. Given private property and absence of interference with the right of free contract, the 'automatic' mechanism without any 'planning' brings about all required adjustments. Anybody who suggests that it is a contradiction to believe in a purposive system of housekeeping which works automatically, i.e. without purpose, merely shows that he does not understand the meaning of the concept 'economy'. The point about the analogy between private and social housekeeping is that a single subject with a consistent set of ends is a fiction. We might also say that we suppose 'all of us' to be the subject: we all pull at a rope in different directions and the result is a social economy.

At this point the theory branches into two versions. According to one, the analogy is also a justification of the actual course of economic events. It amounts to a skilful formulation of the familiar doctrine of harmony. The concept of society furnishes the required unity for the conflicting interests. The price mechanism is justified by the fact that it succeeds in husbanding scarce resources. The analogy is, of course, deceptive. It gives the appearance of unity where there is diversity; it attempts to give purpose to a sequence of events without purpose. It is, of course, true that the sequence of events is the result of a large number of individual volitions and purposes. But it is also determined by a number of legal institutions and arbitrary conditions which are not necessary in the sense in which the economic process is considered to be necessary. Even if these incidental and institutional factors could be conceived to be absent (they cannot), the assumption of a purpose would still be unjustified. The result of what is willed by a diversity of interests cannot be said to have been willed by anyone. The analogy simply postulates a single subject where there is not one, but many. Hence the result cannot be described as collective 'economizing'. To do so is to fall into the trap of the 'communistic fiction'.

The second version is more sceptical about the results of a free pricing system, without abandoning the belief that it is essentially purposive. In some respects, it is said, wrong purposes may be pursued or the right purposes may be pursued inefficiently, but nonetheless, it is a process with a purpose. It is believed to be essential to look upon it in this way in order to discover its deficiencies and their cure. This more widely accepted version is clearly more interesting than the cruder version. It is also more difficult to pin down and to criticize. Even the believers in harmony occasionally criticize the free price mechanism. Since they usually assume free competition, divergencies between the ideal and the actual are bound to arise. But objections to the free pricing system go usually further.

The ideal economic system by which actual events are judged is described in various ways. But there always must be a criterion of social value in order to make sense of such concepts as social economy and social housekeeping. The actual economic system may then be compared with this ideal and one may find that it should be improved. The concepts 'economy' or 'economizing' presuppose a collective subject which acts with a social purpose in view. Only then can purposive collective activity be determined. Now since 'social economy' is the subject matter of the science of political economy, it is, presumably, meant to be a scientific concept. It must therefore be capable of being *objectively* determined, i.e. in such a way as to be valid for everyone. Only thus can economics lead to an objective economic policy, for instance to principles of fiscal policy. Irrespective of how we may judge existing conditions, the concept 'social economy' implies that it is *possible* to judge them *objectively*.

There is also a third possibility. One might retain the terms but not their meaning. Concepts like economy, economic functions, adjustments, equilibrium, etc., could be retained as metaphors without any implication of purpose, in the same way in which chemists used to speak of the affinity of elements. No objection can be raised to such a procedure. But one must be careful with metaphors in economics. In the first place, economic activity is dynamic and there are no constants. Thus if one calculates the elasticity of demand in one set of conditions one should not expect it to be the same in quite different conditions. Hitherto we have not reached sufficiently fundamental factors in economics, and probably never shall, to be able to establish constant coefficients, as it is done in the natural sciences. This lack of fixed points creates difficulties in the formation of concepts, while their existence in the natural sciences makes it less dangerous there to use animistic metaphors. Scientific arguments, at any rate nowadays, are more immune against animistic suggestions.

There is a second reason against the use of such metaphors in economics. Superficially, it appears as if 'social economy' or 'market economy' denote something real. Their metaphorical use must therefore be hedged around with so many reservations that it becomes stylistically cumbersome. If the reservations are then left out, the reader tends to associate the wrong meaning with metaphors, whether the author intends this or not, and the absence of a precise definition makes this much more dangerous.

Superficially, it does look as if there really were a social market economy. We are studying, in the last resort, individuals who act with certain ends in view. It is also true that our resources are insufficient to make economizing unnecessary; it is true that we have certain political aims which we try to realize by combining with other people with similar aims and by exercising political pressure; it is finally true that when we think politically we look upon economic events as a kind of social household, although, indeed, often as bad housekeeping which we should like to reform. More precisely, economic events appear as a potentially efficient system of conducting the nation's affairs, as soon as we put ourselves into the position of a supreme would-be legislator, the subject of directing or preserving the economic process. But as no one, except possibly an economic dictator, actually determines the economic process, this way of looking at the causal sequence of events is false.

We can speak of an individual household because we look upon our own conduct as purposive. The concept of a social household implies similarly a purpose and is therefore political. Without a political valuation, without stating the ends to be pursued, it is meaningless. As we have said above, the concept of a purposive market economy presupposes a subject and a will. If the concept is to be scientific, then objective politics must be possible. If this possibility is denied, and the concept is yet retained, a hopeless muddle results. The deduction of objective politics appears somehow possible, but one cannot say how.

The notion of a market economy as the coordination of activities, directed towards a purpose, a social system of efficient housekeeping, is common to all political doctrines in economics. They claim to tell us what, on certain assumptions, is objectively right; how the affairs of society as a whole can be conducted efficiently. All political doctrines derive their claim to objectivity ultimately from this belief.

Viewed from a different angle, the normative idea of an 'economy' is expressed in the theory of *social value*. Social value determines the valuations of the collective subject, (which is implied in the concept 'economy') and thus provides the standard by which economic events can be judged when they are viewed as a process of social housekeeping. Only a few writers have dealt with the concept of social value systematically. In Britain it is hardly discussed, although terms like 'wealth' and 'welfare' imply social value. Our critical remarks in the following do not aim at a full discussion but merely attempt to consider the idea of 'economy' from a new point of view.

Two examples will suffice: J. B. Clark's theory of social value and v. Wieser's theory of natural value. Both authors are marginal utility theorists.

Optimism, puritanism, and natural law have always been characteristic features of American economics. Carey, for example, criticized the British classics with arguments which at that time would have been hardly possible in any other social setting. Malthus's law of population, for example, is said to be incompatible with his view of the good intentions of Providence, and Ricardo's theory of distribution has not the simplicity which laws of nature have. General Walker's theory of price, like Carey's, is interesting in its own right. What matters for our purpose is that he believed that everyone receives what he deserves according to his contribution to production. J. B. Clark, who, in Europe, is usually considered as America's most eminent economist, elaborated Walker's arguments. He exercised an immense influence on his own and the next generation in America.

J. B. Clark set himself the task of explaining economic activity, and in particular prices under perfect competition, in a manner which would also justify them. More than any other recent eminent economist, he has systematized the idea of harmony. He takes the distribution of property for granted and, implicitly, accepts it as justified. In his book on the labour market and labour disputes he says that 'under perfect competition the reward of each worker is virtually his own actual product'.[2] This ethical interpretation of productivity theory pervades his whole theory of distribution, in spite of occasional suitable assurances that science can only observe and not prescribe. Clark is interesting for our inquiry because he, more than most proponents of the harmony doctrine, attempted to prove his case and was thus forced to an explicit discussion of social value. In various essays[3] he developed a whole philosophical theory, which also appears in his well-known main work on distribution.

Clark's argument is this: Society can be regarded as an organic whole, or even as a single person. If somebody buys or sells, he seems, superficially, to trade with another individual but in reality he trades with the market as a whole. The market is an organism which experiences wants through its component parts, viz., the individuals. It is the expression of the totality of individual wants. It is this social organism which determines price, for under free competition the supply and demand of any single individual does not affect price. Clark explains price by marginal utility and marginal productivity. In virtue of his organic view he can consider the price thus determined as a direct measure of social value. Occasionally he also measures social value in terms of the marginal social labour unit which stands for the marginal sacrifice of 'society as a whole'. The two measures give the same result, because everyone receives for his work exactly the value of his marginal product. In other words, the value of labour's marginal product is equal to its exchange value. The only difference is that the one measure goes 'deeper'.

The whole argument hinges on the view that society is an organism. This view, which Clark had probably adopted from Spencer and in which he was confirmed during his studies in Germany, turns out to be, on closer inspection, an empty phrase. In spite of much elaboration in his writings he never says more than that there is a market and that for some unexplained reason he believes that its prices reflect the wants of society. Clark meets the difficulty of conceiving society as a single subject by repeating that it *is* such a subject. It must, he says, be considered 'literally' as a person or an organism. This, he contends, has hitherto been overlooked in economic theory. Unfortunately, this latter statement is certainly not true.

It is somewhat mysterious how Clark could put forward such a flimsy theory and why it should have been so widely accepted.[4] Later American economists, however, have, on the whole, rejected it.

v. Wieser's theory of 'natural value' is a more thorough piece of work. Its arguments are more widely accepted and have probably had a greater influence than references in the literature to v. Wieser might suggest. The decisive differences between the two theories is that Clark believes in harmony, v. Wieser does not. v. Wieser's intention in his analysis of 'natural value' is to explain, not to justify. Nevertheless, it remains a metaphysical and normative concept and is therefore unfit to explain anything. v. Wieser does not even succeed in giving it a precise meaning.

His theory of natural value is the most coherent attempt to explain the economic process as a social economy. He endeavours to study what economic value would be if it depended exclusively on quantities of utilities and goods as they accrue to the individual. He therefore has to abstract from a number of carefully enumerated circumstances which distort actual prices from what they would be if the market worked perfectly. Thus v. Wieser recognizes that the postulate of a social economy may mean either of two things: One must either, like Clark and other harmony economists, look upon existing economic conditions as the realization of social values, possibly with some reservations about free competition, etc.; or one must examine these conditions in the light of an ideal. v. Wieser sees the ideal in what he calls the communist state.

He also recognizes that there is nothing original in this but that he is merely bringing out certain assumptions more clearly which many economists have shared.[5] He has seen the communistic fiction implicit in most writings on economics, and wants to make it explicit in order to make use of it in his analysis. He does not doubt that it can be used for scientific analysis.

What results does v. Wieser expect from an analysis of natural value and of the ideal market economy? What, to begin with, is the relation between natural value and actual market prices? Natural value, he says, is a 'formative element' (*Bildungselement*) in actual values. But it is not allowed to manifest itself fully because such obstacles as error, deception, compulsion, etc., stand in the way. Above all, the prevailing distribution of property and income is an impediment. Thus there is a second formative element in the determination of prices, viz., unequal purchasing power. He then defines an ideal economic order by abstracting from all social conflicts and believes thus to extract the essence of economic activity: the ideal adaptation of scarce means to competing social wants. In the system of natural value prices are determined only by marginal utilities; actual prices, however, are determined both by marginal utilities and by the distribution of purchasing power.

(This, incidentally, like any notion of a social economy, pre-supposes the possibility of interpersonal comparisons of utility.) Even if ignorance, deception, compulsion, etc., were entirely absent, actual prices would still be distorted natural values because they reflect partly the ruling distribution. But since natural value is one of two elements in the formation of actual prices, an examination of natural value has a bearing upon reality and is not without empirical significance.

v. Wieser's reasoning is clear and consistent. If price formation is to be regarded as a purposive economic process, there must be a purpose. If this purpose is to be determined scientifically, it must be an objectively defined economic ideal. In so far as such an ideal order can be defined (we postpone the discussion of v. Wieser's own definition), and if we assume that the actual order is not utterly unlike the ideal, it seems reasonable to regard actual economic events as a more or less perfect realization of this ideal, i.e. to look upon natural value as a 'formative element' in market values. However this may be, let us assume that it would be possible.

We can now see why v. Wieser uses this device. We want to know, he says, to what extent market values are natural, i.e. how strong the 'formative power' of natural value is. If we know this, we can discover which institutions serve merely 'selfish interests' and which serve the social economy. The latter are *technically* essential. If they were abandoned we would be left without instruments to check and control the economy. By analysing the natural conditions, v. Wieser hopes to discover the *necessary* conditions of social housekeeping, of husbanding scarce resources in the interests of society. What is not natural is also incidental or arbitrary. The word 'necessary' is intended to legitimize the conclusions as scientifically objective.

At this point v. Wieser hesitates in a manner typical of normative writers. They talk about objective values but want to dissociate themselves from political theory. He says that 'natural value is a neutral phenomenon'; that its analysis can neither prove nor disprove socialism. (He speaks of socialism here, not only for the obvious reason that he assumes a communist state. In the same connection he criticizes the whole socialist value theory. His arguments have played an important part in the criticism of Marx.) Natural value is said to be neutral because it can be determined without postulating anybody's right to a definite income. Thus rent and interest can be defined as natural values without any implications about who should receive them. They would also exist in a socialist economy, although they may be differently distributed. (The same argument is used by v. Wieser and many authors after him to criticize Marx's theory of value.) Yet, it is not a convincing proof of the 'neutrality' of natural value. Unless v. Wieser intends to present a purely formal argument without interest, natural values must be determined quantitatively. (The only possible significance of such a formal argument would be the refutation of the socialist theory of labour value as a scientific theory. As a normative doctrine it cannot be refuted in this manner.) But the quantities of natural values are a function of income distribution. Incomes determine demand and supply of goods and factors. In order to determine natural values quantitatively all other economic quantities must have been already determined. That v. Wieser could overlook this can be explained by the fact that the Austrians, in contrast to the Lausanne school, had not advanced to a general equilibrium analysis in which all economic phenomena are shown to be interdependent.

Natural value has not been shown to be a politically 'neutral' concept simply because it can be shown that Marx's theory of labour value does not hold for a socialist economy. Not all politics, nor even all socialism, is Marxism, even although its value theory was a burning question until the end of the nineteenth century. Moreover, we shall see that v. Wieser's definition of the conditions of natural value contains recommendations about, inter alia, income distribution, and that it is presented in a manner which can leave no doubt that it implies a political ideal.[6]

v. Wieser emphasizes repeatedly that the actual market economy diverges from an ideal economy because market values are not exclusively determined by wants and available resources. If we nevertheless want to examine it as a process of 'housekeeping' we must do this in the light of the ideal system of housekeeping in which wants and available resources are the only determinants. Such an ideal is only conceivable if interpersonal comparisons of wants and of marginal utilities are possible.

One should therefore expect that v. Wieser would define his ideal economy as one in which values are determined by marginal utilities, weighted by their social significance. But he does not do this for a good reason. He would have to explain how marginal utilities can be weighted by their social significance. He therefore uses other criteria for the ideal state instead, without explaining how these criteria make social comparisons of marginal utilities possible, and why they should guarantee the ideal social equilibrium between exchange values and marginal utilities, why they should safeguard that natural interpersonal relation between degrees of the satisfaction of wants which is defined as ideal. Yet he must assume that it is done somehow, for this equilibrium between wants and resources is his criterion of *Wirtschaft*, of proper social economy.

He determines the conditions for the system of natural values as follows: a 'perfect communist·state', a society of maximum efficiency in which there is no abuse of administrative power, whose members are entirely unselfish and in which there is neither ignorance nor error. In another passage he stipulates that there should be no inequalities of property, no party divisions, etc.

v. Wieser is not interested in the question whether such a society could really exist. He is content that it can be imagined. Now an assumption can, of course, be as unrealistic as we like. Most abstract assumptions in economics have little bearing on reality. Nor, for that matter, does one body move on the surface of another without friction. But abstract assumptions must be clearly defined if, as analytical tools, they are to be of any use for the determination of other concepts. v. Wieser sets out to obtain a view of the whole economic process. He abstracts, in order to study this process as a deviation from his abstraction. He wants to *determine* the deviations. This can be done only if they are *determinate* deviations from a *determinate* natural state. But when it comes to defining this ideal and the deviations from it, he offers only vague generalities.

It need hardly be said that his description of the natural state is most unsatisfactory. Obviously, even in a communist state individuals would differ in their views on what they consider to be socially useful, i.e. on the proper conduct of the nation's economic affairs. Indeed, v. Wieser admits this possibility later. And it is no solution to postulate unity of social values by postulating 'unselfish' behaviour. For in the first place, he does not define this criterion, and secondly, it is well known that unselfish people are no more prone to agree amongst themselves than others. What does absence of party differences mean in a society in which

M

objectives of economic policy must be determined by collective decisions? The whole argument amounts to the assertion that society must be conceived as a single subject. This, however, is precisely what cannot be conceived. If we tried, we would be attempting to abstract from the essential fact that social activity is the result of the intentions of *several* individuals.

We have discussed v. Wieser's theory in some detail because it exposes clearly the implications of the idea of a social economy. He reasons correctly up to the point at which value judgements must be introduced. His analysis breaks down at this point because values cannot be determined scientifically.

It is, of course, possible to specify the values by which one judges the efficiency of an economic system. But this raises the alternative difficulty of showing that these values are scientific or objective. Yet, without value judgements the whole notion of a social conduct of economic affairs is meaningless. It is v. Wieser's great merit to have seen this clearly.

It is often said that such concepts as *Volkswirtschaft*, social economy, wealth, welfare, etc., are necessary for the definition of the scope and the method of economics. They are therefore often treated in the introductory chapters of systematic treatises. Economics is said to be the science of the wealth of the nation, or of the world as a whole; or the science of how the nations or the world economize their scarce resources to satisfy wants. Scarcity necessitates economy. Anyone who rejects this notion of a social economy has to offer an alternative definition of 'economics'.

An old tradition demands that the sciences be grouped into a logical hierarchy. It divides the world of experience into departments each of which contains one branch of scientific knowledge. The lines of limitation are supposed to be discoverable by logic. They are not a matter of convenience. They are believed to be determined by the peculiar method by which each subject is pursued. Economics, then, is allotted a particular field of inquiry and with it a particular method of research. Its subject is thus delineated by the scope of its method.

These discussions of the scope and method of economics have not been very profitable. Economics, like other sciences, consists of a number of quite different problems thrown together partly by tradition and partly by considerations of what is convenient for research and teaching. Attempts to define its precise scope are bound to be artificial. They are often motivated by the metaphysical intention, not just to give a definition, but to give a definition in such a way that a normative content can be smuggled into apparently scientific propositions.

Such definitions are both unnecessary and undesirable. They are unnecessary for the one concept which an economist need not define precisely is 'economics'. No argument can possibly be affected by such a definition, just as no chemist can draw any scientific conclusions from a definition of the concept 'chemistry'. In economics, as in any other empirical inquiry, we analyse the relations between observable data. We select the data according to their relevance to our problems. These problems happen to fall into our field of inquiry for various historical and practical reasons. We use those methods which promise to yield the quickest and best results.

Even if a strict, non-metaphysical definition were possible, it would still be undesirable. The forces which make for rigid frontiers between the sciences are in any case too strong. They tend to preserve the *status quo* and impede scientific advance. They tend to impose an irrational limitation on the scientific horizon. We can hope for progress in the social sciences only if the frontiers which have been drawn in the past for didactic reasons are removed. The most promising advances to-day are likely to come from an exploration of these borderlands.

The problems raised, but not the science to which they belong, must be clearly defined. A closer examination of these problems will show that they are of the following type: How do individuals behave in certain conditions? What happens on certain assumptions? What effect would a certain measure have on a certain situation? But never: What is 'economics'?

There is only one boundary which must be drawn and which should not be overstepped. But it is common to all sciences and not a frontier between them. This is the frontier between positive empirical knowledge and metaphysical speculations. The social sciences must, above all, be on their guard against normative and teleological speculation. But this boundary does not separate one branch of knowledge from another; on the contrary, such separations only encourage metaphysics.

Chapter 7

THE THEORY OF PUBLIC FINANCE

T HE theory of public finance, even more than any other branch of economic doctrine, suggests the idea of a purposive conduct of economic affairs. In the theory of public finance it is therefore particularly tempting to postulate a single subject and a coherent and objective set of values which guide economic activity. The fiction has almost an appearance of reality in the legal institutions which regulate the behaviour of the state and of the local communities. Here, it would seem, we are obviously concerned with a collective system of economy. The state and the local authorities are collective bodies which try to meet their requirements as efficiently as possible. They economize. Here, at least, there seems to be no reason to depart from the Cameralist tradition.

Moreover, public finance represents economic 'planning', i.e. positive intervention, and not just an automatic mechanism as in the abstract theory of harmony. Therefore the contradictions inherent in the fiction of a single collective subject are less flagrant. Yet, we shall see that it is false to believe that the assumption of a collective subject of economic activity presents fewer difficulties for the theory of public finance than for other branches of economic theory. Here, too, there is a multitude of subjects with conflicting political valuations. Every measure can be considered from as many standpoints as there are social ideals and constellations of interest.

As any other doctrine of economic policy, the theory of public finance is an attempt to assert unity where there is diversity, by postulating an ideal set of values. These postulates are explicit in the so-called principles of public finance and are implicit in the motivation for most fiscal proposals.

In no other field has the intrusion of metaphysics done so much harm as here. With a few exceptions, such as studies of the incidence of taxation and, of course, of the legal aspects which fall outside our inquiry, almost the whole theory of public finance is an elaboration of certain guiding principles, such as 'economy' or 'equity'. These speculations pervade even the theory of incidence and of fiscal legislation where they often obstruct the formulation of meaningful questions. This is particularly dangerous in view of the fact that the significant questions, which have been either obscured altogether or begged by pseudo-solutions, have become increasingly important during the last decades.

The writings on the principles of public finance are legion, and more is still being written. Classification, terminology, and doctrines vary a great deal and have undergone continual change. This is due to the fact that taxation affects political interests particularly strongly. All normative economic doctrines are largely rationalizations of political attitudes and in the theory of public finance probably even more than elsewhere because stronger political pressures are at work here. In so far as one can discern a trend in the development of economic though , fiscal theory has moved more rapidly towards a radical policy than other economic doctrines. The wide range of variations in the theory of public finance is partly also the result of the stronger German influence in this field. It has added 'organic' ideas of the state to the British ideas of natural law and utilitarianism which dominated other branches of economic theory.

Nobody has yet attempted the difficult task of writing an exhaustive critical history of the theory of public finance.[1] We must confine ourselves to a very brief and rough sketch of the general features of this development. We shall dwell at some length only on the more thorough Swedish attempt to formulate principles of taxation on the basis of the Austrian theory of marginal utility. This and a few other exceptions apart, the political conclusions of the theory of public finance are based on even more self-contradictory and on even looser premises than the conclusions in other fields.

One might think that a suitable method of classifying fiscal doctrines would be according to their political recommendations, i.e. according to what distribution of the tax burden they advocate, how they define and limit the scope of public activities, etc. This would seem to be a natural procedure, particularly if we remember that the development of the theory was clearly related to its political tendencies.

Yet, such a classification is impossible. It is characteristic of the theory that concrete conclusions of all types can be and have in fact been derived from any set of principles. Thus regressive, proportional, progressive and degressive taxation have all been justified and have all been refuted both by the principle of ability and by the principle of interest (*Interesseprinzip*). Nowhere has economic doctrine been able to develop political ideas with fewer logical restraints. The confusion is made worse because the discussion takes place, as it were, on two levels simultaneously. There is a dispute about the abstract, metaphysical, rational principles themselves, and about their practical application. For a systematic survey of ideas it is necessary to begin with an analysis of the differences on the first level, viz., those about principles.

All participants in this discussion of principles share the conviction that there must be a highest norm which all budgetary policy ought to obey. This norm is postulated to start with. It is an empty formula, e.g. that taxation must be 'just', that expenditure must be 'economical', that individuals must be treated as 'equals', etc. Almost any phrase will do, if it is sufficiently void of meaning. No concrete empirical meaning is given, and of course no *a priori* meaning can be extracted. The norm is then used as if it were meaningful, i.e. it is asked what practical policies follow from it. A concrete content is read into it, and thus differences of opinion obviously arise.

There is thus not even formal agreement on the abstract premise. Some say taxation ought to be 'economical', others that it ought to be 'equitable'. As a rule, however, disagreement refers to the interpretation of the first principle, in which case we have moved to another level. But some authors find it convenient to strengthen their own interpretations through particular formulations of the highest principle and they are therefore determined to establish, in the first place, that taxation must be, say, 'equitable' and not 'economical', or vice versa. Highest principles are important because they give the resulting interpretations the appearance of scientific objectivity. The tendency is always to keep them sufficiently general to be beyond dispute. This is a widespread practice in economics, but it is best illustrated in the theory of public finance.

In spite of all reservations, it dominates even the more historical and sociological writings such as those of the German school.

v. Tyszka, for example, begins his discussion of the principles of taxation by saying that the idea of equity changes continually and develops with cultural, economic, and social conditions. It is 'relative and historical. . . . The concrete meaning of this abstract concept has changed from age to age.'[2] It is not surprising that he goes on to say: 'We can therefore not simply accept what earlier times have considered to be equitable, but we must ask which system of taxation is compatible with our present idea of equity, in our present political, economic, and social conditions, in short in our civilization?'

After this proposition, which v. Tyszka italicizes, one might expect a sociological analysis of our civilization. But instead we find the following solemn declaration: 'Thus we find *three requirements* for justice in taxation: Taxes must be legal, general, and equitable.'

Disregarding the first requirement, which lies outside the scope of our inquiry, the other two, of which the second is contained in the third (a hierarchy of empty phrases!), have no clear and concrete meaning. They have all the peculiarities of those abstract principles mentioned above. v. Tyszka immediately goes on to interpret them.

It is noteworthy that his interpretation is intended to be a purely logical deduction. Historical and sociological relativism, which played such an important part in his introduction, is no longer mentioned. v. Tyszka seems to believe that he must have allowed for the relativism in his selection of first principles. But this is clearly false for his principles are the same as those which we encounter in other writings. For anybody who does not already associate them with a definite creed, they are completely empty. If they mean anything, v. Tyszka would still have to show that they are in fact the expression of current cultural attitudes.

Perhaps he thinks that the interpretation of his principles is determined by an underlying set of attitudes. This is certainly true; otherwise he could never come to any positive conclusions. But of what use is such reasoning? Can it carry conviction? On what grounds can it claim to be directly inspired by the *Zeitgeist*? Is the civilization which is supposed to inspire it really a unified whole, or are there not powerful conflicts of convictions and interests?

v. Tyszka abandons the historical method after having paid lip service in his introduction. By formulating highest principles which are supposedly open to logical interpretation he removes from the criticism and even the consciousness of the reader the sociological element which, in his own view, determines any positive conclusions.

This is the difficulty which besets constantly the so-called 'socio-political' school of thought, also known as academic socialism (*Kathedersozialismus*), or ethical historicism. Historical relativism is an excellent weapon for the destruction of other people's arguments. When the same critics then go on to indulge in their own doctrinaire speculations, which are usually of the same type as those which they have previously attacked, they have gained a stronghold in the mind of the uncritical reader because of their introductory remarks about historical conditions. If attacked, they can always say they do not claim more than a limited validity for their own conclusions. But the question is whether they can claim any validity at all, and if so, on what grounds. Does not the very idea of an objective sphere of values for any given age manifest the same metaphysical absolutism which they attack in others, however much they stress its historical determination and changing nature?

We have quoted v. Tyszka from amongst many other writers because he illustrates the case particularly well. A similar criticism would apply to the largest part of the German theory of public finance. If even authors of the historical school fall into these traps, the outlook for the pure theorists is worse. The latter often take the highest principles so much for granted that these principles appear only implicitly in the rules of a lower order to which we shall now turn.

Whatever the guise in which the highest principles appear, their interpretation borders on political theory, for we are concerned with the actions of the state and local authorities. Following an old tradition, systems of fiscal theory are divided into two main groups, according to whether they are based on the principle of interest (advantage, benefit) or on the principle of ability. There is an analogous distinction in political theory.

At the end of the eighteenth century, when our inquiry begins, the individualistic principle of interest (benefit, advantage, or *quid pro quo* theory are alternative names) was dominant. It reflected the view that the state is based on a social contract. Rights entail duties and services entail counterservices. The state protects the life and property of its members, and it is therefore the duty of the members to contribute to its expenses. Hobbes, Grotius, Pufendorf, and almost all later philosophers of natural law, developed their fiscal theories from the principle of interest.

The idea of a social contract recurs in various forms. Sometimes the state is considered as a corporation in which the citizens have different shares and therefore different obligations to contribute funds. Or again, the state is compared with an insurance company which insures the citizens against certain risks. It is therefore entitled to impose premia proportional to those risks. The argument is always that we must pay taxes according to our interest in, and the benefits derived from, the activities of the state.

This theory usually led to the demand for taxation *proportional* to property or income.[3] The argument is that citizens have an interest in the activity of the state in proportion to their economic status. The principal task of the state is to protect property. At a time when the wealthier classes were largely exempted from taxation, this was a radical doctrine. Later, the same theory became one of the main conservative arguments against progressive taxation.

The same principle was also used to support quite different recommendations. Occasionally, *regressive* taxation was demanded, i.e. that the poor should carry a proportionally heavier burden than the rich because the state was held to protect not only property but also life and liberty, and these are equally valuable to poor and rich. Or again, especially later, *progressive* taxation was demanded on the ground that risks grow more than proportionally with increasing property and income. Some argued the opposite and came to the opposite conclusions. Sometimes, the demand for progressive taxation was differently motivated. Thus Sismondi argued that the main function of the state is to prevent the poor from robbing the rich. It is therefore right and proper that the rich should pay for their protection. These arguments are intended only as illustrations of the variety of the arguments and their possible interpretations and motivations.

The older version of the principle of interest dominated the theory of taxation for a considerable time. (We shall discuss its modern version later.) It survived until very recently in French thought which is more prone to the ideas of natural law. But generally it has lost ground because it is so obviously unsatisfactory. How can one estimate the interest of individuals? What grounds are there for relating benefit or advantage to property and income? The critics who raised those objections were confirmed in their criticism by the contradictory interpretations of the principle by its exponents.

Some tried to replace interest by costs. Everyone should pay a contribution towards the costs which the state incurs on his behalf. But this argument deprives the principle of its foundations. The important link in the reasoning which shows that costs are proportional to benefit is missing. Moreover, it is not easier to estimate costs than benefits. Public outlays are usually in the nature of joint costs to meet collective wants and can therefore not be imputed without resort to an additional principle which is *a priori* in relation to the principle of costs.

The fundamental question why taxation should be *proportional* to interests or costs was never fully discussed. It seems almost a piece of mathematical mysticism. Suppose we could estimate the advantage accruing to every citizen and thus the total sum of advantages which should be greater than total costs. Total costs are equal to the total taxation required and this we know. We could then argue equally well that everyone should get *the same surplus* of advantage over tax, and that taxation should be distributed accordingly. By further taking account of the special costs incurred by the state on behalf of any one citizen, one could construct a number of simple principles of taxation none of which would be theoretically better or worse than any other. This illustrates the arbitrariness of any principle, quite apart from the difficulty of determining precisely the yardstick and the unit of measure for practical application.

Moreover, the theory accepts the existing distribution of property and income as 'natural'. The institutionalist arguments of the early socialists against the classical theory could also be used against the *a prioristic* conservatism of the principle of interest. We have seen that the social contract, like other liberal constructions, has a very different political meaning according to what are considered to be 'natural' conditions of property and income. Any conclusions can always be rejected by a denial of the 'naturalness' of the initially assumed state of nature.

·   ·   ·   ·   ·

The principle of levying taxes according to the ability to pay is also old. Most modern theorists are content, however, to trace it back to Adam Smith. It is contained in his first maxim of taxation. [4]

On this principle, the benefits derived from services rendered by the state, or their costs, are irrelevant to the theory of taxation. What counts is ability to contribute towards the common costs of promoting the collective interests.

This principle is best suited for an organic theory of the state and it was developed most consistently in Germany. Its proponents usually set out to ask what is 'tax liability' (*Steuerpflicht*) in the abstract, and how it can be justified. Their reply is either nationality, or domicile, or more vaguely, being part of an economic unit. On these 'grounds' the state is held to have a 'right' to raise taxes in order to meet its requirements or, as it is sometimes put, to fulfil its obligations. To this right of the state corresponds a 'duty' of the citizen, viz., the duty to pay tax (*Steuerpflicht*).

Such speculations might be thought to be harmless since they are not concerned with the interpretation of positive law. But the danger lies in the assumption that one can, by interpreting the meaning of liability, or rather of its 'ground', determine scientifically such problems of fiscal policy and legislation as the geographical scope of fiscal authority. These solutions, it should be noted, never pay attention to the effects on price formation of the various alternatives.

After having found, somehow or other, a legal ground and therefore proved tax liability in the abstract, the writers then have to decide on the distribution of those liabilities. It fits well into the general reflections on the relation between state and individual to say that citizens should contribute according to their ability. This, the authors say, is the real meaning of equality and they do not hesitate to go on to increasingly concrete political interpretations. But the principle of ability as such, as we shall see, says no more than that interests or costs should not count.

It is odd that British economists should have accepted a version which is so alien to their political philosophy. One would have expected an elaboration of the principle of interest (benefit, advantage). It is not easy to explain this. We have noted that the theory of ability is easier to handle. It avoids the treatment of the more tricky side of the exchange transaction between the citizen and the state, viz., the service rendered to the citizen by the state.

There is only the contribution rendered by the citizen to the state, which is the payment of a sum of money. This sum is related to his ability to pay, which, at least superficially, seems to be more tangible than his interest. But the fact that the theory is simpler to handle is not a sufficient explanation for its being accepted in Britain. Economists do not usually hesitate to operate with indeterminate or even interdeterminable variables as if they were determined. The whole theory of value is an attempt to provide a basis for such arguments.

It should be noted, however, that Adam Smith introduced the word rather than the theory. The term 'ability' was used by him as a persuasive slogan without much content. Just because this maxim seems beyond dispute it was a particularly suitable cloak for his positive proposals. In substance Adam Smith believed in the principle of interest. He said: 'The expense of government to the individuals of a great nation, is like the expense of management to the joint tenants of a great estate, who are all obliged to contribute in proportion to their respective interests in the estate.' The principle of interest fits perfectly into the view that the whole economy is an expanded family household. He also interpreted his maxim of ability in the sense that everyone should be taxed in proportion to the income which he enjoys under the protection of the state. For Adam Smith the principle of ability had no other function than to lend greater plausibility to his conclusion of proportionality which is derived from the principle of interest.

The other classics took much the same view. Ricardo quoted Smith's maxim with approval without having discussed it. McCulloch advocated proportional taxation on the analogy between state and insurance company, which we have met in connection with the principle of interest. Senior said quite explicitly that taxation rests on a particular kind of barter between the individual and the state in which the latter offers protection against payment which must be proportional to the protection.

Thus it is less difficult to understand how the earlier classics could accept a theory of public finance which seemed to imply an utterly alien political philosophy. They used it only as a disguise for the principle of interest in order to strengthen the authority of their particular interpretation of that principle.

Gradually the view that taxes are a return for services rendered by the state tended to disappear. Instead the view gained ground that taxes should be imposed in proportion to the ability to shoulder them and irrespective of benefits and advantages. The belief gained ground that the interest of the citizens in their state is infinite and not theoretically determinable. Ability, on the other hand, is finite and is theoretically determinable. The principle of interest is thus gradually forgotten or even openly attacked, as, for example, by J. S. Mill.

At the same time, the principle of ability begins to be interpreted in terms of hedonistic psychology. As we have seen, this is in general the fate of economic doctrines in Britain in the nineteenth century. At the end of this process the original principle has been thoroughly transformed. It is altogether different from the principle from which it began to develop or from that which had been developed in Germany. Differences and similarities of the two parallel versions of the principle of ability resemble the differences and similarities of the concepts 'value' and 'right', which we have discussed earlier.

The psychological interpretation of the principle of ability in Britain is a welcome method of adopting a convenient principle without having to swallow more than a minimum of its implicit political theory. By saying that ability is measured by, or even identical with, the subjective sacrifice of paying a tax, the apparently impossible is made possible: German political metaphysics is transformed into good English individualism.

But although it may not be obvious from the positive expositions that the individualistic-utilitarian theory of the state is incompatible with the principle of ability, the contrast is brought to light in those arguments which criticize the principle of interest. Thus J. S. Mill, whose views form an important link in this development, writes: 'Government must be regarded as so pre-eminently a concern of all, that to determine who are most interested in it is of no real importance'.[5] And again: 'The practice of setting definite values on things essentially indefinite, and making them a ground of practical conclusions, is peculiarly fertile in false views of social questions.'[6]

It is remarkable that an English utilitarian should have criticized the principle of interest in these terms. If pursued to its logical conclusions, Mill's criticism would destroy the hedonistic metaphysics on which his whole system of policy recommendations rests. His attack is directed only at the estimation of interest, which he wants to eliminate from the theory. He is, of course, convinced that measuring ability, though difficult, is possible and not subject to similar criticism.

Until J. S. Mill and even Bastable in the earlier editions of his *Public Finance*, the principle of ability was interpreted as the requirement of proportional taxation. In later editions Bastable modified his view somewhat. This interpretation continued the main line of development of the principle of interest. We shall discuss later how proportional taxation was deduced from the higher principles of taxation. Let us first examine in passing some of the qualifications with which the proportionality maxim was gradually surrounded.

According to an old tradition of fiscal theory, a subsistence minimum should be exempt from tax. As we have seen in Chapter 3, according to classical value theory the cost of production of labour is roughly equal to the subsistence minimum. Therefore it was in line with the classical tradition to define the income to which taxation should be proportional as net income, i.e. that portion which exceeds the subsistence minimum. This is the first qualification.

Already James Mill and McCulloch advocated further that earned income should be taxed at a lower rate than income from capital. They justified this by the shorter duration of the former. There should be a kind of depreciation allowance in order to raise income from work to an equal footing with income from capital. J. S. Mill argued for the same discrimination but on somewhat different grounds. This qualification can also be fitted into the main principle without gross inconsistency.

The same is true of J. S. Mill's demand that that part of income which is saved should be exempted from taxation.[7] His reasons were the same as those given to-day, viz., that savings would otherwise be taxed twice: first when they are earned, and again when they yield interest. Mill pointed out that if this rule is followed, exemptions on the ground of the shorter duration of earned income are no longer required; for these exemptions are justified by the necessity for the earned-income receiver to save in order to be on an equal footing with the owner of capital. The theory that only consumed and not total income should be taxed also is old. Hobbes and other exponents of the principle of interest had advocated it, often for the same reasons.

In this way a number of other qualifications to the principle of proportionality can be added, such as obligations towards dependants. One can look upon all these qualifications as steps towards the determination of what should be taxable income. We shall not embark on an exposition of the concept of taxable income or its development. A large and highly controversial literature has been written on this subject. For our purposes it is sufficient to note the extraordinary flexibility of this concept. It can take on almost any content and can yield almost any conclusions. The participants in this dispute do not see that there cannot be a 'correct' definition of taxable income. The word means what we want it to mean. By changing the definition of taxable income we can always change the concrete political meaning of the principles which lay down rules about the relation of income and tax. Hence these rules are as indeterminate as the income concept. In the following discussion we shall, however, disregard this complication in order to bring out more clearly the general doctrinal trend.

Our next question is: how can proportionality be derived from the principle of ability? Until the middle of the nineteenth century this derivation is quite naïve. What should be proved is simply asserted and for the rest the authors rely on analogies used by the exponents of the interest principle. The discussion becomes more serious when the principle of ability is interpreted psychologically. J. S. Mill interprets equality of taxation as equality of subjective sacrifice. [8]

Mill ought next to prove that the subjective utility of income diminishes proportionally to an increase in income. Only then can the psychologically interpreted principle of ability lead to the maxim of proportionality. In fact, he does not prove it. He merely asserts what he ought to prove and asserts it only implicitly. His exposition is essentially a round-about statement of a political creed. He says in his criticism of progressive taxation: 'To tax the larger income at a higher percentage than the smaller, is to lay a tax on industry and economy: to impose a penalty on people for having worked harder and saved more than their neighbours.' [9] But this is not convincing, for the same reasons could be used to urge a poll tax against a proportional tax, since the latter falls also more heavily on the rich than on the poor. Perhaps he had in mind the effects of taxation on saving and enterprise and his argument is directed at the degree of additional taxation of higher income. But proportionality is only one amongst an infinite number of possible gradations. Moreover, such an argument about the effects of taxes would be false because oversimplified. It is probably nearer the truth to look upon his criticism of progressive taxation as the expression of political convictions, as a *bourgeois* irritation at attacks on property. This is confirmed by other passages, e.g. when he denounces progressive taxation as 'not impartial', 'a mild form of robbery', 'obviously unfair', 'legalized theft', etc.

Since both the maxim of proportionality and the principle of equal sacrifice seem obvious to Mill, he concludes that the two are identical. There is no more to it than this circular conviction.

Other authors have attempted to derive progressive taxation from the same psychologically interpreted principle of ability. Their proof often amounts to no more than a reference to the diminishing marginal utility of income. This will not do, for one must already assume that marginal utility decreases very sharply in order to justify proportional taxation. But it has sometimes been maintained that the marginal utility of income does decrease at such a rapid rate that a progressive tax is justified. It is interesting to see how J. S. Mill criticized this view. He was careful to avoid any definite proposition about the diminishing marginal utility of income, although his own maxims imply a definite theory. He merely said that his opponents' assumptions about the shape of the income utility curve are vague and are not supported by evidence.[10]

This is certainly true. But his own proposal of proportional taxation is also only one possible tax rate amongst an infinite number. His proposal, based on equal sacrifice, also assumes that a *definite* shape of the income utility curve has been established. It must have been the abstract and simple nature of proportionality which appealed to Mill and prevented him from seeing that the psychological hypothesis about the diminishing utility of income implied in his own theory also required verification.

In the course of time the maxim of proportionality was gradually replaced by the demand for moderately progressive taxation. Whichever maxim one accepts, it is clear that, in order to maintain the principle of ability as the basis, one must make calculations about how the subjective value of income changes when income rises. These calculations involve interpersonal comparisons. Thus individualist marginal utility theory must be broadened into speculations about social value. Unfortunately, there is no empirical material for such speculations.

But the following difficulty is even more serious: Suppose we had settled the question of the diminishing marginal utility of income, which is, of course, impossible. The principle of ability would still not have been defined. What is the meaning of 'equal sacrifice'? About this there has been continual controversy. Some authors consider it self-evident that the psychological sacrifice should be *absolutely* equal. Others consider it equally self-evident that the sacrifice should be an equal *portion* of the total utility of income. (This latter interpretation is more radical, for it would require tax liabilities to increase more than proportionally to the decreasing utility of increments in income; they would have to increase proportionally to the total utility of income, which, of course, is increasing as long as income has a positive marginal utility.) Later writers dispute over the question what earlier authors like J. S. Mill, who were not sophisticated enough to raise this question, had *really* meant.

It is, of course, impossible to solve this problem. Other interpretations of the demand for equality of sacrifice could be advanced. We shall come across a third. The only common factor seems to be that the word 'equality' is taken as a symbol for some simple arithmetical relation.

There is one important assumption of the principle of ability which is the key to an understanding of later developments. Like the principle of interest it presupposes a correct distribution of income and property upon which the correct tax system is imposed. Whether one arrives at a recommendation of proportional or of progressive taxation, the tax is determined in relation to income and property, which are accepted as given.

It is therefore understandable that some of the earlier writers of both the interest and the ability school had given an alternative formulation to the two principles. It laid down that taxation must not affect distribution. If they then went on to advocate proportional taxation, as they usually did, they meant by this that the *relative* distribution of income and property amongst individuals or families should not be disturbed.[11] This idea was also used to support the maxim of proportionality, of which it is a

N

variation. It seems especially 'natural' to English theory. An obvious analogy can be drawn with classical distribution theory, which is concerned with the relative size of the various types of income. It is, however, not difficult to give an entirely different meaning to the demand for undisturbed distribution. Since taxation necessarily alters incomes and property in some way, the problem consists in changing them as 'equally' as possible. But this condition, as we have seen, is highly ambiguous.

In whichever way this problem is solved, the principle is always that the existing distribution of income and property should be disturbed as little as possible. Every tax system that obeys the principle of equality is believed to fulfil this requirement.

This line of thought is never stated quite so explicitly. It is one of those many tacit, only semi-conscious assumptions. Like the rest of liberal doctrine, it underwent a remarkable transformation which was carried to its logical conclusions by J. S. Mill. A normative 'economic law' is turned into a hypothetical argument. Liberal doctrine was initially a defence of the ruling distribution of income and property which it accepted as 'natural'. Therefore classical liberalism was a laissez-faire or a harmony theory. As we have seen in Chapter 5, under the pressure of the institutionalist criticism of the early socialists, the liberal doctrine gradually underwent a change. The belief that all is in fact for the best, was transformed into a mere hypothesis: the liberal precepts are sound *if* we make the provisional assumption that distribution is correct. The problem of production and exchange was isolated from the problem of distribution. This 'communistic fiction', as we have called it, led eventually to v. Wieser's theory of natural value.

The theory of public finance had the same fate as liberal doctrine in general. James Mill stood for unqualified proportionality, but at the same time he argued for limitations of inheritance and the taxation of 'unearned increments in land values'. The two arguments apply to two different spheres of his thinking which correspond to the distinction between production and distribution. Similarly J. S. Mill rejected with indignation progressive taxation as a penalty on hard work and thrift, a pure theft and a glaring iniquity, but advocated in the same breath radical death duties, taxation of gifts, of unearned value increments, etc. Although he did not emphasize it, it is obvious that his theory of taxation applies only to a hypothetical situation in which distribution is ideal.

This is another instance of the unconscious application of v. Wieser's theory of the ideal economy. We have seen before that v. Wieser was fully aware that his theory of natural value was not original but merely the precise formulation of an old and frequently tacit assumption. In his book, v. Wieser also criticized Sax who attempted to develop fiscal principles on marginal utility lines. v. Wieser's criticism was based on a correct appreciation of the hypothetical nature of the natural state.[12] Sidgwick, who, on the whole, built on Mill's theory of taxation, said explicitly that the principle of ability presupposes acceptance of the existing distribution as just.[13] Wicksell later made this a fundamental assumption of the whole theory of public finance.

The fact that J. S. Mill had not yet seen the full implications of this line of thought explains some peculiarities in his argument. Thus, although he justified death duties with Bentham's argument of the diminishing marginal utility of income and of the desirability of a more equal income distribution, it never occurred to him that progressive taxation could be advocated on the same grounds. But Bentham's principle is more comprehensive and more fundamental than Mill's principle of equal sacrifice, which already assumes correct distribution. Mill's utilitarianism is thus inconsistent on this point. His whole theory of taxation is only ill-digested natural law. Proportional taxation as such must be his highest postulate of equity, for we have seen that he does not succeed in deducing it from the superior principle of ability, and we shall see presently that he cannot deduce this latter principle from the superior maxim of utility. His proposals for distributional reforms through certain tax measures are kept quite independent of his fiscal theory. They are directed against certain incomes, not because they are very high, which would be a sufficient utilitarian reason, but because they are unjust.

These arguments were later taken up and developed by Wicksell. He would have preferred to speak of 'expropriation'. A death duty was, in his eyes, not a proper tax, but the right to joint inheritance by the state. He defended it not on economic, i.e. utilitarian, grounds but by saying that it was sanctioned by the sense of social justice. Since he also wanted to have a 'pure', 'economically objective', theory of public finance, he had to separate the two spheres of justice. We shall return later to this problem and to the question whether such a separation is possible. We have referred to it at this stage because the whole problem is implicit in Mill's theory of taxation. It forms the background of the later development of the English theory of public finance.

It is interesting to contrast the German development with the English. We have seen that a transformation had taken place in England. While the earlier classics had accepted the existing distribution implicitly as justified, J. S. Mill used the assumption of correct distribution only as a working hypothesis. To the earlier English theory of harmony corresponded in Germany the well-known thesis that 'the sole purpose of taxation is to provide the state with the revenue necessary to carry out its tasks, and not to change the existing conditions of distribution'. This proposition, which can still be found in the most recent literature, is unfounded, obscure, and untenable. It is unfounded, for the purpose of any measure is the purpose to which it is put. Whence therefore the *a priori* dictum? It is obscure, for it is impossible to separate one purpose from the other. Irrespective of how the proposition is interpreted, it certainly does not apply to existing tax laws. They always take into account the distributional repercussions, which, indeed, at the prevailing high tax rates, could not be ignored. Finally, the proposition is untenable. An interference with the market of this order of magnitude must necessarily change distribution through its effects on demand and supply. Distribution must change, even at very low tax rates, as a result of the interdependence of all market phenomena. The above maxim appears, incidentally, usually in connection with speculations about the 'ground of tax liabilities' (*Grund der Steuerpflicht*) of the type which we have discussed.

The more modern version, which uses the correct distribution as an assumption for a 'pure' theory of taxation and advocates, or at least allows for, distributional reforms through special taxes, has its counterpart in Germany in Wagner's school, which works with *several* canons of taxation. Only two of these concern us here: the principle of justice and the so-called socio-political principle. This solution has been criticized by many, amongst them, curiously, Wicksell and Lindahl.[14] Their objection is this: if there is a principle of justice, no competing principle can be tolerated. All maxims must be capable of being deduced from the same highest principle whether it is called principle of justice or socio-political principle. A dualism would destroy the normative foundation of the whole argument. We shall meet the same problem and discuss it further in the treatment of the modern marginalist version of the principle of interest.

Let us return to J. S. Mill's theory. We have seen that he advocated proportional taxation on grounds of equal sacrifice. We disregard now the difficulties which arise from the assumption of a correct distribution, from the attempt to combine the demand for proportionality with that for equality of sacrifice, and from the attempt to give meaning to 'equality of sacrifice'. All these difficulties apart, how did Mill justify the principle of equal sacrifice—whatever it may mean?

His reply to the question, why should equality be the maxim, is: 'For the reason that it ought to be so in all affairs of government.' All burdens which the government imposes on its citizens must be distributed 'as nearly as possible with the same pressure upon all, which it must be observed, is the mode by which least sacrifice is occasioned on the whole'. If anybody bears less than his fair share, somebody else must bear more, 'and the alleviation to the one is not, *ceteris paribus*, so great a good to him, as the increased pressure upon the other is an evil'.[15]

The reasoning is typical for the transition from natural law to utilitarianism. In the first place Mill presents the equality as an axiomatic principle of justice. This is impossible for a strict utilitarian because equality is no end in itself. It must be shown to be a means to maximum utility. Mill indeed asserts that equal sacrifice minimizes total sacrifice but he does not prove it. Nor could he prove it. On the Benthamite assumption of diminishing utility of income, which Mill accepts, equal sacrifice would certainly not minimize total sacrifice unless *ceteris paribus* stands for equal incomes. But in that case the whole argument would be pointless for its purpose is to determine the correct tax for *different* income levels. That taxes should be equal for equal incomes is, of course, an assumption underlying the whole argument.

Thus we see that the theory of ability fails all along the line. Neither proportional nor, as some would have it, progressive taxation can be deduced from the requirement of equal sacrifice.

We do not know the shape of the marginal utility of income curve. Nor can we ever know it, for the whole notion is metaphysical. Furthermore we cannot determine the meaning of 'equal sacrifice' unambiguously. It is open to several possible interpretations, each of which is as good or as bad as any other. Moreover, the argument rests on the assumption that the existing distribution is correct. As we shall see, this assumption is logically incompatible with the argument which is based on it. Finally, not only does equal sacrifice not follow from the utilitarian principle of the maximization of utility, it actually contradicts it.

A utilitarian might suggest that all these troubles stem from this last error and that a theory of taxation should be constructed consistently on the utilitarian postulate. Carver and above all Edgeworth tried to do this.[16] Their interpretation of the psychological theory of ability is consistent and thus avoided some of the above-mentioned difficulties. Like much else in British economics, their theory of minimum total sacrifice was an elaboration of one of Sidgwick's arguments.[17] It dominates modern British fiscal theory and was accepted by Marshall, Pigou, Cannan, and others. Pigou has elaborated it into a theoretical system in his recent publication *A Study in Public Finance* (1928). We must confine ourselves to a discussion of its outlines.

From the principle that utility should be maximized the simple rule is deduced that large incomes should be cut down to a certain level and incomes below this level should not be taxed at all. The rule follows directly from the diminishing marginal utility of income. The size to which all incomes should be levelled is determined by requirements of state expenditure.

The extreme ambiguity in this field is illustrated by the fact that even this rule has been presented as a corollary of the principle of equality. It is merely a matter of defining equality in a somewhat different way, not as absolute equality between individual sacrifices, nor as proportionality between sacrifice and net utility from income, but as absolute equality of the *marginal* sacrifice, so that a small increase in taxation would lead to an equal additional sacrifice for everyone.

This tax rule certainly avoids many difficulties. In the first place, it can be subsumed under the guiding economic principle of utility maximization. Next, it removes the untenable dualism which we have found in Mill. Finally, as Edgeworth has pointed out, the shape of the marginal utility curve for income is now irrelevant. No matter at what rate it falls, as long as it does fall, we get the same result.

But especially this last advantage is illusory. In any practical application one would have to examine the effects of such highly progressive taxation on effort, saving, enterprise, etc. This is indeed done by the writers of this school and they conclude that certain modifications are necessary. A balance must be struck between the competing objectives of minimizing sacrifice and minimizing the harmful effects on production. We are left with an insoluble equation with two interdependent minimum conditions. This is not a solution of the problem. Indeed, the problem has not even been stated. One mistakes utilitarian metaphysics for positive knowledge and thus arrives at this particular interpretation of minimum total sacrifice.

We shall not discuss in detail why this interpretation conveys nothing. Two brief comments must suffice which will be useful in the later discussion of the modern version of the principle of interest. In the first place some idea of the shape of the marginal utility of income curve is, after all, necessary just because the rule must be modified for detrimental production effects. Otherwise one does not know what importance to attach to each of the two competing minimum conditions.

Moreover, the scope of public activity and hence the amount of total revenue required is left indeterminate. The theory shares this weakness with all theories of ability. Interest or benefit is a better criterion just because it says something about both expenditure and revenue. The theory under consideration recommends that large incomes should be cut down until sufficient revenue is collected to cover public expenditure. All depends then on the amount of this expenditure. One could, of course, say that public activity should be expanded until social utility is maximized. If this rule is to be added to the other rules, the assumption on which they have been constructed is removed, viz., that a given amount of total taxation is to be raised. We then arrive at a cumbersome formulation of the philosophically dubious *premise* that things should be managed in such a way as to maximize social utility. To this is added some of Bentham's metaphysical psychology which asserts that the utility of income increments declines progressively. As a result, we are asked to bear in mind, in some unspecified manner, the desirability of a more equal income distribution. This is the meagre result of the development of the theory of fiscal principles in England. It could be expounded in greater detail with additional refinements but it would not thereby gain in content.

The theory of minimum total sacrifice, to which the attempt to transform the principle of ability into a consistent utilitarian theory inevitably leads, is quite modern and has become particularly fashionable amongst those writers in the field of public finance who are in close touch with the central development of economic theory. But most of the others have recourse to a more eclectic ability theory. They usually dismiss the principle of interest by pointing out that it is indeterminate. This does not prevent them from advocating taxation according to specific costs in those exceptional instances where these costs are believed to be measurable. In the general part of their discussion they often extend their scepticism to the principle of ability, but as soon as they come to practical problems the scepticism vanishes. Usually, some particular interpretation of the principle of ability is then presented as self-evident, i.e. without proof. Occasionally the shape of the income utility curve is discussed and some particular view is made to appear plausible with the aid of arguments from popular psychology and popular philosophy.

The general attitude is this: We are facing a great number of practical problems of fiscal policy; they must all be solved; the only scientific way of doing this is to apply a general principle from which the solutions can be deduced. The necessity to reach solutions is advanced as an excuse for arguments which are felt to be shaky. As on so many occasions, the metaphysical speculations are thus made to appear eminently 'practical'. They make a 'realistic treatment of fiscal problems' possible. This is the characteristic feature of the general problem which we are examining in this book. The most absurd and useless chimeras appear to be practically significant, simply because they are handled in such a manner that they lead to concrete political proposals.

The Swedish school of public finance probably holds the strongest theoretical position. On the basis of the Austrian marginal utility theory, Wicksell and his pupil Lindahl[18] have made the most penetrating and most consistent attempt to justify fiscal policies rationally. If nevertheless their attempt also fails, it is because they are trying to do the impossible. For an account of the precursors of the theory (Sax, v. Wieser, and some Italians), and of its relation to other theories, we refer the reader to Wicksell's and Lindahl's works.

Wicksell begins his discussion of how fiscal principles can be rationally justified by saying that these questions are ethical and do not concern the economist. But this is no more than a conventional tribute to a traditional phrase. Later sections contain hardly a trace of this ethical relativism. Lindahl is more cautious. He says at the outset that it is the function of science to 'state the facts as they are and to explain their causal connections'.[19] This also holds for the so-called practical sciences. Their peculiarity is merely that they collect and arrange their material in order to meet practical requirements. Lindahl, following Max Weber, explains that these sciences take ends as given from outside and examine the most efficient means of promoting these ends.

In a footnote he emphasizes that it is not the function of science to establish categorical imperatives for our conduct. Yet, he goes on to say, it is neither possible nor desirable for a scientist to avoid subjective value judgements. Every scientist is also a moralist. It is important that his value judgements should not be suppressed but stated frankly. His greater insight into causal connections has given him a 'higher standpoint' from which others can benefit. But only if his aim is generally accepted can he make recommendations without running the danger of being misunderstood.

Whether such a treatment of economic policy in terms of ends and means is possible will be examined in the next chapter. Let us, for the moment, accept Lindahl's method. His next task is to bring out clearly the value premise which, together with an examination of economic facts and their causal connection, is intended to lead to his statement of fiscal principles.

'Such a starting-point for the theory of tax policy is provided by the general demand for justice. It is the task of this theory to elucidate the concept of justice in fiscal matters, and after an examination of the causal connections of fiscal phenomena, to formulate the principles which apply to the various problems. An exposition of the ethical principles of taxation along those objective lines can, of course, be more or less complete, but it should be possible to arrive at agreement in principle. . . . An objective solution along those lines is the first condition for a rational solution of practical conflicts.'[20]

It is not a question of reaching a *compromise* between conflicting interests. As Lindahl emphasizes, the problem is how to give proper *weights* to different interests. These are two entirely different problems. It is, however, an unfortunate fact that justice can mean and has meant so many different things. Lindahl admits this, but adds that the original meaning is the realization of the law as such; not of any positive law but of the ideal 'natural law'. He thus slips into the natural law tautology: 'The meaning of the demand for justice in taxation is that it should be regulated according to the moral rights of the citizens.'[21]

But in spite of his assertion to the contrary, this does not tell us anything about the meaning of justice. Lindahl resorts to the following distinction: 'On closer analysis, the requirement turns out to consist of two components: first, property owned without a just title must go to the community; second, the rest of the tax burden must be distributed in accordance with the thus established just system of property.' The first requirement, which fulfils the 'socio-political' function, 'will change with changing views about the social justice of the ruling distribution of property. . . . Only if we start with a distribution of property which is accepted as just' can we raise the second requirement. 'But it is not up to the fiscal theorist to solve the fundamental social problem, even if an objective solution were possible. . . . Thus the doctrine of just taxation becomes entirely hypothetical.' But although the postulate is hypothetical, Lindahl considers that the *purely fiscal problem* raised by the second requirement of justice can be solved objectively.

He attempts to divest the concept 'justice' of all controversial matters and believes that we are then still left with something, viz., a purely abstract concept of justice which is relevant to a 'pure' fiscal theory.

This is the end of a long development of doctrine. Wicksell wrote: 'Apparently justice of taxation presupposes tacitly a just distribution of income and property, from whichever point of view the problem is judged. Otherwise it would not make sense to speak of equality of service and counterservice or of equality of sacrifice.'[22] The attempt to base a just tax system upon an unjust property system is, as Wicksell once said, an attempt to take a fair share out of an unfair whole.

The notion that it must be possible to develop a pure fiscal theory on the abstract assumption of just distribution is analogous to the doctrine of 'natural value' which we have examined in the last chapter. The pure theory of taxation is, as v. Wieser emphasized, part of the theory of natural social value. Just as natural value is claimed to be of empirical interest because it is one of the forces in the formation of actual prices, so pure fiscal theory is relevant to actual taxation. 'Every system of taxation contains an element of it and these fiscal principles are therefore, unlike the socio-political principles, always relevant and independent of the ethical evaluation of the distribution of property. Even if distribution is unjust, the relation between taxation and a just distribution is not without significance. The solution of this problem is therefore the most important—and the most difficult—task of the practical theory of public finance.'[23]

It is easy to see why the pure theory of public finance chooses 'just distribution of property' as its assumption and not, as v. Wieser in his theory of social value, the 'communistic economy'. It is done in order to keep up the appearance of discussing fiscal theory. In a communistic economy there is no taxation because there is no private ownership. The Wicksell-Lindahl theory of taxation can only be properly understood if seen in this wider context.

The device is to divide the problem into two parts. On the one hand, there is the 'socio-political objective' of taxation which aims at correcting injustices in the existing distribution of property.[24] On the other hand, there is the purely fiscal problem. Its solution presupposes the acceptance of a given distribution.[25] The first problem is outside the scope of our discussion.

The second problem is treated as a problem of exchange or barter. The individual barters with society or, more correctly, with all other individuals. The objects of the transaction are the public services, the price of which is the tax. The whole transaction is explained in terms of 'certain fundamental psychological factors' in the manner of marginal utility theory. This is clearly a version of the interest principle, i.e. of the theory of payment for state services according to benefit, which differs from the older version in that it does not involve a comparison of total quantities of utility or benefit, but of marginal quantities only. The idea of the margin had not been clearly expressed in this connection before Lindahl. It constitutes the originality of his contribution. Wicksell had occasionally alluded to the analogy between taxation and price formation in the market without developing the argument. He emphasized the negative aspect, viz., that no citizen, not even the marginal taxpayer, should pay for more than the utility which he receives from the services of the state. But Lindahl realized that this condition leaves open many possible tax distributions of which only one can be 'just'.[26]

Wicksell and Lindahl pointed out that this refinement of the interest principle, if valid, would have the advantage of solving both the problem of the distribution of the tax burden and the problem of the scope and type of public activity. Any theory of public finance worth its name must do both. The assumption, on which other theories work, that the second problem has already been settled somehow, makes them quite unrealistic. The two problems cannot be separated because they are interdependent. Apart from all other objections, the solutions of the previously discussed taxation theories become entirely indeterminate as soon as one attempts to integrate them into a complete system of fiscal policy.

Previously the question of the nature and scope of public activity had been treated only most superficially. If the question was raised at all, it was only for the purpose of airing political prejudices in technical jargon. The classics spoke of public activity as 'consumption' and this in itself served as an argument for restricting it as a necessary evil as much as possible. The best tax, for them, was therefore the lowest tax. Against this laissez-faire theory List and many authors after him argued that public activity is 'production' and, moreover, a production of 'productive forces'. This classificatory change helped to recruit sympathy for more extensive state activity. It is, in the last resort, the dispute about the 'legal' versus the 'culture' state (*Rechtsstaat versus Kulturstaat*).

Interest in this question of definition subsided later. The new criterion for the direction and scope of public activity was this: public and private activity must both be 'promoted equally'; this must be done in the light of the 'strength of the needs in both directions' so that 'the total result is maximized', or so that 'the cultural level is raised as high as possible'. Empty phrases of this type were used in order to bridge over what was uncomfortably felt as a gap in fiscal theory.

The Wicksell-Lindahl theory is free from this defect. If it were possible to construct a theory of fiscal principles at all, it would have to be along their lines. Just as v. Wieser in his theory of natural social value pursued the normally tacit assumptions of liberal economics rigorously to their conclusions, so Wicksell and Lindahl drew consistently the conclusions of the theory of public finance.

Their principle of taxation in the 'purely fiscal sphere' consists in the requirement that *the marginal value forgone through taxation should be equal to the value of the marginal public service to the taxpayer* in terms of money. The underlying idea is the same as that of liberal economics in general, viz., that everyone tries to buy in the cheapest market, and that more is demanded up to the point at which the utility of a small addition is just outweighed by the sacrifice of paying for it. On the assumption of a just distribution the optimum is reached when prices are in equilibrium.

Again, there is a precise parallel to the 'qualified liberal doctrine' which we have criticized at the end of Chapter 5. Taxation is regarded not as an 'interference' with price formation under free competition, but as an integral part of it, perfectly compatible with its principles. Accordingly, the fiscal optimum is defined as that position in which the money value of the total utility derived by all citizens from state activity is maximized. [27]

To prove his thesis Lindahl turns, true to his programme, to an analysis of the causal connections in the sphere of public finance. He makes several assumptions besides correct distribution, which are analogous to the assumptions of liberal doctrine.

The first is that individuals know what they want and how to get it, that their valuations are 'correct'. Lindahl is clearly aware how dubious this assumption is, especially with respect to public services. The exact calculations of utilities must, he says, often be replaced by a rough guess. But he believes that it is possible even here to indicate how marginal utilities in money terms diminish with increasing supplies. Be this as it may, we shall not cavil at this assumption. There are more fundamental weaknesses.

Another important assumption is the 'equal distribution of political power'. This means that all political parties have an equal opportunity of realizing the rights which are due to them under the prevailing property laws when fiscal legislation is enacted. There must be no 'excess power of certain classes' in the determination of the budget. But what is really meant by 'equal power' does not become clear until after the theory has been interpreted. What is supposed to be an 'assumption' thus turns out to be a particular expression, rather than a premise, of the theory. Its precise meaning is not clear *a priori* for, as Lindahl himself says when criticizing Wicksell, justice is not guaranteed by the negative condition that nobody is taxed against his will.

This 'assumption' contains and postulates already the whole theory. According to the theory everyone should pay tax for the *total* utility of public activity according to his valuation of its *marginal* portion. In this case, says Lindahl, state activity is at a maximum, compatible with the absence of compulsion. But why should this solution reflect the equal distribution of power and result in just taxation in relation to the given distribution of ownership rights? The crucial point at issue is simply taken for granted. We shall, however, postpone for the moment the further discussion of this question.

In the more empirical examination of fiscal policy Lindahl comes up against several difficulties such as revenues accruing to the state from public enterprises; state loans, particularly 'unproductive loans'; the 'purely political' element in the problem, which, in a sense, corresponds to the problem of monopoly in the general liberal doctrine; considerations of the survival of the state and elementary biological and cultural needs; the 'altruistic' interests of citizens, etc. There is, above all, the insuperable obstacle of separating 'socio-political' from purely fiscal taxation. As in all interest doctrines, the reasoning leads to a social contract view of the state. Following Wicksell, Lindahl arrives at the demand for democratic government, a limited veto for minorities, specialization of the budget through linking taxation to particular items of public expenditure, proportional representation, etc. The distinction between tax legislation and legislation in general then becomes important. He discusses older principles of taxation such as ability, modifies and qualifies them, and subordinates them as 'practical' maxims to the highest, so-called 'theoretical' principle of interest—just as Edgeworth had incorporated the older versions of the principle of ability into his theory of minimum sacrifice. In this connection he deals also with certain problems of incidence.

But this is not the place for a discussion of all these interesting arguments. What is inconclusive or faulty in them stems from the manner in which the main problem is stated. Only the central position shall be criticized here.

The decisive question is: what precisely does the assumption of a correct distribution of income and property mean? Must this condition be fulfilled *before* or *after* taxation? Clearly not after taxation, for the theory would then be circular. Taxation would indeed be just, but only because it would be one of the causes of an *ex hypothesi* just situation. Any kind of taxation would by definition fulfil the condition of justice.

Therefore the assumption of a just distribution must refer to the situation before taxation. On Lindahl's own view, before the purely fiscal problem is solved, all unjustly owned property must be transferred to society. Just taxation should be applied to a just system of ownership. This requirement must be taken seriously for the theory demands that 'purely fiscal' taxation should be determined by its marginal utility.

The assumption that ownership conditions before taxation should be just presupposes that they must either be known or at least be capable of being known. Otherwise it is impossible to say whether they are just or whether socio-political corrections should precede purely fiscal taxation.

Now the scope of taxation and of public activity in a modern community is very wide. Even if it were narrower, it would be quite impossible to make even a rough guess of what ownership conditions would be in their absence. Yet such a guess would be a necessary condition for deciding what socio-political taxation should precede fiscal taxation. As we have seen, these reforms must apply to this hypothetical situation, or else the argument becomes circular and 'valid' for any form of taxation. It is clearly circular to assume that socio-political corrections should be applied to the *actual* situation of which purely fiscal taxation of whatever kind is one of the causes. Any correct final situation can be brought about by a number of different combinations of the two types of taxes. Socio-political taxation, which ought to be the *condition* of purely fiscal taxation, would be made to depend upon it.

Moreover, we cannot just assume some abstract pre-tax situation, as we assume 'free competition' for some theoretical arguments. It is not enough to say that in a society of a certain abstract type there is no taxation. The argument must apply to a specific empirical state of affairs: not just *any* situation but *this* situation without tax.

But let us assume, for the sake of the argument, that it would not be impossible to determine the pre-tax situation. The theory then meets an even more decisive difficulty. Granted the assumption of a just distribution, why should the correct tax be determined by marginal utilities? J. S. Mill, it will be remembered, who used the same assumption, though less clearly stated, maintained that the correct tax is one which imposes equal sacrifices on all. Both proposals seem equally arbitrary and equally remote from canons of abstract justice.

Lindahl's solution is, if anything, the more arbitrary of the two. Taxation and the public activity corresponding to its expenditure will *ipso facto* alter the entire economic situation. This should, according to the theory, increase the total utility of each. But it will increase individual utilities by *unequal* amounts. The amount of increase will depend upon the shape of the individual marginal utility curves. It would be different for different persons even if the curves were assumed to be identical, unless it is also assumed that incomes are equal. But on these two assumptions the theory would, on its own premises, be redundant. Moreover, it would be the net increase in *total* utility, and not the marginal quantity, which is relevant for considerations of justice. This is true whatever political value premises we use. Even if we could assume —and we cannot—that the increase in total utility is equal or proportional or in any other way equivalent to the marginal quantity, this would not help, for changes in the absolute size of total utility are not irrelevant for considerations of justice. It is therefore illegitimate to assume that marginal utilities can somehow represent total utilities. Only the latter are the proper concern of value judgements.

It appears therefore that even on its own assumptions and those of subjective value theory, the 'purely fiscal' theory is entirely arbitrary. Even if we assume that the distribution before fiscal taxation is just, it would certainly no longer be just after taxation. The principle has no better claim to be a guide to justice than any other principle, say J. S. Mill's. Worse, the marginal principle cannot be even conceived as a fiscal norm, however much hedged in with assumptions. For even if subjective value theory could evolve a political rule, this would have to aim at a maximization or a just distribution of *total* utilities and not of *marginal* utilities. It should be remembered that we have criticized the theory on its own ground, neither questioning the concept 'subjective value' itself nor the practical applicability of the conclusions.

This criticism cannot be escaped by assuming as given some system of taxation, to which socio-political taxes are applied in order to create a just distribution, after which only a small requirement remains to be covered by a purely fiscal tax. The principle would still be arbitrary, though the political significance of its application would be reduced. By depriving it of significance, one could equally well justify any principle of taxation.

The upshot of all this is that it is in vain to attempt to isolate a purely economic problem from its political setting. Such an attempt leads either to tautologies or to sheer arbitrariness. The fact that it is possible to present a highly sophisticated theory, which appears to be coherent, significant, and convincing until one probes into its principal concepts and assumptions, illustrates the difficulties with which we are faced in the social sciences.

This concludes our general criticism of the theory of public finance. But the preceding discussion is an insufficient safeguard against muddled and biased thinking. In spite of a critical attitude to the manipulation with higher principles one easily lapses into metaphysical habits when problems of detail come under discussion.

It is difficult enough to trace and to discover these elements of political doctrine. They are usually hidden in innocent-looking abstract formulas. One then deduces practical conclusions by omitting essential links in the chain of reasoning and thus the conclusions are made to appear as scientific deductions. We should now proceed to a criticism of the manner in which questions of detail are discussed. But this would go beyond the scope of this book. Anticipating the result of such a discussion, we go on to ask: How should one develop a theory of public finance?

There can hardly be any doubt that it should be a theory of incidence in the widest sense; a study of the *effects* of various possible tax systems.[28] Fiscal theory can make a very important contribution to practical controversies by providing a thorough knowledge of the observable repercussions of alternative tax proposals; their effects on prices, the rate of interest, capital values, wages and other incomes, saving and investment, profits and losses, consumption habits, production techniques, location of industry, size of turnovers, methods of accounting, and of writing off capital, etc. All this can profitably be examined empirically, particularly if the inquiries draw on the available psychological and sociological knowledge, although the data are still inadequate. But a discussion which makes use of the existing, increasingly realistic, theory of price formation would already represent a considerable step forward. This has been shown to be true for many related practical problems.

Hitherto the theory of public finance has not carried out as well as it could have done the important practical task of examining the effects of alternative measures, thus providing knowledge as a basis for political decisions. Bemused by the search for fictitious principles, it has succeeded in little more than in learned expositions and complex proofs of empty catch-phrases. More profitable pursuits have meanwhile been neglected.

It cannot be the task of the scientist to make value judgements and lay down principles of conduct. But even if it were possible to establish value judgements objectively, they would have to refer to the effects of taxation. Therefore the problem of incidence has logical priority also from the point of view of welfare or justice. Unless we know what effects a certain measure will have, the question of welfare or justice does not arise. These effects are by no means obvious. Their intricate connections have to be traced carefully. Thus even if a case could be made out in favour of formulating first principles, they would have no practical significance until the problems of incidence had been solved. In other words, one cannot defend abstract speculations by saying that the problems of incidence are too complex. If the latter should turn out to be insoluble, the whole theory of public finance would have to be abandoned and we would have to act completely arbitrarily.

I do not blame the politicians and tax experts who legislate and administer as best they can. They look abroad to see how similar matters are ordered there: they quote the literature whenever convenient; they form opinions on the nature and on the practical aspects of their problems and then come to some sort of conclusions. The reasons which they advance bear the unmistakable doctrinal imprint of the high principles. Occasionally a problem of tax incidence is touched upon but hardly ever fully discussed. They are usually concerned with specific questions and this explains why they do not put them into the wider setting of tax policy as a whole. Their proposals are probably often based on a more thorough examination of the effects of alternative measures and it is understandable that these considerations are not publicized, for high authority sanctions the view that incidence is a very difficult, or even an insoluble, problem.

We should be grateful to the practical experts and not reproach them. The importance of the problem of the economic effects of taxation is much more acutely felt in practice than in the isolation of academic life. This is also why it is the practical experts who have begun useful studies of incidence. Thus in Britain the heavy pressure of taxation after the war has led to the remarkable investigations of the Colwyn Committee. They belong to the most realistic discussions of this subject ever undertaken. If the method is somewhat crude and the conclusions uncertain, this is due not only to the intrinsic difficulties of the problem, but also to the immaturity of relevant theory. It should have shaped the tools for an analysis and cleared the field of popular metaphysical ideas.

We can do no more than allude briefly to the history of the theory of incidence. The Physiocrats believed that all taxes, wherever they were imposed, would ultimately come to rest on the rent of land. This conclusion followed from their theory of the rôle of land in the process of price formation and of rent as the 'net product' in their peculiar meaning of the term. Adam Smith and Ricardo took up the problem again and treated it more thoroughly. Ricardo particularly, whose sound instinct led him to avoid, whenever possible, discussions of principles, examined the problem of incidence closely. His treatment is still of fundamental importance.

In France the belief in harmony inspired a theory according to which all taxes, irrespective of how and where they are imposed, are eventually distributed equally amongst all classes. Although an unimportant sideline in the development, this theory, like the general belief in harmony, still pervades popular notions.

The more scientific inquiries followed Ricardo's masterly lead. The later classics never went much beyond comments on, and interpretations of, Ricardo. The marginal utility theorists introduced new ideas in this field too and, as in other spheres, many unrealistic artificial assumptions, to which Ricardo had been forced, could thus be abandoned. But the theory remains highly abstract and inapplicable. The most serious defects of the theory are its static assumptions. The real world is never static.

The greatest advance was made in the treatment of the taxation of monopoly profits. After Cournot's pioneering efforts, Edgeworth, Marshall, Wicksell, and some American and Latin authors completed the theory. They developed very elegant theorems which show that in certain monopoly conditions taxation would lead to quite unexpected results. Apart from these theorems of more than curiosity value, one must agree with Wicksell when he says in his valuable study of incidence: 'Modern economists in contrast to Ricardians usually treat this important and difficult subject only cursorily and superficially, which contrasts oddly with their elaborate and careful examination of many less important questions of detail.'[29] Since this was written things have changed to some extent, but not substantially.

Taxation is a most flexible and effective but also a dangerous instrument of social reform. One has to know precisely what one is doing lest the results diverge greatly from one's intentions. The worst is that one may not even notice what is happening. Suppose, for example, that a heavy tax is imposed on large incomes and capital, but some of the details have been regulated in such a way that the tax is shifted. The objective of the tax has not been attained; nevertheless, the tax will have repercussions on the behaviour of the high income receivers, which are undesirable from the value point of view of the tax legislation. The price, as it were, has been paid, but one is cheated of the goods. Yet, the illusion may continue that taxation has met the requirements of redistributional reform. The difficulty is that there is no object of comparison. Had there been a clear understanding of the repercussions, the desired objective might have been achieved, perhaps even without the need to have paid the price. This is a purely hypothetical example, but it illustrates the importance of the problem. Nobody knows much, for example, about the ultimate effects of the present Swedish tax system.

For one thing, the effect of a tax must never be examined in isolation, but must be seen in its setting amongst other measures in the complex system of price formation. A measure has different repercussions according to the nature of other measures applied at the same time. Suppose, for example, that a tax on capital is proposed. The question of incidence will certainly be relevant, even although it may not be discussed in detail when the proposal is debated. But suppose further that, for political reasons, the proposal is confined to the capital of a certain industry. The incidence may now be very different even as far as that industry is concerned.

A proper analysis must consider the tax system as a whole and as an integral part of price formation. One implication of this is that an alteration in an apparently quite insignificant section of a tax bill can shift the whole distribution of the tax burden. To bring about a change in quantity and price relationships, a change at the margin is sufficient. Hence any clause in a tax bill may indirectly affect persons who are not directly affected by it. An analysis of the repercussions must therefore examine the special conditions in each particular case. Every sentence, every word, must be scrupulously weighed. To return to the example of the tax on capital, one would have to pay careful attention to how the law should define real capital liable to tax. One may want to exclude certain types of claims and debts. A different definition might result in different effects, not only for the persons or enterprises which own those special claims or debts. Perhaps quite different groups of persons would have to bear the tax burden in the two cases. 'Common sense' does not take us very far. One has to examine the repercussions on prices in the various alternatives before one can decide upon a policy.

Other difficulties arise because no one country can be examined in isolation, because neither free competition nor complete monopoly prevail, and because the effects of taxation are largely determined by sociological and psychological factors; long-term reactions may be quite different from short-term reactions.

Above all, the process of price formation is dynamic and changes in tax legislation introduce an additional dynamic element. Static models are therefore of little use. 'Income', 'costs', 'profitability', etc., are commonly used as static concepts which have no precise counterpart in the real world. Clearly, the question to what extent dynamic profits and losses should be subsumed under the fiscal income concept and taxed as income cannot be decided by interpreting a principle. But it is equally impossible to settle the question by postulating a political value judgement. Such a judgement would have to be based upon knowledge of the *effects* of defining income in either way.[30] It is false to believe that profits and losses react to taxation in the same way as 'income' and 'costs'. Any political judgement must be based upon a view of the part played by these profits and losses in the whole process of price formation. The problem of incidence is part of the dynamic problem of price formation.

Realistic investigations of the effects of taxes should therefore embrace the whole tax system, should weigh carefully every word and paragraph, should be supported by sociological and psychological research and should be built upon a dynamic theory of price formation. This, I think, is the general trend which the theory of public finance has been following since the end of the First World War and along which it will develop in the future.

Chapter 8

THE RÔLE OF ECONOMICS IN POLITICS

E VEN if one believed that a normative science is possible, our criticism in the preceding chapter would still be valid. For valuations should not be incorporated into economics by means of fallacious arguments. If economic science is to be normative, surely it ought not to be simply bad logic.

There is, on the other hand, wide agreement that economics ought to be 'practical'. How then can the results of economic inquiry be made to serve practical purposes?

In the preceding criticism it was not intended to split hairs. There are cases when economic interests run parallel. We can therefore safely say that whenever interest harmony prevails, economists can make universally valid recommendations.

Some liberal arguments are indeed of this type. Thus if it can be shown that a protectionist measure would promote bribery and corruption,[1] there is a presumption that all respectable citizens would condemn this particular result of a deviation from laissez-faire. Of course, this does not preclude the possibility of other results which are judged differently by the individuals concerned. Those who attach sufficient importance to these other results may even accept the undesirable result as a necessary evil. To take another example, there is often common agreement on certain 'purely legal' aspects of social problems, which do not appear to have important implications for social policy. Perhaps many problems of greater economic significance are also of this kind, particularly in monetary and banking policy. Such problems, though in a sense practical problems, can be treated and solved by theoretical reasoning because there is a harmony of interests.

This must not be taken to be a concession to the so-called 'economic principles'. Why disguise the fact that interests happen to run parallel by a quasi-objective formulation of a 'principle'? It is simpler and more accurate to say that we *presuppose* identical interests and then to submit evidence for this assumption. Indeed, honesty demands that we put it this way, for it may well be that our assumption is wrong. An honest method of exposition should not obscure the points at which criticism may be directed.

As we have seen, the economic reasoning is often obscured by the fact that normative principles are not introduced explicitly, but in the shape of general 'concepts'. The discussion is thus shifted from the normative to the logical plane. On the former there is either harmony or conflict; conflict can only be stated, not solved by discussion. On the logical plane we should define our concepts clearly and then operate with them in a logically correct manner. What is 'correct' and what 'false' can be discussed with the methods of logic, whereas conflicting interests can be recognized, never solved scientifically.

We have seen that the basic concepts are frequently charged with normative implications. Time and again attempts have been made to by-pass interest conflicts by the manner in which those basic concepts are defined. A precise definition of those concepts would, however, reveal that they are logically conditional. No definition can claim absolute and *a priori* validity. All definitions are tools which we construct in order to observe and analyse reality. They are 'instrumental' and have no justification in their own right. By operating with definitions which purport to be universally valid, people have often succeeded in making an implied political principle appear logically 'correct'. Psychologically, it is the other way round. The emotive force which is rationalized in the implied principle makes the normative element that has been disguised in the definition appear to be absolute and 'correct'. The perpetual game of hide-and-seek in economics consists in concealing the norm in the concept. It is thus imperative to eradicate not only the explicit principles but above all the valuations tacitly implied by the basic concepts. Being concealed, they are more insidious and more elusive, and hence more likely to breed confusion.

It would be wrong to believe that the necessity to eliminate normative principles is absent in those fields where identity of interests could possibly be presumed. For monetary policy the assumption of a harmony of interests is, perhaps, more often realistic than for other spheres. This should then be stated and proved. Yet, even here there have been disputes over the 'correct' meaning of such terms as 'value of money', 'inflation', 'natural rate of interest' and 'equilibrium in the capital market'. Such formalistic controversies, which often bar a realistic discussion of the interests involved, cannot, of course, be justified by the assumption of harmony. They do not contribute to our understanding of a harmony, even if it existed.

If there is reason to believe that in a particular case interests are identical, this would have to be ascertained and proved. As a major premise it should not be concealed by an *a priori* principle or a basic concept. The political conclusions are valid only in so far as this premise has been established as a factual basis for analysis. It is certainly not self-evident.

But in most questions of economic policy there are conflicts of interests. This in fact should not be concealed by obscure talk of *a priori* principles. In those cases neither an economist nor anybody else can offer a 'socially' or 'economically correct' solution. No service is rendered to a rational conduct of politics by misusing scientific method for attempts to conceal conflicts. They continue to exist, however vehement the barrage of categorical principles and basic concepts.

It should be one of the main tasks of applied economics to examine and to unravel the complex interplay of interests, as they sometimes converge, sometimes conflict. This ought to be done by economists because the intricacies of the price system are such that interests often run along different lines from those suggested by a superficial examination. It would be of great practical importance to reconstruct precisely the social field of interests. In the first place, we should want to know where interests converge, for in these cases we could make at once generally valid recommendations. We should also want to ascertain where lines of interests intersect. In these cases we could offer alternative solutions, each one corresponding to some special interest. Both types of solution can claim objectivity, not because they express objective political norms, but because they follow from explicitly stated value premises which correspond to real interests. The solutions are of practical interest to the extent to which their value premises are relevant to political controversies, i.e. in so far as they represent the interests of sufficiently powerful social groups.

There has always been a tendency in economics to gloss over interest conflicts. This is quite understandable. The philosophical inspirations of political economy—the philosophy of natural law and its English branch, utilitarianism—stem from a belief in social harmony, and their practical recommendations presuppose such a harmony. We have seen that this is the logical result of their peculiar way of constructing a moral philosophy: in virtue of the idea of harmony both actual and moral conduct can be deduced from 'human nature', or, in utilitarian terminology, from pleasure and pain. In economics the notion of harmony is expressed by the idea that economic activity can be viewed as the process of house-keeping by a single social subject. This leads to the belief that economic problems can be treated 'from an economic point of view'. The whole theory of value is intended not only as an explanation of economic activity, but as the basis for a welfare economics, for a theory of social value. The theory of economic liberalism is built upon this communistic fiction. The theory of public finance is a similar attempt to derive political maxims from the same philosophical premises. Although the terminology changes, the idea of harmony pervades all branches and the conceptual structure of economics.

As we have attempted to show, the dominant idea of the 'common welfare' undergoes changes in the course of time. Since the beginning of the nineteenth century there has been a trend towards greater radicalism. Originally, welfare economics or the theory of social value was usually turned into an unqualified laissez-faire theory according to which all is for the best in the world; the general interest was supposed to require maintenance of the *status quo*, except that any 'unnatural' interventions should be stopped. Under the pressure of socialist and institutionalist criticism, there began a retreat from the conservative interpretation of the doctrine of harmony. Laissez-faire was no longer considered to be in the interest of society under all circumstances. It was thought that there was room for improvement, particularly with respect to income and property distribution. Nevertheless, the conviction persisted that such reforms and the resulting social order are in the interest of society as a whole. Harmony of interests was no longer thought to apply to the *status quo* but to a social order which had to be brought about. J. S. Mill introduced this revolutionary tendency into classical welfare theory. It is equally metaphysical because it rests on the belief that the ideal order can, in principle, be determined and that, if this has not been done yet, it is merely due to imperfect knowledge. The idea that one can judge social policy from a 'purely economic point of view' is thoroughly metaphysical. It assumes tacitly that there is such a thing as the interest of society as a whole, and that particular interests, though superficially antagonistic, are at heart reconcilable. The same tacit assumption confined the discussion of practical problems to those general 'principles' whose rôle we have tried to illustrate above.

The idea of harmony is so compelling that even writers who otherwise attributed a fundamental importance to the conflict of interests did not escape it altogether. For Karl Marx history was a continuous class struggle of the exploited against the exploiters. But there is a vestige of the idea of a common welfare in his thesis that certain social phenomena are the natural result of certain productive conditions, which are realized with maximum efficiency, and develop, in due course, into new productive conditions. In his forecasts particularly the teleological element is most conspicuous. Many modern socialist writers, particularly those who have had contact with orthodox liberal doctrine, have even more definite ideas about the existence of a common welfare.

Similarly, Ricardo's distribution theory was hardly conducive to a justification of the doctrine of harmony. On the contrary, he emphasized that class interests tend to clash and that only very occasionally do they coincide. Indeed, his central question was directed at the forces which determine the shares of the various classes in the total product. One class can improve its lot only by reducing the shares of others. But when he came to more practical political questions he forgot his analysis of the conflict of interests and lapsed into the old laissez-faire tradition.

The historical school provides a third example. Its members started from a criticism of the absolutist and doctrinaire spirit of classical theory. They emphasized that everything is historical and relative. Yet, they believed that it is possible to evolve an objective, though historically conditioned, social policy without ever explaining how this can be done. When it came to practical problems, they too tended to gloss over the fact of conflict.

In modern economics too this historically understandable bias for the assumption of a 'social interest', for something which is 'economically sound', is more apparent in arguments about economic policy and the theories supporting them, such as value theory, than in the more scientific analysis of price formation and distribution. In this latter respect modern economists have followed Ricardo's example. Disregarding the reservation discussed below, it therefore does not seem too difficult to reconstruct the field of economic interests and to fit it into the body of modern economics. Such a reconstruction would be the prerequisite for a 'technology of economics', by which is meant a scientific theory of how policy can serve concrete interests. Only the theory of price formation and distribution would have to be reformulated from this particular point of view. The theory would, as it were, have to be turned round. Instead of answering the question how, in given conditions, prices, incomes, and other quantities are determined, the theory ought to be able to answer the question what interferences, if any, would be in the interests of what groups.

The real difficulty of constructing a technology of economics in this sense would be that we are not entitled to take the existing institutional set-up for granted. By institutional set-up is meant the legal order, and the customs, habits, and conventions, which are sanctioned, or at least tolerated, by that legal order. A purely theoretical analysis of price formation can and, indeed, always has abstracted from institutional changes.

In actual life, however, it is the institutional set-up over which the political struggle is often fought. The scope for discovering the field of economic interests is greatly enlarged if we envisage the possibility of institutional changes. As long as we confine ourselves to the study of wage and price problems in a *given* institutional structure, the interests of one group of workers may conflict with those of another group, they may even coincide with the interests of the employer of this other group. But as soon as we take into account the wider possibilities of institutional change, interests may run along quite different lines. All institutional factors which determine the structure of the market, indeed the whole economic system including its tax and social legislation, can be changed, if those interested in the change have enough political power. Very different interest constellations would be relevant in this wider setting. Moreover, the situation will look different according to whether we examine short-term or long-term considerations.

An inquiry into economic interests should therefore treat the whole institutional set-up as a variable. It should also examine to what extent any groups are sufficiently powerful to bring about institutional changes, and it should finally trace the repercussions of various possible institutional changes throughout the price system.

It may be misleading to speak of an institutional *system*. It is better to speak of the institutional 'condition', or 'situation' or 'set-up'. It should certainly not be thought of as a simple structure, or as in any sense 'systematic'. Nothing has confounded discussions and has muddled political attitudes so much as the traditional method of thinking in terms of 'systems'. To take an example: Our economic 'system' is often described as based upon private property. This generalization, which may have some historical justification if numerous qualifications are added, is quite misleading as it stands, for the relevant social factors can be altered *by degrees* without changing the system as such. Some of the most effective reforms aim at changes within the framework of the existing order of property, such as 'industrial democracy', certain fiscal reforms, etc. On the other hand, one could replace the ruling 'system' by another without substantial changes in the relevant social conditions. Undoubtedly, the unsophisticated person thinks in terms of 'systems' and 'principles'. One of the reasons why metaphysical conceptualism (*Begriffsrealismus*) persists so stubbornly in the social sciences is the influence of public opinion. Popular ideas tend to be formalistic and to mistake the form for reality.[2]

In reality there is no such thing as a 'system'. It is at best an analytical tool for analysing social phenomena. From a system no conclusions can be derived either about what is or about what ought to be. Thus one cannot deduce the right of inheritance from the right of private property. Such concepts as 'right of private property', 'freedom of contract', 'inheritance', etc., so common in abstract economic analysis, are, in this abstract sense, quite unknown to lawyers or sociologists. Thus there has never been a free market in the sense in which the term is used in economics. Long before there was any market to speak of, exchange transactions had been subjected to rules by those in power. These regulations have always been necessarily *material* and not merely *formal*. They have influenced the content and the results of the transactions. The 'system' of private property is modified by every session of Parliament and often by judicial acts. It is the business of the jurists to deal with the institutional set-up in a systematic manner so that the legal practitioners can find their way in it. The political choice is never one between a number of abstract, logically coherent, social orders, as economic theory tends to present it, such as free competition, communism, etc.

Social life is the result of historical development and is anything but a logical system. At every moment we are faced with the choice of either maintaining the social order as it is or of changing it. It can be changed in a number of different directions, in different ways and, above all, to different degrees. This fact makes a technology of economics so extraordinarily complicated. The theory of price formation (including distribution) which should enable us to map out the field of interests, is not yet sufficiently flexible in its institutional basis to allow for a sufficiently wide range of variations. Much remains to be done in this direction by future research.

To sum up: Economists are on safe ground as long as they describe actual events and their causal connections, and as long as they examine the effects of certain clearly defined 'interventions' under specified conditions. In order to make economics into a practical technique or technology, we should have to analyse in detail the field of economic interests. The main obstacle to such an analysis is the fact that the institutional set-up is not given but is changeable in various directions and to various degrees. We must, moreover, know the distribution of power amongst social groups in order to estimate what institutional changes are feasible.

The technology of economics should reflect possible strategies in a 'war game'. It would be of practical importance if it throws light on the possible course of future developments and probable trends. It could also be used to clarify the relation between various programmes and the interests of the groups which sponsor them.

Certain policies may thus be seen to be ill-conceived or doomed to failure from the start. In this way political intentions could be clarified and orientated. Such a study of the politics of economics could claim to be objective, just because it makes no recommendations save those which follow some specified, clearly expressed interest. For the same reason, it could not yield absolutely valid conclusions in the sense of postulates of an economically correct conduct as such, except, possibly, in the limited sphere where interests can be shown to be identical.

Such an economic technology is in the best tradition of political economy, which has always aimed at social policy. It would have to become more relativistic, i.e. it would have to be related to *explicit and concrete value premises*. If this science of economic politics, after thus having been made conditional and relativistic, is to have any practical significance, the chosen value premises must express the interests of all the strong social groups. This requires an analysis of the field of social interests. But the crucial problem is to discover those interests, while taking account of all the institutional changes which are feasible under political pressure.

Were it not for even greater difficulties, the technology of economics might still be expected to make satisfactory headway. But so far we have avoided the most fundamental difficulty. Unfortunately—or perhaps fortunately—human actions are not solely motivated by economic interests. The concept itself, though popular amongst economists, presents, on closer inspection, certain difficulties. Presumably 'economic interest' means the desire for higher incomes and lower prices and, in addition, perhaps stability of earnings and employment, reasonable time for leisure and an environment conducive to its satisfactory use, good working conditions, etc. But even with all these qualificatiors, political aspirations cannot be identified with those interests. People are also interested in social objectives. They believe in ideals to which they want their society to conform.

Citizens do not fight wars merely to protect their economic interests, however much they may overrate their importance. Or again, it would be a mistake to think that the struggle for higher wages or even for security and other material advantages is the driving force of the working-class movement. We must remember its origins in the industrial revolution. At first a new and growing class, it found itself concentrated in industrial urban areas. A standardized way of life was imposed upon it. This class now became aware of certain conflicts and inequalities which had previously, in the patriarchal tradition, been accepted as 'natural'. The age of enlightenment and the French revolution had spread new ideas of law and justice. Out of a feeling of inferiority and maladjustment grew the revolutionary demand for equality and a consciousness of class solidarity. Both found a powerful echo in political democracy as it developed. Demands for higher wages, shorter working hours, etc., are, of course, important as such but they are also an expression of a more general desire for power. They are a plea for justice by an oppressed class. The feeling of being oppressed is the important factor. Even if there were little hope for higher wages, the struggle would still continue. Workers would still demand more power and a voice in management, even if they knew that it would not increase productivity or wages. Ultimately they are after more than money. What counts for at least as much is pride in their work, self-respect, and their dignity as human beings. Probably no big strike can be explained psychologically as merely a strike for higher wages.

In the course of this sociological process different moral standards are developed by different groups. In the eyes of a class-conscious worker, blacklegs are traitors. This moral condemnation is not merely the result of considerations of expediency in the struggle for wages. In the eyes of a typical *petit-bourgeois*, on the other hand, a strike-breaker is almost a hero, a champion of freedom and of the sacredness of free competition.

This is of great importance for our problem. A technology of economics should not be built upon economic interests, but upon social attitudes. 'Attitude' means the emotive disposition of an individual or a group to respond in certain ways to actual or potential situations.

The above illustrations have no more than indicated some emotional sources of social attitudes and some of their extreme manifestations. But it must be stressed that it is generally false to represent political attitudes as interests. Interests are always blended with moral sentiment. The latter may sometimes reinforce an attitude based mainly on interest, thereby checking opposing emotive components of the attitude. At other times the emotional force works in the opposite direction and against the interests. Fortunately there are many people whose attitudes are not identical with their interests.

There are further obstacles to the accurate determination of attitudes. First, we cannot always believe what people tell us. When asked to account for our political convictions, we are liable to use conventional and stereotyped stock phrases which may have little bearing on our actual behaviour. Thus American sociologists have found that people's declarations about their views on the Negro problem have very little to do with their conduct in daily life; or, to take an illustration more familiar to economists: a well-known phenomenon is the businessman who is 'organizing' and monopolizing his markets. Usually he is convinced that his business principles are healthy, that they not only increase his income but also 'adapt' consumption to production and vice versa. He firmly believes that he fulfils an important social function. Yet, the same man will, when more general questions, not immediately related to his own activities, are discussed, express views which seem to come straight from the Physiocrats and Adam Smith. These convictions are held in equally good faith. He will advocate free competition, freedom of business activity, and freedom generally as a principle of economic policy and as a moral right. His professions have no connection with his conduct. The same man might, in practice, propagate large-scale political interventions and regulations. His professed opinions are 'cultural lags', rudiments of conventions, taken over from defunct economic doctrines. Often they are also class slogans, the badges of membership of certain groups in society. The above illustrations must suffice, but the same is also true of other classes. Landowners, just as workers, have their pet slogans.

These phrases, which, of course, enter into political programmes, cannot be used directly by a technology of economics, partly because they are too vague, partly because they have no bearing, or at any rate no unambiguous bearing, upon the actual attitudes of individuals faced with concrete political decisions. But for our purpose it is essential to know just these attitudes as they determine actual behaviour in concrete situations. We certainly cannot infer these responses directly from general professions.

This does not mean that professions which have *no clearly defined* relation to actual attitudes in concrete decisions have *no* bearing *at all* on the latter. Occasionally, though perhaps not often, they are prevalent ideals to which people fail to conform. Just because of their vagueness and their emotive power they are also a particularly suitable medium for political suggestion. But the connection between profession and action is rather complicated and one would have to make detailed psychological inquiries in every case. There are also other much stronger competing motives for the resulting actions. No direct conclusion can be drawn from the way people think and talk to their attitudes.

As long as we confine ourselves to the *actual situation*, we might

P

conceivably be able to infer attitudes from observations of actual behaviour. But since a technology of economics with a claim to yield significant results must include the analysis of *potential situations*, the determination of the relevant interests raises highly complex problems of social psychology.

Even if we succeeded in penetrating through the verbiage to people's probable responses to concrete political situations, this would still not define the relevant field of attitudes. For these responses are largely based upon erroneous ideas of social phenomena and their connections. A technology of economics should not accept attitudes which are based upon erroneous conceptions of the real world. Ideally, it would have to build on attitudes which the individuals with false opinions, given their general emotional dispositions, would have, if they knew all the facts; or, to make the condition more sensible, if they knew all that is actually known by contemporary experts. We are thus faced with the task of inferring from observed actual attitudes those potential attitudes which various groups would take up in potential situations on the unrealistic assumption that they had a clearer understanding of economic phenomena.

But this cannot be done by a logical process. We would have to suppose that there is a logical connection between the valuations of an individual in different situations, i.e. that it would be possible, given his political conviction which is based on certain ideas about the facts, to deduce directly the conviction which would result from other ideas about the facts. But such conclusions require many intermediate steps, some of which are of a psychological character. Again, we are faced with a problem of *social psychology*, not simply of logic.

A passage from Max Weber in which he attempts to define the limits of scientific reasoning in questions of economic policy may serve to illustrate this point. 'The only question is in what sense a scientific discussion about "ought" is possible. First, I can reply to somebody who makes some particular value judgement: You are mistaken about what you really want. If I take your value judgement and analyse it logically, if I show you the ultimate axioms on which it rests, we may discover that they imply certain possible ultimate value judgements which may be incompatible with each other or with your explicit valuation. You may have to compromise or you may have to choose one and sacrifice others, in any case you must choose. To point this out is not an empirical but a logical task.'[3]

This would imply that it is possible to arrive by analysis of a given value judgement at ultimate axioms, which, of course, are not meant to be objective values; they are axiomatic only for the person who accepts the explicit value judgement from which the analysis has started. The 'choice' of the individual would then be merely a particular application of the value axiom thus inferred. The conflicts which Weber has in mind are logical conflicts. In his view there is a logical connection between value judgements in the sense that they can be legitimately criticized by applying the criterion of consistency. It would seem to follow that we could deduce from political valuations based on existing but inadequate conceptions of reality those valuations which would be, or rationally should be, made under more complete and correct conceptions of reality. It would be sufficient to assume as known the valuations and the conceptions of reality in only one situation.

However, Weber is not quite clear on this point. One could also interpret the passage as a refutation of such a method. He implies the existence of a logical incompatibility between ultimate value judgements which are reached by inference, or between some of the latter and the explicit value judgements. In this case the 'choice' would constitute a new and independent valuation.

Whatever Weber meant to say, one thing is certain: in reality there is no logical connection between the valuations of individuals; there is no logical hierarchy dominated by ultimate axioms. What logical hierarchy exists is the result of rationalization, and rationalization alone does not determine human behaviour or attitudes. The desire to think of moral valuations as if they were logically coherent is a legacy from the days of the metaphysical systems. The assumption of logical order was a necessary prerequisite for the attempted scientific treatment of morality. Quite apart from the question whether there ought to be a logical order of value judgements, we cannot, for our purpose, assume one. Otherwise, the technology of economics might lapse again into the traditional debate about first principles. It should confine itself to empirically observable group attitudes, including potential attitudes which would become actual in certain carefully specified conditions.

This criticism of Weber does not mean that there is no connection at all between the attitudes of a group in different situations. If that were so it would be impossible, in principle, to map out the relevant attitudes, and a technology of economics would be a nonsense attempt. Clearly there are such connections, but they are psychological, not logical. In the case of a single individual the connection between different attitudes in different situations is called 'personality' or 'character'. Our problem is therefore part of the psychology of character and, since we are concerned with social groups, it is a problem of the social psychology of the character of groups. The technology of economics is a branch of modern, psychologically orientated sociology.

It is doubtful whether sociology will be able to provide us in the foreseeable future with a firm foundation for the technology of economics. We shall have to be content for a long time with somewhat vague generalizations. It is, however, of interest that such generalizations are being attempted, even although they are still qualified in numerous ways. Thus inquiries into, say, the character psychology of the working class or the farmers, in a country, however tentative, would provide a basis for an empirical treatment of political problems in terms of the actual valuations of these important social groups. Two requirements ought to ensure that the technology of economics will not end up in traditional metaphysics; first, it should always formulate its value premises explicitly in concrete terms and relate them to the actual valuations of social groups; second, in formulating the relevant attitudes, the above-mentioned problems of social psychology should not be neglected. If the results are likely to be vague and unsatisfactory for a time, we should bear in mind Sidgwick's plea to make our concepts and assumptions as precise as possible, even if that deprives our conclusions of precision. It is easy enough to get clear and precise results as long as the manner in which they are reached is sufficiently obscured.

Hitherto we have assumed the relevant attitudes to be given and fixed, so that we can use them as a starting-point for our technology of economics whenever we succeed in discovering them. The final difficulty is that those attitudes themselves are subject to change.

In earlier times this complication was less important. Attitudes once formed changed only gradually. Politicians had not yet discovered that long-term policies can aim not only at making use of existing, but also at creating new attitudes. Modern developments of communication and psychological techniques made such policies possible. Moreover, the experiences of the war have greatly stimulated the growth of propaganda.

Attitudes can be consciously created in two ways, according to which generation is to be influenced. The most effective propaganda for the long run must aim at the young generation. Modern child psychologists are inclined to believe that with suitable methods a child's attitudes to life can be moulded within limits wide enough for any practically relevant purpose. They also maintain that neutral education is a contradiction in terms. Every generation creates, consciously or unconsciously, the outlook on life of the next. The older generation might be so clumsy that the result of its education, through negative suggestion, resentment, etc., diverges widely from its intentions.

As we would expect, the two dictatorships, Russia and Italy, were the first to learn the lesson of conscious indoctrination. The calculated political indoctrination in those two countries is perhaps the most interesting part of the social experiments of communism and fascism. Its success or failure may have wider implications than many are now inclined to believe. Next to Russia and Italy, the United States of America practises most consciously political indoctrination. This may seem odd, for America is, in a sense, the most individualistic nation in the world. But she has had to absorb and assimilate people from many different countries. As a result of this, there is hardly another nation in the world, with the exception of Russia and Italy, where, in spite of great differences in cultural heritage and of large geographical distances and social gulfs, the young grow up with more uniform and standardized convictions and attitudes.

At the same time adult opinion is also worked upon. The development of advertising techniques and the need to maintain domestic morale in the war have led to the refinement of propaganda. Every channel of communication can be used, openly or secretly, for exercising political influence. The most effective propaganda first stirs up emotions, and then uses the receptivity thus created for moulding attitudes by suggestion.

This fact will probably become increasingly important in the future and will weaken the basis of a technology of economics by making it more difficult to determine the relevant attitudes. Economics as a science is not concerned with the political problem of moulding attitudes. It cannot pronounce on questions of value. The technology of economics must take certain attitudes as given and cannot lay down what they ought to be. It can, however, help to keep the political struggle more honest. In so far as the public pay any attention to it, it may prevent their attitudes from being based on false notions about the facts and particularly about the relations between economic interests. A situation in which intellectual sanitation of this kind would be even more important than to-day may arise if the state, or powerful groups which control sufficient material resources and have command over the necessary techniques, should want to use the propaganda machine in order to pervert public opinion. The experiences of war propaganda and of modern elections suggest that this would not be impossible. In the light of such attempts the politics of open class interests, so much decried in quieter conditions, would appear to be a more honest method.

In such conditions the social sciences would be put to a critical test. Propaganda which aims not only at changing emotional attitudes of the citizens but also at distorting their conception of reality—and this is the essence of modern propaganda—must come into conflict with the scientific ethos, from whichever political party these attempts may come. The most effective resistance would be instruction and education in the social sciences with a strong practical orientation. In such conditions, if not before, would it be shown how dangerous it is not to be clear about the character and the foundations of social knowledge. There are forces in society which work against the scientist's desire for clarity, and they may find the so-called fundamental concepts and principles useful instruments for their purposes. It will then become even more urgent for those who stand for lucidity and honesty to deprive these speculations of their scientific pretensions.

Only if economists are modest in their claims and renounce all pretensions to postulate universal laws and norms can they promote effectively their practical objectives, viz., to keep political arguments rational, that is to say, to base them on as complete and as correct a knowledge of the facts as possible.

But is not the proposition that politics ought to be rational in this sense and that economists ought to support this endeavour itself a normative principle? And is it not arbitrary at that? Why not sacrifice 'truth' to higher values?

The answer to this question is that the possibility of scientific endeavour depends upon the tacit assumption that rational argument is desirable.

Appendix

RECENT CONTROVERSIES

by PAUL STREETEN

JUST as Kepler was inspired by the doctrine of harmony in the spheres to discover the laws which govern the orbits of the planets, so the early economists were inspired by the doctrine that there is a harmony of interests in society to formulate economic laws. This doctrine runs through the development of economic theory and pervades the structure of its language and thought.

In his critical analysis of the political element in the growth of economic theory Dr. Myrdal traces the influence of this doctrine from the philosophers of natural law, through the utilitarians and the classical economists, to the neo-classical writings of Lindahl, v. Wieser, Fisher, and Pigou. He shows that the doctrine is often implicit and hardly conscious to its exponents, that it is qualified in response to criticisms, but that nevertheless, the common element in the different versions is clearly recognizable.[1]

Recent controversies in welfare economics have been conducted without much regard to their historical antecedents. The intentions and the arguments in these controversies are essentially repetitions of classical and neo-classical controversies. Those in the classical tradition, at least since J. S. Mill, attempt to define a sphere in which interest harmony prevails; the critics reject these attempts, although they are often found to accept them in parts implicitly.

Recent discussions have usually taken Professor Lionel Robbins's *An Essay on the Nature and Significance of Economic Science* (1st ed., 1932) as their starting-point. Yet, Professor Robbins's main points, for which he claims no originality,[2] are old. Professor Robbins argued (1) that interpersonal comparisons of utility or satisfaction are value judgements and therefore unscientific; (2)

that (partly) because such interpersonal comparisons are value judgements what goes under the name of welfare economics is a 'normative study', containing 'propositions involving the word "ought" [which] are different in kind from propositions involving the word "is"'.[3] And (3) that welfare economics is therefore not the proper study of economists *qua* economists.

Jevons, Böhm-Bawerk, Walras, Fisher, Pareto, and Davenport, among others, have, as Dr. Myrdal shows, put forward similar, arguments. Proposition (1) is an important (though perhaps not an essential) part of Dr. Myrdal's criticism of social value. It has been rejected, most recently again by Mr. I. M. D. Little.[4] But although it can reasonably be denied that interpersonal comparisons of satisfactions, happiness, or welfare are value judgements, it is clear that, even if they can be made descriptively, they cannot provide *per se* the 'scientific' basis for social policies.

Proposition (3) was rejected by those who refused to give up welfare economics as a proper pursuit for economists. It is also frequently violated by the proponents of a 'neutral' economic 'science' themselves. One school of the rehabilitators of welfare economics accepted, the other school rejected, proposition (2).

The recent attempts to reconcile scruples about interpersonal comparisons with a resuscitation of welfare economics are reminiscent, and in some instances a repetition of, the older controversies discussed by Dr. Myrdal. In the thirties and forties of this century, just as in the discussions of the last century, one school of rehabilitators attempted to separate production (including exchange) from distribution, and thus 'efficiency' from 'equity' or 'justice', and to render pronouncements on 'efficiency' (= on the sphere of production) non-controversial (= subject to interest harmony). The critics again emphasized that 'efficiency' and 'justice' cannot be separated conceptually and that interest conflicts cannot be sidestepped by such devices.

The rehabilitation of welfare economics was attempted along two main lines. Hotelling, Kaldor, Hicks,[5] and with certain important reservations, Scitovsky, building on Pareto's foundations, were responsible for one attempt which has come to be known, mostly amongst its critics, as the 'New Welfare Economics' or the Compensation Principle. They accept proposition (1) but reject (2)[6] and (3). Bergson, Samuelson, Tintner, and others developed an alternative method known as the 'Social Welfare

Function'. They too accept proposition (1) but in contrast to the new welfare economists they also accept proposition (2), i.e. they assert that welfare economics is a normative study, in the sense that ethical premises are essential (although not in the sense that these premises can be 'discovered' by economic science). They reject, of course, proposition (3) and believe that welfare economics can and should be studied scientifically by economists.

The Compensation Principle

Just as the classics, the 'new' welfare economists distinguish between distribution and production, and believe that it is possible to make recommendations concerning the latter, without committing oneself to judgements on the former. The purpose of the distinction is again to achieve harmony ('scientific agreement' as it is sometimes called) at least with respect to some types of policies.

The 'new' welfare economists suggest that we should speak of an 'improvement in efficiency', or an 'increase in real income', even though some may be harmed, if it *would be possible* to compensate those who are harmed out of the gains of those who are benefited, and still leave some better off.

Onr eflection, however, it is clear that what is claimed to be a criterion for an economic improvement is neither a necessary nor a sufficient condition. Improvements are possible in which the proposed test does not hold, and it is not true that whenever the condition is fulfilled the situation is actually better. It fails as a guide to policy because it states both too little and too much. Too little, because we require additional criteria for choosing among different income distributions, and too much, because not all policies that obey the rule are improvements.

The critics of the compensation principle (Samuelson, Reder, Baumol, Little,[7] and others), like some early socialists and other critics of classical theory, stressed that distribution cannot be ignored when efficiency is under discussion.

The following three alternative arguments were advanced in defence of the compensation principle, against the criticism that the compensation which *might* be paid does not determine the welfare which *does* exist. (*a*) It is true that in particular cases the result of following the principle might be a worse state. But if the principle were accepted, as a general guide consistently and over a sufficiently long period of time, everybody would most probably gain and hardly anybody would lose. (*b*) It is true that potential overcompensation does not guarantee an actual improvement. Let us therefore every time actually compensate all losers. (*c*) The principle does not claim to be a categorical command. Let politicians, governments, reformers, the common man, or even the economist (but not in his capacity as economic scientist) decide on how to correct faulty distribution. The principle brings out the *economic aspect* of changes in which other aspects play important parts. For many purposes it is sufficient to be able to tell what *could* be done and neither necessary nor desirable to say what *should* be done.

The Long Run Argument

Defences (*a*) and (*c*) are, of course, of ancient and respectable lineage. Arguments of the type (*a*) have been used frequently by free-traders. They admit that there are cases in which theoretical analysis could show that free trade would not produce the best results; but by and large, if it is accepted as a general principle, the results will be better than if we take any other course. Edgeworth used the same type of argument in favour of the greatest happiness principle. 'Moreover, each party may reflect that, in the long run of various cases, the maximum sum-total utility corresponds to the maximum individual utility. He cannot expect in the long run to obtain the larger share of the total welfare. But of all principles of distribution which would afford him now a greater, now a smaller proportion of the sum-total utility obtainable on each occasion, the principle that the collective utility should be on each occasion a maximum is most likely to afford the greatest utility in the long run to him individually.'[8]

Professor Hicks, following the classical tradition, argued that 'there would be a strong probability that almost all [inhabitants] would be better off after the lapse of a sufficient length of time' if 'the economic activities of a community were organized on the principle of making no alterations in the organization of production which were not improvements in this sense, [i.e. potential overcompensation] and making all alterations which were improvements. . . .'[9]

Against this type of argument Mr. Little has pointed out that there is no reason to believe that the distribution effects will be random. If they are not, we have no right to assume that everyone will be better off after a sufficient length of time. Secondly, this defence of the compensation principle entails the interpersonal comparisons which the criterion is intended to eliminate. For if the time is long the individuals in the community will have changed and we would have to compare the welfare of individuals of different generations. Even if we look at the same generation intertemporal comparisons for the same individual give rise to the same difficulties as interpersonal comparisons. Furthermore, to say that most people will have gained after a time and that the losses of those who have not will be negligible involves both interpersonal comparisons of utility and a value judgement.

Actual Compensation

The criticism of defence (a) suggests defence (b). Changes in which some people gain and no one loses must surely be improvements on some widely accepted value premises. Let us therefore always compensate.

In spite of its plausibility this defence is not valid. In the first place, actual compensation is impracticable. We do not know enough about individuals' preferences. Even if we knew everything it would be administratively impossible. Not only would it be costly but it would cause further changes, the losers of which would again have to be compensated, etc. But even if we could ignore these objections, there are difficulties of applying the rule of *actual* compensation which lie deeper. Its use would betray a conservative bias, because the basis of comparison is the *status quo*. A policy based upon such a rule may involve changes which would preclude other changes which would have been more desirable.

Institutional Defence

It is possible to defend the compensation principle on other grounds than either (a) confidence in probable long-run *actual* compensation of all losers if all 'improvements' allowing *hypothetical* compensation are carried out, or (b) the requirement of *actual* compensation of all losers on each occasion. One could argue that whenever economists recommend changes that make compensation possible, it is up to others to decide upon what distributional corrections are indicated. ('Others' does not exclude economists themselves in some function other than that of economists.)

This division of labour may take either of two forms. We may say that the recommendations of economists stand without qualifications if we can be certain that those concerned with correcting the distribution have the will and the power to act appropriately. This may be called the institutional defence. Or we may say that the recommendations of economists are concerned only with one aspect of complex problems and that the acceptance of those recommendations depends upon judgements of all relevant aspects, giving each its due weight. Only after those competent or eager to judge distributional and other value aspects have made their contribution can the qualified 'economic' recommendations become full-blooded recommendations. This may be called the 'economic aspect' defence.

It appears that the new welfare economists must have meant to say something like what is implied by either of these two defences and that their critics misinterpreted them to some extent. They were concerned more with *potential* than with *actual* increases of economic welfare and with conditional rather than categorical recommendations.

Professor Scitovsky ascribes the institutional defence to Mr. Kaldor, and he himself subscribes to it. Those who rely on this argument are free to admit that 'efficiency' and 'justice' are not two separate things, that the question-begging analogy of the cake (production) and its slices (distribution) is misleading, and that 'economic welfare' or 'social income' embrace both. But they can still insist that economists can neglect one aspect of an indivisible whole as long as somebody else looks after it.

The institutional defence of the compensation principle has, however, its own difficulties. In the first place, to delegate authority for just and equitable arrangements to public authorities implies itself a value judgement: the judgement that their will should be done. Scitovsky believes that socialist economies, and present-day Britain in particular, are probably cases where Parliament can be relied upon to maintain equity and promote justice by correcting distributional evils brought about by the market.[10] But there are many people, both inside and outside Britain, who would dispute this. Some believe that distributional corrections are unfair, others that the government is not truly guided by considerations of justice but is, at best, stupid, at worst the tool of self-seeking pressure groups. The economist who is asked to substitute for judgements about desirable distribution judgements about desirable institutional arrangements to bring about good distribution is not on safer, more neutral or more scientific ground. Even an ideal socialist government would act against the convictions of those whose ideal is not the socialist principle of distribution. The belief that such satisfactory institutions are possible is just another version of the doctrine of the harmony of interests.

The 'Economic Aspect'

These objections do not hold against those who say that tests for changes in potential social income bring out the economic aspect in complex problems which have many other aspects besides. Interest groups, irreconcilably divided on matters of distribution, could still consult economists about the 'economic aspect' of their programmes.

Those who take this view might say: It is not the job of the economist to make recommendations, but his analysis may help others to arrive at their recommendations. Economic analysis can help individuals or a group to think clearly about the features of a situation which are relevant to their choice. Although economists cannot say which of two situations is better, they can throw light on certain features, and thus help others to make their decision. Obviously, potentialities are relevant.[11]

The objection to this line of argument is, however, that judgements on the aspect of potential real income and judgements on the aspect of distribution cannot be made independently but are interdependent. Distributional value judgements depend upon what is available for distribution, and the satisfactions derived from a collection of goods depend upon the desires generated by a particular distribution.

Moreover, and equally fatal to any attempt to separate 'aspects', judgements about distribution are not independent of the way by which a situation is reached. The fact that people have enjoyed certain things in the past and have built expectations and plans on this enjoyment, even though it may be judged to be wrong, renders the situation different from one in which they have never enjoyed these things. A scale of values for different distributions, even more than a scale of preferences for different compositions of goods, largely depends upon what *others* enjoy and upon what people have come to expect as their due in the *past*.

The attempt to isolate aspects of 'utility', 'satisfaction', 'welfare', 'happiness', etc., from the social setting which determines them (above all income distribution) may be for some purposes heuristically useful, but as a picture of reality and as a basis for recommendations it is misleading because it ignores the social determination of wants and hence of real income.

The recognition that wants and desires are not ultimate, independent, autonomous data, but the product of social relations[12] also casts doubt on the belief that the more fully desires are met by an economic system, the more efficient it is. The optimum which can be derived from given resources on the definition of welfare economists (that organization of production in which there is no further opportunity for 'improvements' according to the compensation principle) is an optimum only in a limited and trivial sense. The wants which the organization meets optimally are in a wealthier community largely its own creation. A different collection of goods, produced in a different manner, would result in a different set of wants and, if it met those new wants optimally, would also be an optimum.[13]

Sociologists have observed and common experience confirms that it is not only true that we do, and try to get, what we like, but also that we like what we have to do and what we have to get. 'The facts of life and situations come first, and attitudes are simply ways of adjustment and adaptation.'[14]

All this is still based on the value judgement that individual wants only ought to count. Even on that postulate the 'optimum' is ambiguous for two reasons: First, because there is an infinite number of optima according to the initial income distribution, even if wants are *constant*; second, because there is an infinite number of sets of wants, each created by the economic set-up (the distribution and the social structure resulting from this distribution) which also ministers to them.

In order to rank situations in an order of better and worse, we would next have to value and appraise these wants. Then a further range of optima is opened up according to the values which are postulated. A policy which frustrates individual wants might maximize the war potential; or a policy which satisfies the manifest satisfactions of people might also result in neuroses, suicides, and road deaths which are not deemed a price worth paying.

It would be a misunderstanding to interpret this argument as a justification for state intervention or as a threat to liberty. For a paternalistic society which imposes restrictions will, of course, not merely remove some wants but will also create new ones, e.g. the desire for a removal of restrictions. This would lead to new conflicts. The argument merely shows that it is circular to select one set of desires which are largely moulded by the prevailing social setting as an ethical premise to justify this setting.

The Social Welfare Function

Another school attempted the rehabilitation of welfare economics along different lines. They proposed that a set of ethical judgements (including judgements about distribution) should be provided from 'outside' economics. It would then be possible to order various economic situations in such a way as to make any one unambiguously better or worse or indifferent to another. On certain additional assumptions economists can then deduce from this set of value judgements optimum conditions.

Dr. Myrdal's discussion in Chapter 8, though written long before the term 'Social Welfare Function' had been coined, is an illuminating criticism of this type of approach. The Social Welfare Function is a highly formal construction which abstracts from some of the most important facts of social life and choice. No political programme or individual value standard would fit the model of a Social Welfare Function of the required type. There is always interaction between programme and prognosis, between values and analysis of their implications and consequences in a given social setting. The standards are changed in the light of what the analysis shows is possible; and the data which any analysis has to take as given, change with the changing standards of people. Convictions are modified by facts and social facts change with changing convictions. Social Welfare Functions are never 'given' in the abstract.[15]

Recent controversies have been conducted along the same lines as those which date back at least to J. S. Mill. Critics of the traditional abstractions have always stressed that 'efficiency', 'wealth', 'real income', 'economic welfare', etc., cannot be isolated from those conflicts to which distribution gives rise. Income refers to a collection of heterogeneous goods which we render homogeneous by weighting them by their market prices. Any change in this collection (except in the trivial case where there is more of all or at least no less of any good, or in a one-commodity world) involves weighting. But prices, which are usually used as weights, are the result of income distribution. Judgements based upon the assumption of a harmony of interests ('objective', 'scientific', unequivocal judgements) are not possible except in some trivial cases.

The critics have therefore always tended to stress the institutional background and limitations of the activities in which harmony was supposed to prevail. Private property, the law of contract and inheritance, and monopoly, made it necessary to modify recommendations which ignored these disturbing factors. Many critics, however, accepted fundamentally the classical doctrine of harmony and social value. They believed that once these 'disturbances' are removed, the classical doctrine comes into its own. Early socialists like Thompson and Hodgskin, American institutionalists like Veblen, and contemporary Liberal-Socialists like Lerner and Meade, stand in this tradition. So does the Keynes of later days (though not the Keynes of *The End of Laissez-faire*). Keynes added to the institutional 'disturbances' the rate of interest, which interferes with the smooth working of the classical model. He was also a critic of the classical tradition in his recommendation that not merely distribution, but also production cannot be safely left to itself. Production has to be stimulated by state activity. In this respect he is more akin to advocates of 'production policy' like List than to the English classical economists. But Keynes, like so many other critics, stood in the classical utilitarian tradition in his belief that a government can and ought to control economic life according to rational principles and thereby advance the general well-being. Opposed to this Anglo-Saxon conviction is the Continental thought of Marx, or Schumpeter, or Dr. Myrdal, who, each on different grounds, reject such concepts as 'utility', 'social welfare' or the 'common well-being' as metaphysical nonsense. Their attacks are directed at the various versions of the notion of interest harmony, both as a meaningful concept and as a desirable objective. They not only point out the existence of conflict but often welcome it as a condition of life.

Q

NOTES

1. *Essays on Some Unsettled Questions of Political Economy*, 1844.
2. *An Introductory Lecture on Political Economy*, 1826.
3. Article 'Political Economy' in the *Encyclopædia Metropolitana*, 1836; it appeared separately in a second edition in 1850. Also: *Four Introductory Lectures on Political Economy*, 1852; and *Industrial Efficiency and Social Economy*, ed. Levy, New York, 1928.
4. *Political Economy*, 6th ed., 1872, p. 3.
5. *The Character and Logical Method of Political Economy*, 1857; *Essays in Political Economy, Theoretical and Applied*, 1873; and *Some Leading Principles of Political Economy, Newly Expounded*, 1874.
6. *The Character and Logical Method of Political Economy*, 3rd ed., 1888, p. 34.
7. *Op. cit.*, p. 32.
8. *The Postulates of English Political Economy in Economic Studies*, posthum. ed., ed. Hutton, 1879. We quote from the 2nd ed., 1895. Bagehot contends: 'But the aim of that science is far more humble; it says these and these forces produce these and these effects, and there it stops. It does not profess to give a moral judgement on either; it leaves it for a higher science, and one yet more difficult, to pronounce what ought and what ought not to be.' (P. 27.)
9. *Principles of Political Economy*, 1883.
10. *Scope and Method of Political Economy*, 1891.
11. *Principles of Political Economy and Taxation*, 1817, ed. Gonner, 1903; Ricardo's Preface to the 1st ed., p. 1.
12. 1821, pp. 1 ff.
13. *Lehrbuch der politischen Ökonomie*, Heidelberg, 1826–37.
14. Cp. Senior, *Four Introductory Lectures*, 1852, pp. 57 ff. and *passim*.
15. '. . . The science of political economy may be divided into two great branches—the theoretic and the practical. The first, or theoretic branch, that which explains the nature, production, and distribution of wealth, will be found to rest on a very few general propositions, which are the result of observation, or consciousness, and which almost every man, as soon as he hears them, admits, as familiar to his thoughts, or at

least, as included in his previous knowledge. . . . The practical branch of the science, that of which the office is to ascertain what institutions are most favourable to wealth, is a far more arduous study. Many of its premises, indeed, rest on the same evidence as those of the first branch; for they are the conclusions of that branch:—but it has many which depend on induction from phenomena, numerous, difficult of enumeration, and of which the real sequence often differs widely from the apparent one.' Senior, *An Introductory Lecture on Political Economy*, 1826, pp. 6 f. Cp. Senior, *Political Economy*, 1850 (6th ed., 1872, p. 124).

16. Mill writes: 'Science is a collection of *truths*; art, a body of *rules*, or directions for conduct. The language of science is, This is, or, This is not; This does, or does not, happen. The language of art is, Do this; Avoid that. Science takes cognisance of a *phenomenon*, and endeavours to discover its *law*; art proposes to itself an *end*, and looks out for *means* to effect it.' *Essays on Some Unsettled Questions of Political Economy*, 1844 (quot. from 3rd ed., 1877, p. 124).

17. It is noteworthy that Bentham, the chief representative of the early utilitarians, makes much the same distinction between 'science' and 'art'.

18. 'The problem whether political economy is to be regarded as a positive science, or as a normative science, or as an art, or as a combination of these, is to a certain extent a question merely of nomenclature and classification.' J. N. Keynes, *Scope and Method of Political Economy*, 1891 (quot. from 3rd ed., 1904, p. 35). The question really is 'whether it shall be systematically combined with ethical and practical enquiries, or pursued in the first instance independently. The latter of these alternatives is to be preferred on grounds of scientific expediency. Our work will be done more thoroughly, and both our theoretical and practical conclusions will be the more trustworthy, if we are content to do one thing at a time.' *Op. cit.*, p. 47. Keynes is here merely summarizing the results reached by the classical writers in their discussion of this issue.

19. *Principles of Political Economy, with some of their Applications to Social Philosophy*, 1848; quot. from Ashley's ed., 1920.

20. *Economics of Welfare*, 1920, p. 5.

21. *Principles of Economics*, 1902–12, tr. from the Dutch. The source of this and of the following quotation is Pierson's Introduction.

22. Pierson continues: 'To have forgotten this is the chief error of those whose views we are now opposing. Economics, they say, teaches us *what is*; economic politics, *what ought to be done*. What ought to be done? May the economist ever presume to dictate to the legislator what he ought to do? It is clear that the so-called precepts of economists can never go beyond something like the following: Assuming that the State

is prepared to take for its guiding principle the material welfare of the people, it must adopt such or such a course of action. But no dictum of this kind can be justified without invoking some general economic law, and showing how that law will operate in a given set of circumstances. Everything will depend on the argument, and all else will be of secondary importance. Once it has been clearly proved, for example, that a curtailment of freedom of trade is prejudicial to wealth, it adds little to the strength of the proof to conclude with a warning to the legislator that if he desires to safeguard material interests, he must adopt free-trade principles.' *Op. cit.*, p. 5.

23. His chief contributions in this field are the following: *Die Objektivität sozialwissenschaftlicher und sozialpolitischer Erkenntnis* (1904) and *Wissenschaft als Beruf* (1919). These were both reprinted, together with other papers, in the miscellany published after his death, *Gesammelte Aufsätze zur Wissenschaftslehre*, Tübingen, 1923. Parts of his writings have been translated into English. See 'Science as a Vocation', in *From Max Weber*, Essays in Sociology, translated by H. H Gerth and C. Wright Mills, London, 1947, p. 129; *Methodology of the Social Sciences*, Glencoe, Illinois.

On one, though not unimportant, point Weber seems to hesitate in drawing the full consequences of his critical approach to the value problem; see below, Chapter 8, pp. 202 ff.

24. *Essays*, 1844 (quot. from 3rd ed., 1877, pp. 123, 125 and *passim*). Cf. the works by Senior referred to above.

25. *Theory of Political Economy*, 1877; quot. from 4th ed., 1911, p. 267.

26. Cf. for instance Sidgwick, the last great utilitarian. He speaks of 'principles which appear certain and self-evident because they are substantially tautological. . . . One important lesson which the history of moral philosophy teaches is that, in this region, even powerful intellects are liable to acquiesce in tautologies of this kind, sometimes expanded into circular reasonings, sometimes hidden in the recesses of an obscure notion, often lying so near the surface that when once they have been exposed, it is hard to understand how they could ever have presented themselves as important.' *Methods of Ethics*, 1874; quot. from 6th ed., 1901, p. 375. In this passage Sidgwick is taking exception, in particular, to certain natural law trends in intuitionist moral philosophy.

27. *Den aeldre Nationaløkonomis Opfattelse af de sociale Spørgsmaal*, Copenhagen, 1896. The quotation in the text refers to the economic theory of the harmony of interests.

NOTES TO CHAPTER 2, PAGES 23–55

1. Bentham's *Collected Works*, ed. by Gowring, vol. x, pp. 214–15.
2. *Introduction to the Principles of Morals and Legislation*, p. 1.

3. The only difference is that the concept 'national income' usually disregards the cost side, i.e. the computation of disutilities. Such a procedure is, of course, illegitimate if the concept is to be used as an index of economic welfare. The inconsistency is partly due to the neo-classical tendency to confine its calculations to positive utility items. This tendency in turn can be explained by the original opposition of the neo-classical to the classical value theory, which explained value essentially in terms of costs.

4. This creates certain difficulties. The problem arises whether future generations should be given the same weight as the present generation or perhaps less. If the latter, there would be an ethical equivalent to a positive rate of interest, i.e. a time discount. This view also corresponds more closely to Bentham's method of looking upon 'propinquity' as a 'dimension' of pleasure and pain. The first alternative, on the other hand, seems sounder in principle and has been generally accepted by later utilitarians.

5. Bentham and J. S. Mill extended the concept to embrace in their pleasure calculus the whole organic nature. The handling of this extreme extension of the 'sum total' proves most conclusively not only that utilitarianism rests ultimately on an *a priori* principle, but also that its limits are defined in all directions by such 'self-evident' principles.

Mill wrote: 'This, being, according to the utilitarian opinion, the end of human action, is necessarily also the standard of morality; which may accordingly be defined, the rules and precepts for human conduct, by the observance of which an existence such as has been described [a state as free as possible of pain and as full as possible of pleasure] might be, to the greatest extent possible, secured to all mankind; and not to them only, but, so far as the nature of things admits, to the whole sentient creation.' *Utilitarianism*, 1850, 2nd ed., 1864, p. 17.

Sidgwick shared this view. In his *Methods of Ethics*, 1874, 6th ed., 1901, pp. 414 ff., he considered correctly any limitation as arbitrary and irrational, but he also pointed out that any more general formulation of the criterion increases enormously the difficulties of actually calculating the sum total of happiness. The difficulties of computing the happiness of one's fellow human beings for any given course of action are serious enough, without having to take into account the whole organic nature. Even the most orthodox hedonist would have to admit that the evidence for forming a judgement about any course of action would be very restricted. Sidgwick concluded by asserting that one has to confine oneself to humanity 'for practical reasons'. But in that case it is difficult to see why an argument which has been so mutilated 'for practical reasons' should lead to such unconditionally valid moral imperatives, even if the calculation itself is flawless.

Indeed, Edgeworth, one of the most conscientious thinkers, could not accept this view. 'We may not refuse once more to touch this question, however unwelcome to the modern reader; otiose to our unphilosophical aristocrats, and odious to our democratical philosophers.' He arrived at the same conclusion as Sidgwick, but for a different reason: '. . . it may be admitted that there is a difference with respect to *capacity for happiness* between man and the more lowly evolved animals; and that *therefore* . . . the interests of the lower creation are neglectable in comparison with humanity, the privilege of man is justified.' He adds, with great perspicacity, that a utilitarian who admits the practical conclusion but rejects the premise of the unequal capacity for happiness must appeal to an *a priori* principle of reason. The so-called utilitarian must then be 'gently reminded that this affirmation of first principles not subordinate to the Utilitarian Principle is exactly what the great utilitarian called "ipse-dixitism";' we are up against the vicious circle of the natural law argument. (*Mathematical Psychics. An Essay on the Application of Mathematics to the Moral Sciences*, 1881, p. 130.) Suppose one does not accept Edgeworth's premise as empirically true. It does indeed appear to be a fallacy for it is much more like a 'first principle'. In this case, Edgeworth's criticism could be applied to his own argument.

6. 'Assuming, then, that the average happiness of human beings is a positive quantity, it seems clear that, supposing the average happiness enjoyed remains undiminished, Utilitarianism directs us to make the number enjoying it as great as possible. But if we foresee as possible that an increase in numbers will be accompanied by a decrease in average happiness or *vice versa*, a point arises, which has not only never been formally noticed, but which seems to have been substantially overlooked by many Utilitarians. For if we take Utilitarianism to prescribe as the ultimate end of action, happiness on the whole, and not any individual's happiness unless considered as an element of the whole, it would follow that, if the additional population enjoy on the whole positive happiness, we ought to weigh the amount of happiness gained by the extra number against the amount lost by the remainder. So that, strictly conceived, the point up to which, on Utilitarian principles, population ought to be encouraged to increase, is not that at which average happiness is the greatest possible,—as appears to be often assumed by political economists of the school of Malthus—but that at which the product formed by multiplying the number of persons living into the amount of average happiness reaches its maximum.' *Methods of Ethics*, 1874, 6th ed., 1901, pp. 415 f.

7. *Utilitarianism*, 1850, 2nd ed., 1864, pp. 92 f. The expression in brackets is not really a qualification. If it were one, how could a com-

putation ever be made? See on Mill's treatment of 'higher' and 'lower' pleasures below, pp. 49 f.

8. *Op. cit.*, p. 93; note.

9. 'The first and most fundamental assumption, involved . . . in the very conception of "Greatest Happiness" as an end of action, is the commensurability of Pleasures and Pains. By this I mean that we must assume the pleasures sought and the pains shunned to have determinate quantitative relations to each other; for otherwise they cannot be conceived as possible elements of a total which we are to seek to make as great as possible.' Sidgwick, *Methods*, p. 123.

10. Edgeworth alluded to the idea that the doctrine of harmony makes utilitarian reasoning easier because it removes the necessity for direct interpersonal comparisons and calculations of utility; cf. his 'Theory of Distribution', *Quarterly Journal of Economics*, February 1904, reprinted in *Papers Relating to Political Economy*, 1925, vol. I, p. 58: 'When competition is no longer umpire, the economist must abandon—if he ever maintained—the position of extreme solipsism which Jevons . . . has propounded' (i.e. that pleasures and pains of different individuals, hence subjective utility, value, etc., are incommensurable quantities). Cf. Chapter 4 below.

11. *Op. cit.*, p. 11.

12. *Op. cit.*, p. 12. This argument has a long line of ancestors and goes back to Plato.

13. *Op. cit.*, p. 14.

14. *Op. cit.*, pp. 14 f.

15. *Op. cit.*, p. 15.

16. *Methods*, p. 121. The above interpretation of Mill's view on 'higher' and 'lower' pleasures is not the one commonly accepted. It is generally held, also by Sidgwick, that Mill really abandoned the utilitarian principle of insisting only on quantitative differences of satisfactions. The evidence produced is usually Mill's dictum, which would be paradoxical for a consistent utilitarian, that it 'is better to be a human being dissatisfied than a pig satisfied; better to be Socrates dissatisfied than a fool satisfied. And if the fool, or the pig, are of a different opinion,' Mill goes on to argue, 'it is because they only know their own side of the question. The other party to the comparison knows both sides.' (P. 14.)

It seems to me that the paradox disappears when we look at the curious meaning of 'satisfaction' or 'content' in this context. Just before this passage Mill warns us not to identify *happiness* (defined on utilitarian lines as presence of pleasure and absence of pain) with *content*. Of the latter he says: 'It is indisputable that the being whose capacities of enjoyment are low, has the greatest chance of having them fully satisfied', which does not mean, of course, that he realizes the maximum net sum of happiness. On the contrary, the intelligent human being has a chance of a greater amount of happiness just because of his greater knowledge of possible 'higher' pleasures. There is further internal evidence for this interpretation, which cannot be discussed here.

Edgeworth suggests in his *New and Old Methods of Ethics* that there is another way of distinguishing between higher and lower pleasures without sacrificing their comparability. He thinks of the difference as that of orders of magnitude. This would, of course, make a comparison in any individual case impossible. '. . . Lower pleasures are related to the higher, somewhat as differentials to an integral, incommensurable indeed, yet capable of being equated after infinite summation.' If this were the case, computation would be possible, if not individually, at any rate for society. Cf. *op. cit.*, p. 26.

17. *Op. cit.*, pp. 52 f.
18. *Methods*, p. 412.
19. *Op. cit.*, p. 201.
20. *Op. cit.*, pp. 406 ff.
21. *Op. cit.*, p. 422.
22. 'We cannot, of course, regard as valid reasonings that lead to conflicting conclusions; and I therefore assume as a fundamental postulate of Ethics, that so far as two methods conflict, one or other of them must be modified or rejected.' *Op. cit.*, p. 6. Cf. also the special meaning which Sidgwick gives to the term 'method' in his introductory chapter.
23. *Autobiography of John Stuart Mill*, 6th ed., 1879, p. 66.

NOTES TO CHAPTER 3, PAGES 56–79

1. J. S. Mill, *Principles of Political Economy*, 1848; ed. by Ashley, 1903, vol. III, p. 436.
2. F. v. Wieser, *Der natürliche Wert*, Vienna, 1889, *Natural Value*, translated by C. A. Malloch, London, 1893, p. xxx.
3. G. Cassel, *Nature and Necessity of Interest*, 1903, p. 71.
4. Cf. e.g. F. Knight's review of Cassel's *Theoretische Sozialökonomie* in *Quarterly Journal of Economics*, 1921. Knight, who is certainly the last to defend traditional marginal utility theory, replies to Cassel (p. 146): 'But should it not be kept in mind also that the ultimate object of economic theorizing is a criticism in ethical and human terms of the workings of the economic machine, and that a theory of value as well as price is indispensable?'
5. This is clearly a gap in the theory of price formation which the classical economists must have seen. Senior tried to fill it by an analysis of wages, linking the argument, to some extent, with Adam Smith's.

Senior distinguished three elements in wages: (1) wages proper which are the reward for the average type of unskilled labour; (2) interest on capital invested in labour, such as training, and (3) rent on superior innate ability. Occasionally there is a more psychological explanation: then wages proper are that part of total wages which is proportional to the disutility of effort, and skill is defined as the ability to achieve more without a corresponding increase in disutility, or without extra expenditure on training.

This theory is, of course, only an application of the classical theory of distribution to wages. It is taken over by Mill and Cairnes and is then elaborated by Marshall. We shall not criticize it here. For our purpose it is only important to note one point: If the scale of values applied to different kinds of labour is made dependent upon price formation, the foundation of the classical theory of labour cost is destroyed. For it must assume either complete homogeneity of labour or an independently given scale of values. In other words, this gap in the theory of price formation is inevitable and cannot be filled without abandoning the explanation of price formation in terms of labour costs. A similar criticism applies to Cairnes's theory of 'non-competing groups' which, however, was dictated by somewhat different considerations.

6. Malthus's search for a concept of real value different from Ricardo's—about which more shall be said below—starts from this very point: '. . . whenever two elements enter into the composition of commodities, their value cannot depend exclusively upon one of them, except by accident, or when the other can be considered as a given or common quantity. But it is universally acknowledged, that the great mass of commodities in civilized and improved countries is made up at the least of two elements—labour and profits; consequently, the exchangeable value of commodities into which these two elements enter as the conditions of their supply, will not depend exclusively upon the quantity of labour employed upon them, except in the very peculiar cases when both the returns of the advances and the proportions of fixed and circulating capitals are exactly the same.' T. R. Malthus, *The Measure of Value*, 1823, p. 13.

7. Ricardo did not approve of the attempts of his enthusiastic disciples to give empirical validity to his abstractions. James Mill wrote in his *Elements of Political Economy*, 1821, 2nd ed., 1824, pp. 97 ff.: 'If the wine which is put in the cellar is increased in value one-tenth by being kept a year, one-tenth more of labour may be correctly considered as having been expended upon it.' This type of argument is repeated several times in his book. Bailey remarked in his *A Critical Dissertation on the Nature, Measures and Causes of Value*, 1825, p. 219: 'Now if any one proposition can be affirmed without dispute, it is this, that a fact can

be correctly considered as having taken place only when it really has taken place.' McCulloch, whose faith in the labour cost theory is unshakable, uses even odder analytical devices.

We shall have to say more about Senior's attempt to treat the sacrifice of saving like the disutility of labour. Senior's theory, which is inspired by Malthus's criticism, has been anticipated by Ricardo in his *Principles* and even more in his correspondence. But it cannot be incorporated in his theory of exchange value because it is incompatible with the labour cost hypothesis.

8. Other commodities occasionally called monopoly goods are excluded from the cost-price theory proper. In analogy to his theory of different qualities of labour, Ricardo points to their scarcity and to the wants and purchasing power of those who demand them, i.e. to the law of supply and demand. He does not explain how their exchange values are determined.

9. There is a rudimentary theory of abstinence and of the relation of saving to the interest rate. It precedes, of course, logically, the wages fund theory whose beginnings can also be found in Ricardo. Although the number of workers is related to the stock of capital in the wages fund theory, the question how the amount of capital is determined remains open.

10. Their number is determined according to the Malthusian theory of the connection between the reproduction rate and the wage rate on the one hand, and the cost of subsistence on the other. This theory too precedes logically the wages fund theory and for the same reasons. Cf. footnote above.

11. Yet, Malthus had actually moved in this direction and he has a strong claim to being a forerunner of modern economic theory. But he never went beyond tentative beginnings which were lost again as his discussion went further. He had a keen sense for the weaknesses of Ricardo's theory, but he never succeeded in refuting it convincingly because he, perhaps even more than Ricardo, was befogged by the metaphysical idea of an intrinsic and absolute value. The only difference between him and Ricardo in this respect is that he applied the notion differently. This was the topic of their disputes. In his criticism too it prevented Malthus from following rigorously the implications of his own reasoning.

Moreover, Malthus lacked Ricardo's logical subtlety, although he had as good or perhaps even a better scientific intuition. But he was prone to non sequiturs and contradictions of which Ricardo would never have been guilty. They irritated Ricardo and other critics. Unfortunately this is also true of those parts of his work in which his intuition yielded the most brilliant ideas. Malthus has therefore never been properly appreciated as a theorist, and as more than a population expert, statistician, and historian. It would be a rewarding task to examine his theory of price formation with special attention to his ingenious intuition of the essential issues. Cf. *inf.*

12. 'It is a direct inference from the explanation of value in the preceding chapters, as denoting a relation between two commodities, a relation incapable of existing when there is only one commodity, that it cannot exist between a commodity at one period and the same commodity at another period. We cannot ascertain the relation of cloth at one time to cloth at another, as we can ascertain the relation of cloth to corn in the present day. All that we can do is to compare the relation in which cloth stood at each period to some other commodity.' *A Critical Dissertation on the Nature, Measures and Causes of Value*, 1825, pp. 71 ff.

13. 'When Mr. Ricardo tells us, that a commodity always produced by the same labour is of invariable value, he implicitly maintains all I have been attempting to disprove. By the epithet invariable he clearly means, that its value at one time will be precisely the same as its value at another, not in relation to other commodities, for he supposes all other commodities to vary, but in relation to itself. He distinctly states, that if equal quantities of gold could always be obtained by equal quantities of labour, the value of gold "would be invariable, and it would be eminently well calculated to measure the varying value of *all other things*", whence it follows, that this invariableness must be intended to be affirmed of the value of gold compared with itself, and not of any relation between gold and some other commodity.' *Op. cit.*, pp. 74 f. Bailey exposes brilliantly the metaphysics of classical value theory. (One must remember that the value of labour is also a variable in Ricardo's theory.)

14. Thomas de Quincey, *Dialogues of Three Templars on Political Economy*, 1824, published in vol. *X of Thomas de Quincey's Works*, New York, 1877. Cf. also his *The Logic of Political Economy*, 1844, pp. 45 ff.

15. Ricardo quotes Adam Smith: 'Labour was the first price—the original purchase-money that was paid for all things.' And: 'in that early and rude state of society, which precedes both the accumulation of stock and the appropriation of land, the proportion between the quantities of labour necessary for acquiring different objects seems to be the only circumstance which can afford any rule for exchanging them for one another'. *Principles of Political Economy and Taxation*, 1817, ed. by Gonner, London, 1929, p. 7.

16. Ricardo tries to prove that labour cannot command the full equivalent of the real value which it bestows upon commodities. Profit intervenes. The capitalist draws his profits by paying out wages whose real value is less than the real value which the workers bestow upon the

commodity. The real value of labour itself, which, as usual, determines its exchange ratio with other commodities, consist of the costs, measured in terms of labour, incurred in reproducing and rearing workers. These costs vary partly with their habits—although Ricardo usually assumes unchanged habits—partly with technology, stock of capital, etc.

Thus it is not the real value of labour which is invested in commodities but only labour itself. The two would only coincide in the absence of profit. The workers would receive in wages the full real value of their labour. In equilibrium the costs of reproducing workers, i.e., the real value of labour, would be equal to the value created by labour.

17. *Principles of Political Economy*, 1820, 1st ed., p. 62 and other places.

18. *Op. cit.*, p. 60, 1st ed.

19. *A Critical Dissertation*, etc., p. 254.

20. *An Essay Concerning the True Original, Extent and End, of Civil Government*, 1690. Works in 9 volumes, London, 1824, vol. IV.

21. In accordance with the attitude to natural law of the maturer utilitarians, Sidgwick criticized this argument: 'But this must be admitted to be a rather desperate device of ethico-political construction: on account of the fatal facility with which it may be used to justify almost any arbitrariness in positive law.' *Methods*, p. 280, note.

22. *Op. cit.*, pp. 353, 4 f.

23. Cf. below, Chapter 5.

24. *Wealth of Nations*, 1776, ed. by Cannan, 1903, vol i, p. 32.

25. 'Labour is either bodily or mental . . . and it is necessary to include in the idea, not solely the exertion itself, but all feelings of a disagreeable kind, all bodily inconvenience or mental annoyance, connected with the employment of one's thoughts, or muscles, or both, in a particular occupation.' Mill, *Principles*, ed. Ashley, 1909, p. 22.

26. 'Equal quantities of labour at all times and places, may be said to be of equal value to the labourer. . . . Labour alone, therefore, never varying in its own value, is alone the ultimate and real standard by which the value of all commodities can at all times and places be estimated and compared. It is their real price; money is their nominal price only.' A. Smith, *Op. cit.*, p. 35. Criticizing Adam Smith, Ingram denies that this proposition has any meaning: 'This sentence, which on close examination will be found to have no definite intelligible sense, affords a good example of the way in which metaphysical modes of thought obscure economic ideas. What is a "quantity of labour", the kind of labour being undetermined? And what is meant by the phrase "of equal value"?' *A History of Political Economy*, 1888, ed. by Ely, 1915, p. 92, footnote.

27. McCulloch also says that the 'performance of labour must un-

avoidably occasion the *same sacrifice*' at all stages of economic development. *Principles of Political Economy*, Edinburgh, 1825, p. 116 f.

28. For example: '. . . cost means sacrifice, and cannot, without risk of hopelessly confusing ideas, be identified with anything that is not sacrifice. It represents what man parts with in the barter between him and nature, which must be kept eternally distinct from the return made by nature on that payment.' J. E. Cairnes, *Some Leading Principles of Political Economy*, London, 1874, p. 60.

29. 'The sacrifices to be taken account of, and which govern exchange value, are, not those undergone by A, B, or C, but the average sacrifices undergone by the class of labourers . . . to which the producers of the commodity belong.' J. E. Cairnes, *Some Leading Principles of Political Economy*, 1874, p. 95. Cairnes is here also, and mainly, concerned with the sacrifice of saving by capitalists. See below.

30. 'But any other cause limiting supply is just as efficient a cause of value in an article as the necessity of labour to its production. And, in fact, if all the commodities used by man were supplied by nature without any intervention whatever of human labour, but were supplied in precisely the same quantities as they now are, there is no reason to suppose either that they would cease to be valuable, or would exchange in any other than the present proportions.' *Political Economy*, 1836, 6th ed., 1872, p. 24.

31. Marshall, *Principles of Economics*, 1890, 8th ed., 1922, V, III, 2. Cf. Myrdal, *Prisbildningsproblemet och föränderligheten*, Uppsala and Stockholm, 1927, pp. 32 ff.

32. *Letters of David Ricardo to Thomas Robert Malthus, 1810–1823*, ed. by Bonar, Oxford, 1887, p. 237.

33. *Letters of David Ricardo to John Ramsay McCulloch, 1816–1823*, ed. by J. R. Hollander, Publications of the American Economic Association, vol. X, New York, 1895, p. 72. My italics.

NOTES TO CHAPTER 4, PAGES 80–103

1. There is a nice anecdote, told by Hayward in his obituary of Sidgwick in the *International Journal of Ethics*, vol. XI, 1901, p. 187. 'Sidgwick had just completed his *Methods of Ethics*. There lay the manuscript, accepted by Messrs. Macmillan. The author looking upon it said to Mr. Browning: "I have long wished and intended to write a book on Ethics. Now it is written. I have adhered to the plan I laid out for myself; its first word was to be 'Ethics', its last word 'Failure'."

In later editions these words lost their characteristic positions, but they seem to strike the keynote of the book.

2. Cournot hardly attempts to say anything about the 'profounder' problems of value. When he says that it is the task of political economy

to observe and to describe but not to criticize nature's immutable laws, this does not mean very much. It is, after all, the assumption of value theory that economic values are proper objectives of scientific inquiry and that objective judgements about economic value are possible.

3. *Theory of Political Economy*, 1871, 4th ed., 1911, pp. xxix ff.

4. *Wealth of Nations*, 1776, ed. by Cannan, 1904, p. 30.

5. 'The exchange-value of a thing may fall short, to any amount, of its value in use; but that it can ever exceed the value in use implies a contradiction; it supposes that persons will give, to possess a thing, more than the utmost value which they themselves put upon it, as a means of gratifying their inclinations.' *Principles of Political Economy*, 1848, ed. by Ashley, 1920, III, I, 2.

6. Jevons is most explicit: 'The reader will find, again, that there is never, in any single instance, an attempt made to compare the amount of feeling in one mind with that in another. I see no means by which such comparison can be accomplished. . . . Every mind is thus inscrutable to every other mind, and no common denominator of feeling seems to be possible. But even if we could compare the feelings of different minds, we should not need to do so; for one mind only affects another indirectly. Every event in the outward world is represented in the mind by a corresponding motive, and it is by the balance of these that the will is swayed. . . . Thus motives in the mind of A may give rise to phenomena which may be represented by motives in the mind of B; but between A and B there is a gulf. Hence the weighing of motives must always be confined to the bosom of the individual.' *Theory of Political Economy*, 1871, 4th ed., 1924, p. 14.

7. Wicksteed says: 'We may now return to our curves with a clear conscience, knowing that for any object of desire at any moment there actually exists a curve could we but get it.' *The Alphabet of Economic Science*, 1888, p. 55.

'It cannot be theoretically impossible to conceive of such a thing as an accurate measurement of satisfaction, even though its practical measurement should always remain as vague as that of heat was when the thermometer was not yet invented.' *Op. cit.*, p. 15.

8. *Theory of Political Economy*, 1871, 4th ed., 1911, p. 18.

9. *Op. cit.*, p. 11, and other passages.

10. 'I have granted that we can hardly form the conception of a unit of pleasure or pain, so that the numerical expression of quantities of feeling seems to be out of the question. But we only employ units of measurement in other things to facilitate the comparison of quantities; and if we can compare the quantities directly, we do not need the units. Now the mind of an individual is the balance which makes its own comparisons, and is the final judge of quantities of feeling. . . . Pleasures,

in short, are, for the time being, as the mind estimates them; so that we cannot make a choice, or manifest the will in any way, without indicating thereby an excess of pleasure in some direction.' *Op. cit.*, p. 12.

11. 'The theory turns upon those critical points where pleasures are nearly, if not quite, equal. I never attempt to estimate the whole pleasure gained by purchasing a commodity; the theory merely expresses that, when a man has purchased enough, he would derive equal pleasure from the possession of a small quantity more as he would from the money price of it. Similarly, the whole amount of pleasure that a man gains by a day's labour hardly enters into the question; it is when a man is doubtful whether to increase his hours of labour or not, that we discover an equality between the pain of that extension and the pleasure of the increase of possessions derived from it.' *Op. cit.*, pp. 13 f.

12. Wicksell, *Lectures on Political Economy*, ed. by L. Robbins, 1934, vol. I, p. 43.

13. *Methods*, p. 124 and *passim*.

14. It is interesting, in this connection, that the earliest critics saw in the theory of marginal utility what we have called a behaviourist theory of choice (*Wahlhandlungstheorie*) and used exactly the same arguments against it which will be used below against this latter version. Thus Cairnes wrote about Jevons's theory: 'What does it really amount to? In my apprehension to this, and no more—that value depends upon utility, and that utility is whatever affects value. In other words, the name "utility" is given to the aggregate of unknown conditions which determine the phenomenon, and then the phenomenon is stated to depend upon what this name stands for.' Jevons's theory was believed to say no more than this: 'that value was determined by the conditions which determine it—an announcement, the importance of which, even though presented under the form of abstruse mathematical symbols, I must own myself unable to discern'. *Some Leading Principles of Political Economy*, 1874, p. 15.

Ingram took the same view in *A History of Political Economy*, 1888, ed. by Ely, 1915, p. 228 and *passim*. Cairnes, Ingram, and other early critics of marginal utility theory had, however, directed their criticism also against the mathematical method generally and the discussion went soon into other channels. The marginalists met the criticism by claiming to be proponents of logical and mathematical method and their tautological psychology thus escaped its well-deserved criticism.

15. *Positive Theorie des Kapitales*, Innsbruck, 1888, 4th ed., 1921, vol. I, pp. 232 f. These reflections were added to the third edition and are not in William Smart's English translation of the earlier edition.

16. Cf. e.g. 4th ed., vol. II, Exkurs X, *Betreffend die "Messbarkeit" von Gefühlsgrössen.*

17. Cf. *Cours d'Économie Politique*, Lausanne, 1896–7, and *Manuel d'Économie Politique*, Paris, 1909.

18. *Theory of Political Economy*, 1871, 4th ed., 1911, pp. 88 f.

19. *Principles of Economics*, 1890, 8th ed., 1922, Appendix T, 3, and *passim.*

20. *Cours d'Économie Politique*, Lausanne, 1896–7, pp. 46 ff.

21. 'A Statistical Method for Measuring "Marginal Utility" and Testing the Justice of a Progressive Income Tax' in *Economic Essays Contributed in Honor of John Bates Clark*, New York, 1927, p. 157, note. The inverted commas in the title of the essay indicate that Fisher, with the now traditional horror of anything associated with hedonism, would prefer to substitute for 'utility' or 'marginal utility' such terms as 'want or 'want for one more'.

22. *Op. cit.*, pp. 179 ff.

23. Fisher continues: 'Philosophic doubt is right and proper, but the problems of life cannot, and do not, wait. . . . So economists cannot afford to be too academic and shirk the great practical problems pressing upon them merely because these happen to touch on unsolved, perhaps insoluble, philosophical problems. . . . By common sense we cut our gordian knots.' This is one way of getting away from epistemology. For the economist who is not courageous enough to make this jump, he has an *argumentum ad hominem* which would have particular force in times of crisis: 'Even the philosophic doubter, if himself taxed unfairly, would be apt to know it! He would scarcely be satisfied if told that any comparison between his tax burden and others is meaningless because his mental phenomena and others' are incommensurable.' *Op. cit.*, pp. 180 f.

NOTES TO CHAPTER 5, PAGES 104–139

1. In the chapter 'On Machinery' which he added to the third edition of his *Principles*, Ricardo stressed—probably under socialist influence—especially R. Owen's—the conflict between workers and capitalists more than his assumptions required. Cf. Wicksell's criticism in his *Lectures*, I, 1.

Ricardo's argument concludes: 'All I wish to prove, is, that the discovery and use of machinery may be attended with a diminution of gross produce; and whenever that is the case, it will be injurious to the labouring class, as some of their number will be thrown out of employment, and population will become redundant, compared with the funds which are to employ it.' *Principles of Political Economy and Taxation*, 1817, ed. by Gonner, 1911, pp. 381 f. This does not merely refer to transition effects. Senior tried to criticize Ricardo but he did not quite succeed. Mill followed Ricardo but his arguments are not very clear. It is an important point because Ricardo's proposition negates the basis of liberalism, viz., that total production is maximized if capitalists are left free to invest according to their own interests.

2. This argument was refined later. See particularly Edgeworth's *Mathematical Psychics*, 1881, pp. 124 f., where he stresses that utilitarianism is concerned with happiness, not with the means to happiness, and the criterion is social maximization of happiness. Bentham is right if the capacity to enjoy happiness is equal for all men, i.e. if the utility of a pound is the same for everyone when income is distributed equally. But if the capacity to enjoy is unequal, both happiness and means to happiness must be distributed unequally, and unequally in two different ways. Edgeworth argues against certain authors who claim that if capacities to enjoy are unequal, means to happiness should not, but happiness itself should still be equally distributed. Cf. Sidgwick's *Methods*, p. 416 and *passim*. Sidgwick is not altogether consistent here. He admits that the principle of the distribution of happiness cannot be derived from the utilitarian formula. The formula must be replaced by an *a priori* principle of 'justice'. But on reflection this must turn out disastrous for the utilitarian theory of a social sum of hedonistic quantities. *Either* these are commensurable quantities, then a rational principle of distribution is implied in the idea of a summation; any other solution would not yield maximum total utility. *Or* they are incommensurable, then no utilitarian calculus is conceivable. Nevertheless, J. S. Mill and others argue similarly. It is a delicate point and Edgeworth's attempt at a stricter formulation is understandable.

3. Article 'Government', in *Encyclopaedia Britannica*.

4. *Inquiry into the Principles of the Distribution of Wealth Most Conducive to Human Happiness*, etc., 1824.

5. *Labour Defended against the Claims of Capital*, etc., 1825.

6. Perhaps the most lucid account of classical liberalism based on the division of labour is James Mill's in his admirable *Elements of Political Economy*, 1821. Here is one of many passages, referring particularly to international trade, which illustrates the point: 'Now it is certain, as has been already abundantly proved, that no commodity which can be made at home will ever be imported from a foreign country, unless it can be obtained by importation with a smaller quantity of labour, that is, cost, than it could be produced at home. That it is desirable to have commodities produced with as small a cost of labour as possible, seems to be not only certain, but admitted. This is the object of all the improvements that are aimed at in production, by the division and distribution of labour, by refined methods of culture

R

applied to the land, by the invention of more potent and skilful machines. It seems, indeed, to be a self-evident proposition, that whatever the quantity which a nation possesses of the means of production, the more productive they can possibly be rendered, so much the better: for this is neither more nor less than saying, that to have all the objects we desire, and to have them with little trouble is good for mankind. Not only is it certain, that in a state of freedom no commodity which can be made at home will ever be imported, unless it can be imported with a less quantity or cost of labour than it could be produced with at home; but whatever is the country from which it can be obtained with the smallest cost of labour, to that country recourse will be had for obtaining it, and whatever the commodity by the exportation of which it can be obtained with the smallest quantity of home labour, that is the commodity which will be exported in exchange. This results so obviously from the laws of trade, as not to require explanation. It is no more than saying, that the merchants if left to themselves, will always buy in the cheapest market, and sell in the dearest. It seems, therefore, to be fully established, that the business of production and exchange, if left to choose its own channels, is sure to choose those which are most advantageous to the community. It is sure to choose those channels, in which the commodities which the community [!] desires to obtain, are obtained with the smallest [social!] cost.' *Op. cit.*, pp. 158 f.

Or to quote Ricardo: 'Under a system of perfectly free commerce, each country naturally devotes its capital and labour to such employments as are most beneficial to each. This pursuit of individual advantage is admirably connected with the universal good of the whole. By stimulating industry, by rewarding ingenuity, and by using most efficaciously the peculiar powers bestowed by nature, it distributes labour most effectively and most economically: while, by increasing the general mass of productions, it diffuses general benefit, and binds together by one common tie of interest and intercourse, the universal society of nations throughout the civilized world. It is this principle which determines that wine shall be made in France and Portugal, that corn shall be grown in America and Poland, and that hardware and other goods shall be manufactured in England.' *Principles*, etc., p. 114. Ricardo actually speaks here only of foreign trade which is not relevant in this connection. But he, like Mill, believes that the same principles apply to domestic trade and production and says so explicitly just before this passage. Cf. Ricardo's interesting criticism of Say, *op. cit.*, pp. 303 f.

7. 'It is used to escape the awkwardness, if it be not something more, of estimating exertions of a country in units of labour or of capital—a mode of procedure which leaves it open to the critic to speak of the

omitted element as if it were an essential condition.' *Theory of International Trade*, Dublin, 1887, 2nd ed., 1897, p. 24.

8. *Defence of Usury*, 1787, 3rd ed., 1818.

9. *Op. cit.*, p. 82; in the chapter on wages he says, for instance: 'These then are the laws by which wages are regulated, and by which the happiness of far the greatest part of every community is governed. Like all other contracts, wages should be left to the fair and free competition of the market, and should never be controlled by the interference of the legislature.'

10. Yet, even they had been anticipated by the Physiocrats. Particularly Turgot's arguments resemble Ricardo's. Some obscure hints can also be found in Adam Smith.

11. 'Nevertheless so full was his mind of the terror of the French revolution, and so great were the evils which he attributed to the smallest attack on security that, daring analyst as he was, he felt himself and he fostered in his disciples an almost superstitious reverence for the existing institutions of private property.' *Principles of Economics*, 1890, 8th ed., 1922, app. B 4 note.

12. Cf. e.g. *An Inquiry into the Nature and Progress of Rent and the Principles by which it is regulated*, 1815, pp. 47, 48 and *passim*, in his writings on rent and tariffs.

13. See e.g. L. v. Mises, *Liberalismus*, Jena, 1927.

14. *Elements of Political Economy*, 1821, 3rd ed., 1826, p. 21.

15. *Principles of Political Economy*, 1848, ed. by Ashley, 1920, V, XI, 12.

16. *Op. cit.*, IV, VII, 7.

17. 'The laws and conditions of the *Production* of wealth partake of the character of physical truths. There is nothing optional or arbitrary in them. Whatever mankind produce, must be produced in the modes, and under the conditions, imposed by the constitution on external things, and by the inherent properties of their own bodily and mental structure. . . . It is not so with the *Distribution of wealth*. That is a matter of human institution solely. The things once there, mankind, individually or collectively, can do with them as they like. . . . The distribution of wealth, therefore, depends on the laws and customs of society. The rules by which it is determined are what the opinions and feelings of the ruling portion of the community make them, and are very different in different ages and countries; and might be still more different, if mankind so chose.' *Op. cit.*, II, I, 1, my italics.

18. What has come to be known as the 'New' Welfare Economics' has continued in this tradition. See appendix by the translator (added 1950).

19. The philosophy of pragmatism is, in this connection, a modern,

perhaps more relativistic, version of utilitarianism. Similarly, psychological behaviourism, if it purports to be more than a method, if it presents itself as a philosophy, amounts to no more than a mechanistic version of the old psychology of associations.

20. *Theory of Political Economy*, 1871, 4th ed., 1911, p. 27.

21. *Op. cit.*, p. 146.

22. In his discussion of non-arithmetic mathematics and its significance for the pleasure calculus and marginal utility theory, he says: 'The criterion of a *maximum* turns, not upon the *amount*, but upon the *sign* of a certain quantity.' *Mathematical Psychics*, 1881, p. 6 and *passim*.

23. *Defence of Usury*, 1787, 3rd ed., 1818, pp. 3, 4.

24. See e.g. *Essays in Political Economy*, 1873, p. 251.

NOTES TO CHAPTER 6, PAGES 140–155

1. There are, of course, conflicts in a family household too, but they are presumed to be resolved by an arbiter. The head of the family is making the valuations. His position is sanctioned by civil law; it is, for example, *his* income of which he disposes for his own and his dependants' welfare. At any rate this is the assumption of the economists who employ this analogy. When the autocratic view of society is rejected, the analogy between family and society does no longer hold.

2. J. B. Clark, *The Possibility of a Scientific Law of Wages*, Publications of the American Economic Association, vol. IV, 1889, p. 62.

3. 'The Philosophy of Value', in *The New Englander*, New Haven, 1881, *The Philosophy of Wealth*, Boston, 1886, and 'The Unit of Wealth' in *Festschrift für Karl Knies*, 1896.

4. Anybody interested in an aftermath of Clark's metaphysical optimism should read the unfortunate book by the eminent, to-day perhaps underestimated, Harvard economist Carver, *The Religion Worth Having*. He develops Clark's theory to its most philistine conclusions. The social value of an individual is his production minus his consumption. This plausible but somewhat obscure moral theory is then elaborated in technical terms and applied to various fields, e.g. religious activity. The book is very amusing and anybody unfamiliar with utilitarian tendencies in economics might mistake it for a brilliantly written satire. But the author, at any rate, is quite unconscious of its humour.

5. 'Most theorists, particularly those of the classical school, have tacitly made similar abstractions. In particular, that point of view from which price becomes a social judgement of value, really amounts to a disregard of all the individual differences which emerge in purchasing

power, and which separate price from natural value. A great many theorists have thus written the value theory of Communism without being aware of it, and in doing so have omitted to give the value theory of the present state.' *Der natürliche Wert*, Vienna, 1889, translated by Christian A. Malloch, *Natural Value*, London, 1893, ed. by William Smart, p. 61, note.

6. It soon becomes obvious that v. Wieser is not very serious with the claim to neutrality. In the next paragraph he says: 'So little is natural value a weapon against socialism, that socialists could scarcely make use of a better witness in favour of it. Exchange value can have no severer criticism than that which exposes its divergencies from the natural measurement, although, indeed, this forms no particular proof for the essence of socialism.' *Op. cit.*, p. 63.

NOTES TO CHAPTER 7, PAGES 156–190

1. It is a great loss to the subject that Edwin B. Seligman never accomplished this task in the comprehensive manner which it deserved. For decades he had devoted a large part of his time to the study of the history of public finance. His interest in the subject had been one of the guiding forces in the collection of his great library which now belongs to Columbia University. As his young friend during his last years, I saw that there was also an element of personal tragedy for Seligman in his failure to carry out his intention. But towards the end of his life he somehow always found something else to which he could devote his time. These were very often pursuits for which he was less superbly equipped but which he took up, I suspect, in order to escape the challenge to write the great history of public finance for which he had prepared himself in the course of his whole life. (Footnote added 1950.)

2. *Grundzüge der Finanzwissenschaft*, Jena, 1920, pp. 67 ff.

3. For an exhaustive discussion see Seligman's *Progressive Taxation in Theory and Practice*, Baltimore, 1894, enlarged edition, Princeton, 1908.

4. *Wealth of Nations*, 1776, ed. by Cannan, 1904, vol. II, p. 310.

5. *Principles of Political Economy*, 1848, ed. Ashley, 1920, V, II, 2.

6. *Op. cit.*, V, II, 2.

7. Cf. e.g. *op. cit.*, V, II, 4.

8. 'Equality of taxation, therefore, as a maxim of politics, means equality of sacrifice. It means apportioning the contribution of each person towards the expenses of government, so that he shall feel neither more nor less inconvenience from his share of the payment than every other person experiences from his. This standard, like other standards of perfection, cannot be completely realized, but the first object in

every practical discussion should be to know what perfection is.' *Op. cit.*, V, II, 2.

9. *Op. cit.*, V, II, 3.

10. 'Whether the person with £10,000 a year cares less for £1,000 than the person with only £1,000 a year cares for £100, and if so, how much less, does not appear to me capable of being decided with the degree of certainty on which a legislator or a financier ought to act.' *Op. cit.*, V, II, 3.

11. James Mill, for example, says: 'A tax operating fairly, ought to leave the relative condition of the different classes of contributors the same after the tax as before it.' *Elements of Political Economy*, 1821, 2nd ed., 1824, p. 268.

12. *Natural Value*, pp. 236 ff.

13. *The Principles of Political Economy*, 1883, p. 262.

14. Lindahl, *Die Gerechtigkeit der Besteuerung*, Lund, 1919, pp. 6 ff.

15. *Principles of Political Economy*, 1848, ed. Ashley, 1920, V, II, 2.

16. Edgeworth, 'The Pure Theory of Taxation', *Economic Journal*, vol. VII, 1897; 'The Incidence of Urban Rates', *Economic Journal*, vol. X, 1900; and 'The Subjective Element in the First Principles of Taxation', *Quarterly Journal of Economics*, vol. XXIV, 1910. All these articles in *Papers Relating to Political Economy*, 1925, vol. II.

Carver, 'The Ethical Basis of Distribution and its Application to Taxation', *Annals of the American Academy of Political and Social Science*, vol. VI, 1895; 'The Minimum Sacrifice Theory of Taxation', *Political Science Quarterly*, vol. XIX, 1904; *Social Justice*, Cambridge, 1915.

17. *The Principles of Political Economy*, 1883, p. 262 and *passim*.

18. Wicksell, *Finanztheoretische Untersuchungen*, vol. II, Jena, 1897, and Lindahl, *Die Gerechtigkeit der Besteuerung*, Lund, 1919.

I am greatly indebted to my friend Erik Lindahl for many profitable discussions on this subject. Our differences have in no way diminished the value of these discussions. If my criticism is sound and decisive, much of the credit is due to him.

19. *Op. cit.*, p. 2.

20. *Op. cit.*, p. 4.

21. *Op. cit.*, p. 9; the following quotations, *ibid.*, ff.

22. *Finanztheoretische Untersuchungen*, Jena, 1897, quoted by Lindahl, *op. cit.*, p. 100.

23. *Op. cit.*, pp. 10–11.

24. *Op. cit.*, p. 101.

25. *Op. cit.*, p. 12.

26. Cf. Lindahl's criticism of Wicksell, *op. cit.*, p. 138.

27. *Op. cit.*, p. 92, note. The particular formulation of liberal doctrine to which Lindahl's theory of public finance is linked is untenable not

only for the reasons discussed at the end of Chapter 5. Those who say that, if the present distribution is accepted, maximization defines the optimum ignore the fact that distribution itself is altered by the various alternatives. In other words, the problems cannot be separated in this manner by just assuming correct distribution and deriving an optimum in the maximization of production, even if such a maximum were possible. The political value judgement must, as we have seen in Chapter 5, refer to various *combinations* of production and distribution. We shall see that there is an analogous fallacy in fiscal theory.

The chances of establishing a maximum in production are not enhanced by Lindahl's insistence on measuring everything in money terms. The value of money must then be determined and we are faced with the same index number problem which we discussed in Chapter 5.

28. There are, of course, also other problems such as the inquiry into the legal institutional set-up and into the historical, sociological, and psychological forces which have brought it into being and are likely to determine fiscal policy in the future. These problems are outside the scope of this book. The more effectively these studies can be immunized from the infection of speculation about fiscal principles, the more fertile will they be. It is true that human attitudes tend to be rationalized in those fiscal principles (the whole theory is an ambitious attempt of such a rationalization), but this does not mean that they constitute a profitable starting-point for an inquiry. It would be like saying that religions or primitive magic can only be studied by accepting their beliefs as a method of inquiry. This would not take us very far. A study of political attitudes, here as anywhere else in politics, must start with the knowledge of their non-rationality. This is the great advance in the type of sociological method which is beginning to gain ground.

29. *Zur Lehre von der Steuerinzidenz*, 1895, p. 6. Reprinted in *Finanztheoretische Untersuchungen*, Jena, 1896, p. 1.

30. Cf. Myrdal, *Prisbildningsproblemet och föränderlighten*, Uppsala and Stockholm, 1927, p. 45.

NOTES TO CHAPTER 8, PAGES 191–207

1. Cf., for example, Seligman, *Principles of Political Economy*, New York, 1904, 6th ed., 1920, p. 4. Also Bastable, *The Theory of International Trade*, Dublin, 1887, and many other writers.

2. Lawyers know also that no one is more legalistic than the non-lawyer. An example is provided by the essentially non-formalistic idea of bona fide. Its extensive use in commercial life is of fairly recent origin. It is still primarily a lawyer's doctrine, although one might expect that it would appeal particularly to the common man's dislike

of formalism and to his sense of equity. But this is due to a mistaken notion about the common man. He, more than the expert, is prone to think in legalistic forms and stereotyped conventions.

3. Max Weber, *Verhandlungen des Vereins für Sozialpolitik in Wien*, 1909, p. 582, reprinted in *Gesammelte Aufsätze zur Soziologie und Sozialpolitik*, Tübingen, 1927, p. 416.

NOTES FOR APPENDIX, PAGES 208–217

1. Of course, the classical economists and the utilitarians were not crude harmony theorists. Professor Viner and Professor Robbins have stressed this point again recently. Bentham 'did prescribe limits for the field of governmental intervention in economic matters, but these limits were not . . . very narrow ones, and in any case were not so narrow as to give scope to the doctrine of the natural harmony of interests, *in the sense of a harmony preordained or inherent in the nature of man living in a society unregulated by government*'. J. Viner, 'Bentham and J. S. Mill', *American Economic Review*, March 1949, p. 369 (my italics). Yet Bentham did believe in harmony in a different sense. According to him, private and sectional interests are not the 'real' interests, but result from imperfect insight. If everybody had full knowledge of his true interests no conflict could arise. Bentham must make this assumption in order to define objectively the 'public interest', which the reformer or legislator has to promote. Otherwise it would not be desirable to maximize the sum of happiness. Bentham appears to have been inconsistent here. He held both that the maximization of individual happiness spells conflict, and that it is desirable for each, and particularly the task of the legislators, to maximize the social sum of happiness.

2. Robbins, *Essay*, p. 151, footnote, where he quotes Cantillon and Ricardo to the effects that economists, as scientists, cannot give advice on what people ought to do.

3. Robbins, *Essay*, p. 149 and chapter VI. To say that welfare economics is a 'normative' study is in some contexts equivalent to saying that recommendations involve disagreement and conflict, i.e. to deny harmony. E.g. *op. cit.*, pp. 139–40.

4. I. M. D. Little, *A Critique of Welfare Economics*, chapter IV, p. 57. In his view that interpersonal comparisons of happiness are judgements of facts he has found important support from Professor D. H. Robertson who, however, prefers to compare economic welfare rather than happiness. Cf. 'A Revolutionist's Handbook', *The Quarterly Journal of Economics*, February 1950, p. 6, and 'Utility and All That', *Manchester School*, May 1951.

5. N. Kaldor, 'Welfare Propositions and Interpersonal Comparison of Utility', *Economic Journal*, September 1938, pp. 549–52. J. R. Hicks,

'The Foundations of Welfare Economics', *Economic Journal*, December 1939, pp. 696–712. T. Scitovsky, 'A Note on Welfare Propositions in Economics', *Review of Economic Studies*, vol. IX, 1941.

6. See, for example, J. R. Hicks, article 'Demand' in *Chambers's Encyclopaedia*: 'It is possible to construct a theory of welfare economics which assumes no more than the consistency of preference scales.'

7. P. A. Samuelson, 'Welfare Economics and International Trade', *American Economic Review*, 1938, pp. 261–6; *The Foundations of Economic Analysis*, 1947, pp. 249–52; M. W. Reder, *Studies in the Theory of Welfare Economics*, 1947, pp. 94–100; W. J. Baumol, 'Community Indifference', *Review of Economic Studies*, 1946–7, vol. XIV (1), pp. 44–9; I. M. D. Little, *A Critique of Welfare Economics*, 1950, chapter VI.

8. F. Y. Edgeworth, *Papers Relating to Political Economy*, vol. II, pp. 102–3.

9. J. R. Hicks, 'The Rehabilitation of Consumer's Surplus', *Review of Economic Studies*, (1940–1), vol. VIII, p. 111.

10. 'I would conclude, therefore, that while the new welfare economics has, in Kaldor's argument, provided the economist with a guide to policy in some communities, this guide has no universal validity. . . .' T. Scitovsky, 'The State of Welfare Economics', *American Economic Review*, June 1951.

11. If this argument is valid it would support the claim to superiority of the compensation principle over the social welfare function. In order to arrive at a social welfare function, situations have to be ranked in an order of preference. There is no scope for judging certain aspects only.

12. In particular the 'insatiability of wants', almost axiomatic in welfare economics, is the product of Western competitive economic activity. It is alien to many other communities and even to some groups inside competitive societies.

13. There is the quite separate possibility that one may agree that unfulfilled desire is an evil and yet believe that the solution is, not to satisfy, but to kill it.

14. F. Zweig, *Women's Life and Labour*, 1952.

15. One aspect of this difficulty, which is usually ignored by economic theory, has been stressed repeatedly by Professor Frank H. Knight. Human association and the formulation of programmes serve only to a limited extent the purpose of achieving any given ends. To a large extent they are a matter of formulating and improving the 'rules of a game'. Another aspect is that ends emerge and are modified as a result of the examination of appropriate means.

The Social Welfare Function fits best the case of an absolute dictator. In a free society, the means-ends pattern does not fit the facts of social activity.

INDEX

Ability, principle of, 160, 163 ff.
Abstinence, theory of, 75–6
Acquisitiveness, 44–5
Advantage, principle of, *see* Interest, principle of
Altruism, 46–7, 49
American school, 4, 128, 148, 149
Aristotle, 59
Associationism, 15, 35, 36, 42–3, 46
Attitudes, 159, 239
   creation of, 204–5
   social, 200 ff.
Austrian school, 85, 128, 152

Bacon, 23, 35, 45, 96
Bagehot, W., 3, 7, 9, 218
Bailey, 66, 70, 77, 83, 225, 227
Bain, Alexander, 34, 98
Bargaining, collective, 125
Bastable, 114, 166
Bastiat, 121
Baumol, W. J., 210
Beccaria, 36
Behaviourism, 236
Benefit, principle of, *see* Interest, principle of
Bentham, J., 14, 15, 24–7, 34, 36, 37, 38, 42, 48–9, 51, 52, 56, 70, 76, 89, 97, 98, 109, 110, 111–12, 114, 117, 118, 137, 171, 175, 219, 221, 240
Bergson, 209
Birth control, 39
Blanc, Louis, 123
Böhm-Bawerk, 16, 98, 209
Bona fide, 239–40
Bonum communionis, 37
Branting, H., xiii
Butler, 34, 45

Cairnes, J. E., 3, 7, 9, 32, 74, 123, 138, 225, 229, 231
Cambridge school, 35, 127
Cameralists, 16, 29, 140, 156
Canard, 6
Cannan, 38, 78, 127, 174
Capital,
   taxation of, 89
   and value, 62, 75
Capital movements, 4
Carey, 121, 148
Carlyle, T., 36, 49
Carver, 130, 174, 236
Cassel, G., vi, 13, 19, 34, 58, 92, 99, 224
Character, 204
Christianity, 46
Clark, J. B., 10, 32, 101, 148–50, 236
Clarke, Samuel, 35, 45
Coleridge, 36
Colwyn Committee, 187
Common sense, 11, 44, 142–3
Communist state, 150, 153
Communistic economy, 179
Communistic fiction, 54, 101, 115, 133, 145, 150, 170, 194
Compensation principle, 209 ff.
Competition, free, 4, 10, 104, 125–6, 135, 138, 146, 149, 201
Comte, A., 36, 45, 123
Content, and happiness, 223–4
Contract,
   free, 124
   social, 30, 71, 161
Cost, and value, 60 ff., 80
Costs, 64, 68, 70, 74, 75–6, 80, 101
Cournot, 32, 83–4, 99, 188, 229

243